Anonymous

Joint Rules

Rules and Orders of the Senate and House of Representatives and of the State Library, and Legislative Directory: Biennial Session, 1878

Anonymous

Joint Rules

Rules and Orders of the Senate and House of Representatives and of the State Library, and Legislative Directory: Biennial Session, 1878

ISBN/EAN: 9783337213831

Printed in Europe, USA, Canada, Australia, Japan

Cover: Foto ©Suzi / pixelio.de

State of Vermont.

JOINT RULES, RULES AND ORDERS

OF THE

Senate and House of Representatives

AND OF THE STATE LIBRARY,

AND

LEGISLATIVE DIRECTORY:

BIENNIAL SESSION,

1878.

Prepared pursuant to an Act by the General Assembly,

BY

GEORGE NICHOLS, SECRETARY OF STATE.

MONTPELIER:
J. & J. M. POLAND, STEAM BOOK AND JOB PRINTERS.
1878.

JOINT RULES

OF THE

SENATE AND HOUSE OF REPRESENTATIVES.

1.

A Joint Assembly shall be formed by an union of the Senate and House of Representatives in the Hall of the latter, at such time and for such specific purpose only as may be expressed in a concurrent resolution of both Houses; and may adjourn from time to time during the session of the General Assembly. The President of the Senate shall in all cases preside over, and the Secretary of State, or in his absence, the Secretary of the Senate, shall officiate as Clerk; and the rules of the Senate as far as applicable shall be observed in regulating the proceedings of every Joint Assembly.

2.

The proceedings of every Joint Assembly including the resolution ordering the same, shall be recorded by the Clerk in a book kept for that purpose, which shall be preserved in the office of the Secretary of State, a copy of which shall be furnished to the Governor by the Secretary of State, and shall also be published with the Journal of the proceedings of the House of Representatives.

3.

At the commencement of each session the following Joint Standing Committees, consisting of two Senators and three Representatives, shall be appointed by the presiding officers of the two Houses respectively, to wit:

A Committee on Joint Rules.

A Committee on the Library.

A Committee on the Reform School.

A Committee on the State Work House.

4.

A Joint committee of three Senators and three Representatives shall be appointed by the presiding officers of the two Houses respectively, to whom may be referred all documents transmitted by the Governor for the use of the General Assembly, who shall report thereon to that House from which they were received.

5.

The committees of the Senate and House of Representatives, to whom the same subject matter shall have been referred, may, for the purpose of facilitating business, meet together as a joint committee, and make a joint or separate report to either or both Houses, as they may think expedient.

6.

In every case of disagreement between the Senate and House of Representatives, if either shall request a conference and appoint a committee for that purpose, and the other House shall also appoint a committee on its part, such committee shall meet at a convenient hour, to be agreed upon by their chairman, in the conference room, and state to each other, verbally or in writing, the reasons of each House for its vote on the subject matter of disagreement, confer freely thereon, and make a report of their doings to their respective Houses as soon as may be.

7.

Committes of Conference shall consist of an equal number from each House, and shall return the papers referred to them to that House which last voted upon the subject matter of disagreement.

8.

After each House shall have adhered to the vote of disagreement, a bill or resolution shall be lost.

9.

When bills and resolutions are on their passage between the two Houses, they shall be verified by the attestation of the Secretary or Clerk of each House respectively, and all joint resolutions shall be fairly engrossed, after their passage, in the House in which they originate, and shall, when finally passed, be signed by the presiding officer of both Houses, in the same manner as bills.

10.

When a bill or resolution, which shall have passed one House, is rejected in the other, notice thereof shall be given to the House in which the same shall have passed; and all such rejected bills or resolutions, with the accompanying papers, shall be returned to and left in the custody of the House which first acted on them.

11.

Each House shall transmit to the other, all papers on which any bill or resolution shall be founded; and should any bill or resolution pass both Houses, the same papers shall be delivered to the Governor.

12.

No bill, which shall have passed one house, shall be sent for concurrence to the other on the last day of the session.

13.

A two thirds vote of all present shall be required for the suspension of any joint rule.

RULES AND ORDERS

OF THE

SENATE.

RULES AND ORDERS OF THE SENATE.

1.

The credentials of Senators shall be presented to the Secretary or Assistant Secretary previous to ten o'clock on the morning of the first Wednesday of October, at which time the Senate shall be called to order. The names of the Senators shall be called over, and when a quorum shall have taken their seats, they shall take the following oath, viz: "I ——, Senator of the County of ——, in the State of Vermont, October Session, 18——, do solemnly swear that I will be faithful and true to the State of Vermont, and that I will not, directly or indirectly, do any act or thing injurious to the constitution or government thereof as established by convention. So help me God. And I also solemnly swear that, as a member of this Senate, I will not propose or assent to any bill, vote, or resolution, which shall appear to me injurious to the people, nor do or consent to any act or thing whatever, that shall have a tendency to lessen or abridge their rights and privileges, as declared by the Constitution of this State; but will in all things conduct myself as a faithful, honest representative and guardian of the people, according to the best of my judgment and abilities. So help me God." Whereupon they shall, on nomination of the President appoint a *Canvassing Committee*, consisting of one Senator from each county, to join such committee as the House of Representatives may appoint, whose duty shall be to receive, sort, and count the votes for Governor, Lieutenant Governor, and Treasurer; and shall, in like manner, appoint a committee of one Senator from each county to join such committee as the House of Representatives may appoint, whose duty shall be to canvass the votes for County and Probate officers, and make report thereof to the Joint Assembly of both Houses.

2.

The Senate shall meet every day (Sundays excepted) at ten o'clock in the morning, and two o'clock in the afternoon, unless otherwise specially ordered.

3.

The President having taken the chair, and a quorum being present, the journal of the preceeding day shall be read, and all errors therein corrected.

4.

In case no quorum shall assemble within fifteen minutes after the time to which the Senate was adjourned, those present shall have the power to send the Sergeant-at-Arms, or other officer, after the absentees, and compel their attendance.

5.

Whenever the Senate shall assemble, according to adjournment, or at the commencement of a session, and the President shall be absent, it shall be the duty of the Secretary, if present, if not, of a Senator, to call to order; and the Senators present, if a quorum, shall by ballot elect a President *pro tempore*.

6.

No Senator shall be absent without leave, unless he is sick, or otherwise necessarily detained.

7.

No Senator shall audibly speak to another, or otherwise interrupt the business of the Senate, while the journal or other public papers are being read, or while a Senator is orderly speaking in debate.

8.

Every Senator, when he speaks, shall, standing in his place, address the President, and when he has finished shall sit down.

9.

No member shall speak more than twice on the same question, without leave of the Senate; and Senators who have once spoken, shall not again be entitled to the floor (except for the purpose of explanation,) to the exclusion of another who has not spoken.

10.

In all cases, the Senator first arising and addressing the President (subject to the restriction of rule 9,) shall be entitled to the floor, and when two or more arise at the same time, the President shall name the one who is to speak.

11.

When a Senator shall be called to order he shall sit down; and every question of order shall be decided by the President without debate, subject to an appeal to the Senate.

12.

If a Senator be called to order for words spoken, the exceptional words shall be immediately taken down in writing by the Senator calling to order, that the President may be better enabled to judge of the matter.

13.

The first hour of each morning's sitting may be devoted to the reception and disposal of petitions, memorials and remonstrances, motions, resolutions, and the introduction of bills; after which the orders of the day, or other proper business, shall be announced, always commencing with the unfinished business of the last sitting. The first hour of the afternoon's sitting may be occupied in receiving and disposing of reports of committees, and in completing the business of the morning hour; at the expiration of which, the Senate will again take up the orders of the day.

14.

Reports of committees may be signed by any member in behalf of the committee, and shall be by him presented to the Senate, when the call for reports is made. The signer of each report shall be held responsible for the accuracy of its statements, and the propriety of its language, and when the same shall be under consideration, he shall be further liable to give additional statements of facts or other explanations, in answer to the call of any Senator.

15.

The proceedings of the Senate, except when acting as in Committee of the Whole, embracing the titles of bills and such parts thereof as may be affected by the proposed amendments, and also the names of the Senators, and the votes which they give on every question decided by yeas and nays, shall be, by the Secretary, accurately and concisely inserted in the journal.

16.

The Senate shall biennially, within the first four days of actual sitting, elect, by ballot, a Secretary, and an Assistant Secretary, who shall be severally sworn to the faithful discharge of their duties, and shall hold their offices until superseded by a new election. The Assistant Secretary shall be, *ex officio*, engrossing clerk.

17.

The Senate shall at each biennial session appoint the following committees, to consist of three members each, except that the committees on the Judiciary and on Railroads shall consist of seven members each, and the committees on Claims, and on Education shall consist of five members each:

A Committee on Rules.
A Committee on Finance.
A Committee on Judiciary.
A Committee on Claims.
A Committee on Education.
A Committee on Agriculture.
A Committee on Manufactures.
A Committee on Elections.
A Committee on Military Affairs.

A Committee on Railroads.
A Committee on Highways and Bridges.
A Committee on Banks.
A Committee on Land Taxes.
A Committee on Printing.
A General Committee.
A Committee on Federal Relations.
A Committee on the State Prison.
A Committee on the Insane Asylum.
A Committee on Grand List.

18.

All bills after the second reading, and all petitions, memorials, remonstrances, resolutions and other papers, calling for legislative action (except such as have been reported by a committee), on objection being made, shall be referred by the President to appropriate committees.

19.

Before any resolution, any petition, or other paper addressed to the Senate, shall be received and read, whether the same shall be introduced by the President or a Senator, the title shall be fairly endorsed thereon, and a brief statement of its objects or contents shall be made by the introducer.

20.

Every motion shall be reduced to writing by the mover, if required thereto by the President or a Senator, and a motion to lay another motion, the latter not being in writing, on the table, or otherwise to dispose of it, shall not be in order.

21.

Every bill, shall receive three readings before it is passed; the President shall give notice at each reading whether it be the first, second, or third; the last of which reading of public bills shall be at least twenty-four hours after the first reading, unless the Senate unanimously direct otherwise; provided, that the bills may be read the second time by their title. Resolutions requiring the approbation and signature of the Governor shall be treated in all respects as bills; and the third reading of all bills of a public nature shall be ordered for some particular day. Each and every nomination made by the Governor, to be confirmed by the Senate, shall lie over at least twenty-four hours between such nomination and the confirmation thereof.

22.

On motion of a Senator, public bills, after the second reading, may be referred to a committee of the whole.

23.

No amendment to a bill originating in the Senate shall be received at the third reading, but the bill may be committed to a Senator for amendment at any time before its passage.

24.

Motions on bills and resolutions shall be sustained in the following order,: 1. To postpone indefinitely. 2. To lay on the table. 3. To commit. 4. To amend.

25.

A call for the previous question shall not at any time be in order. A motion to adjourn shall always be in order.

26.

If the question in debate contains several points, the same may be divided on the demand of a Senator. A motion to strike out and insert shall not be divided, but the rejection of a motion to strike out and insert one proposition shall not preclude a motion to strike out and insert a different one, or a motion to simply strike out; nor shall the rejection of a motion simply to strike out, prevent a subseqnent one to strike out and insert.

27.

In filling blanks, the largest sum and the longest time shall be first in order.

28.

When the reading of a paper is called for, and the same is objected to by a Senator, the question shall be determined by a vote of the Senate.

29.

The yeas and nays shall be taken on the call of a Senator, and every Senator present shall vote unless excused by the Senate; but no Senator shall be compelled to vote who was absent when the question was stated by the President, nor shall any one be permitted to vote who was absent when his name was called, nor after the decision of the question has been announced from the chair.

30.

No Senator in the minority, nor one who did not vote on the decision of the question, shall have a right to move a reconsideration thereof; nor shall any motion for reconsideration be in order unless made before the close of the next day of actual sitting of the Senate, after that in which the vote was taken, and before the bill, resolution, report, amendment, address, or motion upon which the vote was taken, shall, in the regular progress of business, have gone out of the possession of the Senate.

31.

On all questions, in the decision of which a simple majority is required, when the Senate is equally divided, the Secretary shall take the casting vote of the President. In all such cases a motion for reconsideration, if made in time, shall be in order from any Senator who voted on the question.

32.

The President shall have the right to call upon any Senator to discharge the duties of the Chair, whenever he shall find it necessary temporarily to retire; but such substitution shall not extend beyond more than one adjournment.

33.

The Senate having taken the final vote on any question the same shall not again be in order during the same session, in any form whatever, except by way of reconsideration; and when a motion for reconsideration has been decided, that decision shall not be reconsidered.

34.

No proposition to amend the rules of the Senate, or the joint rules of both Houses, shall be acted on until the same shall have been before the Senate at least twenty-four hours; and no rule of the Senate shall be suspended except by the vote of three fourths of the members present.

35.

Messages shall be sent to the House of Representatives by the Secretary or Assistant Secretary.

36.

Reporters may be placed on the floor of the Senate, under the direction of the Secretary, with the approbation of the President.

37.

No person shall be admitted within the lobby of the Senate Chamber except the Governor, Treasurer of the State, Secretary of State, Auditor of Accounts, members of the other House, Judges of the Supreme Court, Circuit Judges, Senators and Representatives in Congress, Ex-Governors and Lieutenant Governors, Ex-Judges of the Supreme Court, Ex-Senators of the State Senate, District Judge and Attorney of the United States, members of other State Legislatures, Clerk and Assistant Clerk of the House of Representatives, and the Secretary of Civil and Military Affairs, and such ladies and gentlemen as the President or a Senator may introduce.

38.

When in session the Senators shall sit with their heads uncovered.

39.

Upon any disorderly conduct in the gallery, the President may order the same to be cleared.

40.

Whenever a bill or resolution is laid on the table, by order of the Senate, and shall have remained on the table twenty-four hours, it shall be subject to be taken up by the Chair, and presented for the consideration of the Senate, without a call or order on the subject.

41.

There shall be one Door-Keeper, one Assistant Door-Keeper, and two Messengers of the Senate.

42.

CHOICE OF SEATS.

At nine o'clock on the morning of the first day of the Senate, and before the session shall be called to order, the Secretary shall place in a box prepared for the purpose, fourteen ballots, designating by name the several counties in the State, and shall proceed to draw therefrom, impartially, one ballot at a time until all are drawn. And as each ballot is drawn, the Senator or Senators from the county designated by such ballot, shall, personally, if present, or may by proxy, if absent, select his or their seat or seats. If any Senator or Senators, from any county so drawn, should not be present, either personally or by proxy, at the time of such drawing the county next drawn shall have preference.

43.

The subject matter of each and every bill and resolution shall be briefly indicated in its title by the mover; and every bill and resolution shall be properly folded, and the name of the mover legibly written at the bottom of the same, before its introduction.

44.

After the second reading of any bill of public character, the Secretary shall cause not less than three hundred copies of the same to be forthwith printed for the use of the General Assembly, and he shall furnish five copies thereof to the Librarian.

RULES AND ORDERS

OF THE

HOUSE.

RULES AND ORDERS

OF THE

HOUSE OF REPRESENTATIVES.

Rule 1.

At half-past eight o'clock on the morning of the second day of the session, and before the House shall be called to order, the Clerk shall place in a box prepared for that purpose, ballots designating by name the several towns in the State; and shall also place in a like box for that purpose, ballots designating by number the several seats in the House; and shall proceed to draw therefrom impartially one ballot at a time from each box; and as such ballots are drawn, the member from the town designated by such ballot shall occupy the seat drawn in connection with such town, unless application shall be made to the Clerk within twelve hours from the time of such drawing, to exchange seats with some other member or to take some vacant seat after all the members shall have drawn.

Rule 2.

The House shall meet every day (Sundays excepted), at ten o'clock in the morning, and at two o'clock in the afternoon, unless otherwise specially ordered.

RULE 3.

OF COMMITTEES.

At the commencement of each session the following Standing Committees shall be appointed, viz: A committee of three members, to report rules of the House.

A committee consisting of seven members, who shall take into consideration all matters relating to the election of members; to be denominated the Committee on *Elections*.

A committee of seven members, to whom shall be referred all matters relating to the Government of the United States, and the relations of this State to it; to be denominated the Committee on *Federal Relations*.

A committee consisting of nine members, who shall take into consideration all matters affecting the revenue of the State—shall, from time to time, inquire into the state of the Treasury; ascertain the amount of debts due the State, and the claims against it; report the amount of taxes necessary to be raised for the support of Government, and inquire whether any, and if any, what measures ought to be adopted, the better to equalize the public burdens, secure the accountability of public agents, and otherwise improve the financial concerns of the State; to be denominated the Committee of *Ways and Means*.

A committee consisting of seven members, who shall take into consideration all matters relating to the militia; to be denominated the Committee on *Military Affairs.*

A committee consisting of nine members, who shall take into consideration all matters relating to the Judiciary; to be denominated the *Judiciary Committee.*

A committee consisting of seven members, to take into consideration all literary and scientific subjects; to be denominated the Committee on *Education.*

A committee consisting of nine members, who shall take into consideration all claims against the State; to be denominated the Committee of *Claims.*

A committee consisting of nine members, who shall take into consideration all matters relating to Railroads; to be denominated the Committee on *Railroads.*

A committee consisting of seven members, who shall take into consideration all matters relating to Highways, Bridges and Ferries; to be denominated the Committee on *Highways, Bridges and Ferries.*

A committee consisting of seven members, who shall take into consideration all matters relating to Banks; to be denominated the Committee on *Banks.*

A committee consisting of seven members, who shall take into consideration all matters relating to Domestic Manufactures; to be denominated the Committee on *Manufactures.*

A committee consisting of one member from each county, who shall take into consideration all matters relating to Agriculture; to be denominated the Committeee on *Agriculture.*

A committee consisting of one member from each county, who shall take into consideration all matters relating to Land Taxes; to be denominated the *Land Tax Committee.*

A committee of one member from each county to make up the Grand List.

A committee of one member from each county, to take into consideration all subjects referred to a member from each county; to be denominated the *General Committee.*

A committee of one member from each county, whose duty it shall be to receive and distribute all public documents and papers, printed for the use of the members; to be denominated the *Distributing Committee.*

A Committee consisting of seven members, to take into consideration all matters relating to the State Prison; to be denominated the Committee on the *State Prison.*

A committee of seven members, to whom shall be referred all bills and other matters relative to private corporations, for which there may be no other appropriate committee; to be denominated the Committee on *Corporations.*

A committee of seven members, to whom shall be referred all bills and other matters relative to town lines; to be denominated the Committee on *Town Lines.*

A committee consisting of one member from each county, to take into consideration all matters relating the mileage and debentures of the members of the House; to be denominated the Committee on *Mileage and Debentures.*

A committee consisting of seven members, to take into consideration all matters relating to the Public Buildings; to be denominated the Committee on *Public Buildings.*

A committee consisting of five members, to take into consideration all matters relating to the Insane Asylum, to be denominated the committee on *the Insane.*

RULE 4.

No committee shall sit during the session of the House, without leave from the House.

RULE 5.

All committees shall have a right to report by bill.

RULE 6.

All committees shall be made by the Speaker, but any appointment made by him may, on motion of a member, be overruled by the House; in which case the House shall, on nomination of a member immediately fill the vacancy.

RULE 7.

Any member shall be excused from service on any committee upon his own request, if, at the time of his appointment, he shall be a member of two other committees.

RULE 8.

When the House shall have ordered the appointment of a committee, the Speaker shall be entitled to one recess of the House in which to make the appointment.

RULE 9.

OF THE RIGHTS AND DUTIES OF THE SPEAKER AND OTHER MEMBERS.

The Speaker shall take the chair at the hour to which the House stands adjourned, call to order and proceed to business; causing the journals of th previous day to be read at the opening of the House on each day, unless otherwise ordered by the House. He shall preserve order, and may speak on questions of order in preference to any other member, rising from his seat for that purpose; and shall decide on all questions of order, subject to an appeal to the House.

Rule 10.

In case of any disturbance or disorderly conduct in the gallery or lobby, the Speaker may cause the same to be cleared.

Rule 11.

If any member, in speaking, or otherwise, transgress the rules of the House, the Speaker shall, or any other member may, call to order, in which case, the member so called to order shall immediately sit down, unless permitted to explain; and the House shall, if appealed to, decide the same without debate. If the decision be in favor of the member called to order, he shall be at liberty to proceed; if otherwise, and the case require, he shall be liable to the censure of the house.

Rule 12.

No member shall speak more than twice to the same question without permission from the House; nor shall he speak the second time while the floor is claimed by a member who has not spoken to the question under consideration.

Rule 13.

No member shall absent himself from the service of the House unless he have leave of absence, is sick, or unable to attend.

Rule 14.

The yeas and nays shall be ordered on any question, on demand of a member, and when taken, and also on a division of the House, every member present, except the Speaker, shall vote, unless excused by the House; but no member shall be compelled to vote who was not present when the question was stated from the Chair; nor shall any one, in taking the yeas and nays, be permitted to vote, except by unanimous consent, who was not within the bar of the House when his name was called; and when any member shall ask leave to vote, the Speaker shall propound to him the question: "Were you within the bar of the House when your name was called?" Nor shall any member be permitted to vote on any question in which he is immediately or directly interested.

Rule 15.

In all cases of ballot by the House, the Speaker shall vote; in other cases he shall not be required to vote, unless the House be equally divided, or unles his vote, if giveu to the minority, will make he division equal; and in case of such equal division, the question shall be lost. And no member, or or other person, shall visit or remain by the Clerk's table while the yeas and nays are being called, or the ballots are being counted.

Rule 16.

No member in the minority or who did not vote on any question, shall have a right to move a reconsideration thereof, nor shall a motion for reconsideration be in order, unless made before the close of the next day of actual session after that on which the vote was taken.

Rule 17.

Every member, on presenting a resolution, shall state, shortly, the object of it, and be held responsible for the propriety of expression therein used.

Rule 18.

Every motion shall be reduced to writing by the mover, if required by the Speaker, or any other member.

Rule 19.

The Speaker shall have a right to call upon any member to discharge the duties of the chair, whenever, from indisposition or other cause, he shall find it necessary temporarily to retire from it; and when the House shall go into Committee of the Whole, the chairman shall be named by the Speaker.

Rule 20.

All petitions shall be referred to a Committee without reading, unless the reading be demanded by a member.

Rule 21.

The House having once decided on any question, it shall not again be brought before the House by any member thereof, in any form whatever, during the same session.

Rule 22.

When a motion shall be made for a call of the House, the call shall be ordered, if said motion is sustained by a majority of the members present.

RULE 23.

No motion to amend the rules of the House shall be acted upon until it shall have been before the House at least twenty-four hours.

RULE 24.

The Governor, Lieutenant Governor, the Treasurer, and Secretary of State, Auditor of Accounts, Secretary of Civil and Military Affairs, and members of the State Senate, Senators and Members of Congress, the Judges of the Supreme and Circuit Courts, the District Judge, Collector, Attorney, and Marshal of the United States, Members of the Council of Censors, and such as have previously held those offices; the clergy, and such as may be introduced by a member, shall be admitted to seats on the floor of the House.

RULE 25.

Counsel may be admitted to advocate any cause if permitted by three-fourths of the members present.

RULE 26.

No bill shall pass the House until it shall have been read three several times, the last of which shall be at least twenty-four hours after the first reading, and the third reading of all bills of a public nature shall be ordered for some particular day.

RULE 27.

Every bill originating in the House shall be engrossed before it is read the third time, and at the third reading it shall not be amended in the House unless by unanimous consent; but it may be committed to a member for amendment.

Rule 28.

All bills shall be read a second time by their titles only, unless the reading shall be demanded by a member; and all bills after the second reading, and all petitions, memorials, remonstrances, resolutions and other papers, calling for legislative action (except such as have been reported by a committee), no objection being made, shall be referred by the Speaker to appropriate committees.

Rule 29.

No bill for the charter, re-charter, or increase of capital of any bank, or for the alteration of county or town lines, or the removal or alteration of shires, shall be entertained by the House, unless it is made to appear to the committee to which it may have been referred that the required notice has been given.

Rule 30.

The subject matter of each and every bill shall be briefly indicated in the title by the mover, at the time of its introduction; and every bill and resolution shall be properly folded, and the name of the mover, and the town he repesents, shall be legibly written on the bottom of the same before it shall be offered.

Rule 31.

A two thirds vote of all present shall be required for the suspension of any rule of the House.

Rule 32.

MOTIONS.

A motion to adjourn shall always be in order, and shall be determined without debate.

RULE 33.

Motions on bills and resolutions shall be sustained in the following order:

1. To dismiss.
2. To postpone to a day certain.
3. To lay on the table.
4. To commit.
5. To amend.

RULE 34.

If the question in debate contains several points, the same shall be divided on the demand of a member. A motion to strike out or insert shall not be divided, but the rejection of a motion to strike out and insert one proposition shall not preclude a motion to strike out and insert a different one, or a motion simply to strike out prevent a subsequent one to strike out and insert.

RULE 35.

In filling blanks, the largest sum and the longest time shall be the first in order.

RULE 36.

ORDER OF BUSINESS.

The first hour of each morning's sitting may be devoted to the reception and disposal of petitions, memorials, remonstrances, motions, resolutions and the introduction of bills; after which the orders of the day, or other proper business, shall be announced, always commencing with the unfinished business of the last sitting. The first hour of the afternoon's sitting may be occupied in the receiving and disposing of reports of committees, and in completing the business of the morning hour; at the expiration of which, the House will again take up the orders of the day.

Rule 37.

REPORTS.

Reports of committees may be signed by any member in behalf of the committee, and may be made to the House by any member of the committee in person, or by laying the same on the Speaker's table during the afternoon hour. The signer of such report shall be held responsible for the accuracy of its statements, and the propriety of its language, and when the same shall be under consideration, he shall be further liable to answer all proper calls of any member of the House, for additional statements of facts.

Rule 38.

All bills and other matters reported to the House by committee requiring the action of the House, shall be taken up and considered in the same order in which they are reported, unless the House should otherwise direct.

Rule 39.

All incidental questions of order, arising after a motion is made for the previous question, and pending such motion, shall be decided, whether on appeal or otherwise, without debate.

Rule 40.

After the second reading of all bills of a public character, the Clerk shall cause not less than three hundred copies of the same to be forthwith printed for the use of the members of the General Assembly.

Rule 41.

All messages from the House of Representatives to the Senate, shall be transmitted by its Clerk, or one of his assistants.

RULES AND BY-LAWS

OF THE

STATE LIBRARY.

RULES AND BY-LAWS OF THE STATE LIBRARY.

1.

The Library shall be kept open each day, at suitable hours, of every session of the Legislature and Constitutional Convention, when the Librarian or his Assistants shall be present. And no person shall be allowed access to the Library at any time except in the presence of the Librarian or his Assistants.

2.

Books may be taken from the Library by the Governor and Lieutenant Governor; the Secretary of Civil and Military Affairs; members of the Senate and House and their Clerks; members of the Constitutional Convention and its Clerks; Heads of Departments; Judges of the Supreme Court; Trustees of the Library; Secretary and members of the Board of Education.

3.

The right to take and keep books by the members and Clerks of a Legislature, or Constitutional Convention, is limited to the time said Legislature or Convention may be in session, and no other person shall keep a book from the Library more than twenty days.

4.

The Librarian shall keep records in which he shall enter all books taken from the Library; and every person taking a book shall be responsible for its return agreeably to the rules of the Library until the Librarian shall cancel the charge. And no book shall be taken from the Library until the same has been so charged.

5.

Every book placed on the shelves of the Library shall be stamped on the outside and inside, when practicable, with the words, "Vermont State Library," in such a manner as to be indelibly inscribed.

6.

The Librarian in suitable books shall keep a record of all the transactions of the Library in the purchase and exchange of books, and also of all the expenses of the Library, for the examination of the Trustees and the Committee on the Library.

7.

The Librarian, in the discharge of his duties, shall in all matters be subject to the control of the Trustees of the Library, and shall keep a full record of all their proceedings.

8.

The Library and Library Rooms shall be under the control and charge of the Librarian, and he shall carefully preserve the books and all other property belonging to the Library; and if any loss or damage to the same shall happen from his want of care, or any violation of the rules of the Library, by him permitted, he shall be personally responsible for the same.

9.

If on notice to any person that the time for which any book or books have been drawn from the Library by such person, has expired, such person shall neglect to return such book or books to the Library for more than three days after such notice, such person shall be liable to pay the State double the value of such book or books, which value shall be estimated at the cost of replacing the same.

10.

If any person shall take from the Library any book or other article belonging to the same, without being properly authorized so to do, such person shall be liable to pay to the State double the value of such book or other article, and shall also pay a penalty of ten dollars.

11.

If any person shall have in his possession any book or other article belonging to the Library, and shall neglect to return the same to the Library on demand, such person shall be liable to pay to the State double the value of such book or other article, and also a penalty of ten dollars.

12.

If any book shall be damaged while the same shall be drawn from the Library by any person, such person shall be liable to pay to the State the amount of such damage.

11.

12.

OATHS.

THE following oaths are required to be administered by the Constitution of the State of Vermont, and by statutory provision, to officers under the civil government thereof, to wit:

The Representatives, having met and chosen their Speaker and Clerk, shall, each of them, take and subscribe the following oaths, or affirmations, (except when they shall produce certificates of their having heretofore taken and subscribed the same,) to wit:

You do solemnly swear (or affirm) that, as a member of this assembly, you will not propose or assent to any bill, vote, or resolution, which shall appear to you injurious to the people, nor do or consent to any act or thing whatever, that shall have a tendency to lessen or abridge their rights and privileges, as declared by the Constitution of this State; but will in all things conduct yourself as a faithful, honest representative and guardian of the people, according to the best of your judgment and abilities. So help you God (in case of an oath); under the pains and penalties of perjury (in case of an affirmation).

Rule 1 of the Senate requires the following oath to be taken by the members of that body, to wit:

I, ———, a Senator from the County of———, in the State of Vermont, October session, 18——, do solemnly swear that I will be true and faithful to the State of Vermont, and that I will not directly or indirectly, do any act or thing injurious to the Constitution or Government thereof, as established by convention. So help me God. And I also solemnly swear that, as a member of this Senate, I will not propose or assent to any bill, vote or resolution, which shall appear to me injurious to the people, nor do or consent to any act or thing whatever, that shall have a tendency to lessen or abridge their rights and privileges, as declared by the Constitution of this State; but will in all things conduct myself as a faithful, honest representative and guardian of the people, according to the best of my judgment and abilities. So help me God.

Every officer, whether judicial, executive, or military, in authority under this State, shall take and subscribe the following oaths or affirmations of allegiance to this State, and of office, (unless he shall produce evidence that he has before taken the same, except military officers, who are to take only the oath of allegiance, and such as shall be exempted by the Legislature.)

OATH OR AFFIRMATION OF ALLEGIANCE.

You do solemnly swear (or affirm) that you will be true and faithful to the State of Vermont, and that you will not, directly or indirectly, do any act or thing injurious to the Constitution or Government thereof, as established by Convention. So help you God (if an oath), under the pains and penalties of perjury (if an affirmation).

OATH OR AFFIRMATION OF OFFICE.

You———, do solemnly swear (or affirm) that you will faithfully execute the office of ———for the ———of ———, and will therein do equal right and justice to all men, to the best of your judgment and abilities, according to law. So help you God (if an oath), under the pains and penalties of perjury (if an affirmation).

The form of oath to be administered to persons appointed in pursuance of the provision of law, to perform any duty or execute any office, commission, or trust whatsoever, where an oath is required, and no specific form is provided, is as follows:

OATH TO BE ADMINISTERED TO COMMITTEES, ETC.

You solemnly swear that you will faithfully execute the office (duty or trust) of——— to the best of your judgment and abilities, according to law. So help you God.

REGULATIONS

IN THE

DEPARTMENT OF THE CLERK.

HENRY N. NEWELL, *Clerk.*
WILLIAM W. STICKNEY, *First Assistant Clerk.*
OLIN MERRILL, *Second Assistant Clerk.*

To insure a systematic and correct performance of the duties in this Department, the Clerk of the House of Representatives establishes the following Regulations:

DUTIES OF ASSISTANTS.

First Assistant Clerk.—It shall be his special duty:

I.

To officiate at the Reading Desk when required by the Clerk, and in case of his absence to perform his duty generally.

II.

To file all bills, resolutions, etc., disposed of by the Speaker.

III.

To distribute to the proper committee or officer, all bills, petitions and other papers referred.

Second Assistant Clerk.— It shall be his special duty:

I.

To make copies of all resolutions instructing committees.

II.

To make all proper entries in the Senate and House bill-books, and send to the printer all bills to be printed.

HENRY N. NEWELL, *Clerk.*

HOUSE OF REPRESENTATIVES,
Montpelier, Oct. 2, 1878.

LIST OF THE

EXECUTIVE AND LEGISLATIVE DEPARTMENTS

OF THE GOVERNMENT

OF THE

STATE OF VERMONT,

AND OFFICERS CONNECTED THEREWITH, WITH PLACES OF RESIDENCE,

1878.

Executive Department.

His Excellency, REDFIELD PROCTOR,

of Rutland,

GOVERNOR.

Pavilion, 27.

Frank C. Partridge, Middlebury, *Messenger.*

Needham's.

Secretary of Civil and Military Affairs,

HARRY P. STIMSON, Rutland.

Pavilion, 66.

Frank G. Butterfield, Rockingham, *Clerk.*

Mrs. Newcomb's.

His Honor, EBEN P. COLTON, Irasburgh,

LIEUT. GOVERNOR.

Pavilion, 60.

JOHN A. PAGE, Montpelier,

TREASURER.

at Home.

JOHN W. PAGE, Montpelier ....*Clerk.*

at Home.

Secretary of State,
GEORGE NICHOLS, Northfield.
Pavilion, 44.
CHARLES W. PORTER, Montpelier, *Deputy.*
Pavilion, 91.
FRED A. WOODBRIDGE, Vergennes, *Clerk.*
A. Davis',
EUGENE W. J. HAWKINS, Starksboro, *Eng. Clerk.*
Bishop's, 62.

Auditor of Accounts,
JED. P. LADD, Alburgh,
Pavilion, 69.

Sergeant-at-Arms,
TRUMAN C. PHINNEY, Montpelier.
at Home.
ERASTUS S. CAMP, Montpelier.........*Assistant.*
at Home.
BURLEIGH F. SPALDING, Glover,.........*Clerk.*
Riverside.
John F. Mead, Randolph,.............*Messenger.*
Mrs. Newcomb's.
George P. Miner, Manchester,..........*Messenger.*
H. D. Hopkins'.
George D. Tuttle, Rutland,............*Messenger.*
H. D. Hopkins'.
Herman D. Hopkins, Jr., Montpelier...*Messenger.*
at Home.
Edward L. Smith, Montpelier..........*Messenger.*
at Home.

Inspector of Finance,
WILLIAM H. DUBOIS, Randolph.

Commissioner of the Insane,

HARVEY S. CALDERWOOD, St. Johnsbury.

Superintendent of the State Prison,

HENRY P. SPENCER, Windsor.

Directors of the State Prison,

CYRUS M. SPAULDING, Jericho;
ELON G. PETTIGREW, Ludlow;
CYRUS JENNINGS, Hubbardton.

Trustees of the Vermont Reform School,

CHARLES ROGERS, Wheelock;
VICTOR ATWOOD, St. Albans;
HERRICK STEVENS, Vergennes.

State Library.

HIRAM A. HUSE, Montpelier, *Librarian.*
at Home.

JAMES W. FARGO, Randolph............ *Assistant.*
Bishop's, 25.

THOMAS L. WOOD, Randolph .... *Assistant.*
Bishop's, 61.

Edwin H. Johnson, Burlington,........ *Messenger.*
J. P. Dewey's.

State Cabinet.

HIRAM A. CUTTING, Lunenburgh, *Geologist and Curator.*
Mrs. Charles Reed's.

MILITARY DEPARTMENT.

Adjutant & Inspector General,

JAMES S. PECK, Montpelier.

At Home.

Quarter Master General,

LEVI G. KINGSLEY, Rutland.

Judge Advocate General,

JOEL H. LUCIA, Vergennes.

GOVERNOR'S STAFF.

Surgeon General.

JOHN A. MEAD, Rutland.

Aides-de-Camp,

Colonel George W. Hooker, Brattleboro.
" Willard Farrington, St. Albans.
" Henry A. Fletcher, Cavendish.
" Thaddeus M. Chapman, Middlebury.

Additional Aides-de-Camp,

Colonel Walter Scranton, Vergennes.
" Carlos D. Williams, Northfield.

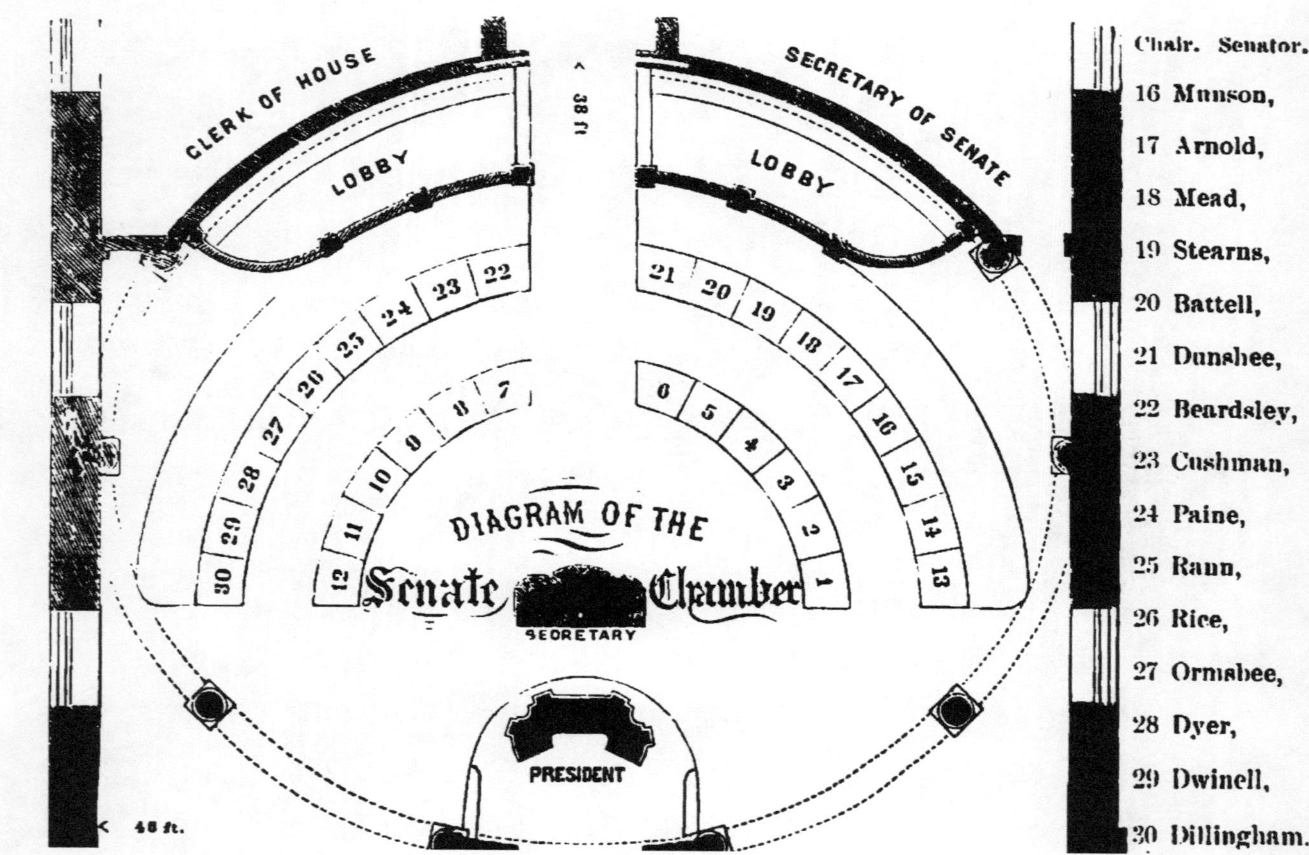

Chair.	Senator.
16	Munson,
17	Arnold,
18	Mead,
19	Stearns,
20	Battell,
21	Dunshee,
22	Beardsley,
23	Cushman,
24	Paine,
25	Rann,
26	Rice,
27	Ormsbee,
28	Dyer,
29	Dwinell,
30	Dillingham.

Legislative Department.

SENATE,

Arranged Alphabetically by Counties; with Senators' Names, Residences, Rooms, the Number of their Chairs, respectively; and the Officers of the Senate.

His Honor, EBEN. P. COLTON, Lieut. Governor, *President.*

Counties.	Senators.	Residences.	Rooms.	No. of Chair
Addison	Noble F. Dunshee.....	Bristol	Pavilion, 54..........	21
"	Joseph Battell..........	Ripton	Pavilion, 91..... ...	20
Bennington	Loveland Munson......	Manchester.......	Pavilion, 13..........	16
"	William B. Arnold	Pownal....	American, 31........	17
Caledonia	Sumner S. Thompson...	Lyndon	Riverside, 11	15
"	Henry C. Belden.......	St. Johnsbury....	Pavilion, 46..........	14
Chittenden	Henry Ballard..	Burlington.......	Pavilion, 114.........	1
"	Chester W. Witters.....	Milton..........	Pavilion, 115........	2
"	Cicero G. Peck.........	Hinesburgh......	Pavilion, 71..........	3

Essex	Charles W. King	Lunenburgh	American, 48	4
Franklin	Albert Sowles	St. Albans	Pavilion, 56	8
"	E. Henry Powell	Richford	Pavilion, 65	7
"	Chester K. Leach	Fletcher	American, 55	9
Grand Isle	George W. Beardsley	Alburgh	Bishop's, 38	22
Lamoille	Richard F. Parker	Wolcott	Pavilion, 89	13
Orange	John B. Mead	Randolph	Mrs. Newcomb's	18
"	John C. Stearns	Bradford	Pavilion, 117	19
Orleans	Isaac N. Cushman	Irasburgh	E. R. Skinner's	23
"	Benjamin F. Paine	Jay	L. G. Camp's	24
Rutland	Horace H. Dyer	Rutland	Pavilion, 25	28
"	Ebenezer J. Ormsbee	Brandon	Pavilion, 21	27
"	Levi Rice	Tinmouth	J. L. Tuttle's	26
"	Charles A. Rann	Poultney	Mrs. True's, 22	25
Washington	William P. Dillingham	Waterbury	Pavilion, 58	30
"	Albert Dwinell	Calais	Pavilion, 88	29

Counties.	Senators.	Residences.	Rooms.	No. of Chair
Windham......	Alvin B. Franklin......	Newfane.........	Mrs. True's, 28......	6
"	Dan P. Webster........	Putney..........	Pavilion, 109	5
Windsor	John F. Deane.........	Cavendish........	S. P. Redfield's	12
"	Nelson Gay............	Stockbridge......	Pavilion, 111........	10
"	William C. Danforth....	Barnard.........	Pavilion, 110........	11

OFFICERS OF THE SENATE.

Names.	Residences.	Offices.	Rooms.
FREDERICK W. BALDWIN, . .	Barton, . . .	*Secretary*, . . .	Riverside, 10.
CHAUNCEY W. BROWNELL, Jr.,	Burlington, . .	*Ass't Secretary*, .	Riverside, 10.
LEWIS B. HIBBARD, ...	Cavendish, . .	*Chaplain*, . . .	Mrs. Hibbard's.
ELBRIDGE M. BUCK, ...	Cavendish, . .	*Doorkeeper*, . .	Bennett's.
ALVIN D. WHITE, ...	Huntington, .	*Ass't Doorkeeper*,	Bishop's, 62.

CHARLES A. DINSMORE, . .	Woodstock, . .	*Page*, ...	A. S. Needham's.
EVERETT C. BENTON, . . .	Guildhall, . .	*Page*, ...	Riverside, 21.

REPORTER.

ROBERT ROBERTS, ... Burlington, ... Anson Davis'.

HOUSE OF REPRESENTATIVES,

Arranged with reference to towns; Names of Members, their Rooms, the Number of their Seats, respectively; and the Officers of the House.

HON. JAMES L. MARTIN, Londonderry, *Speaker.*

Towns.	Counties.	Representatives.	Rooms.	No. of Seat.
Addison........	Addison.........	Benjamin C. Hayward..	H. S. Harwood's....	36
Albany.........	Orleans.........	Enoch C. Rowell	Chas. Hathaway's....	108
Alburgh........	Grand Isle.......	Henry Mott............	Pavilion, 121........	55
Andover	Windsor	Frederick A. Way.....	E. S. Camp's........	67
Arlington	Bennington.....	Charles A. Derrick.....	American, 60........	175
Athens.........	Windham........	Othniel R. Edwards.....	Orrin Daley's.......	128
Bakersfield	Franklin........	Elisha H. Beals	Bishop's, 40.........	169
Baltimore.......	Windsor.........	Ervin C. Sherwin.......	Bennett's...........	144
Barnard	"	Charles W. Black.......	American, 52........	126

Barnet	Caledonia	William E. Peck	Pavilion, 77	153
Barre	Washington	J. Henry Jackson	At home	197
Barton	Orleans	Ira D. R. Collins	L. G. Camp's	229
Belvidere	Lamoille	William Winthrop	Union House, 18	47
Bennington	Bennington	Benjamin F. Morgan	H. D. Hopkins'	28
Benson	Rutland	Rollin E. Brown	Hathaway's	235
Berkshire	Franklin	Daniel Moren	Bishop's, 44	86
Berlin	Washington	John E. Benjamin	At home	66
Bethel	Windsor	Marcus A. Moody	Bishop's, 16	233
Bloomfield	Essex	Milton Cook	W. H. Barnes'	75
Bolton	Chittenden	Walter H. White	Edwin Morse's	14
Bradford	Orange	Joseph W. Bliss	Bishop's, 26	202
Braintree	"	George L. Spear	Pavilion, 45	30
Brandon	Rutland	Nathan T. Sprague	Pavilion, 14	46
Brattleboro	Windham	William H. Rockwell	Pavilion, 64	172
Bridgewater	Windsor	George E. Smith	L. G. Camp's	232

Towns.	Counties.	Representatives.	Rooms.	No. of Seat.
Bridport	Addison	Frank A. Williams	Mrs. True's, 30	193
Brighton	Essex	Asa B. Garland	J. F. Stone's	123
Bristol	Addison	George F. Meader	American, 52	72
Brookfield	Orange	Not represented.		
Brookline	Windham	Samuel B. Higgins	Bishop's, 41	121
Brownington	Orleans	Gilbert J. Gross	L. G. Camp's	209
Brunswick	Essex	James M. Gilkey	Riverside, 22	93
Burke	Caledonia	Daniel S. Townshend	Orrin Daley's	64
Burlington	Chittenden	Bradley B. Smalley	Pavilion, 40	226
Cabot	Washington	True A. Town	J. F. Stone's	109
Calais	"	Benjamin P. White	Pavilion, 57	39
Cambridge	Lamoille	William Melendy	Bennett's	154
Canaan	Essex	George Hilliard	J. F. Stone's	25
Castleton	Rutland	John Howe	J. L. Tuttle's	131

	Cavendish	Windsor	Henry A. Fletcher	Americau, 29	179
	Charleston	Orleans	Charles S. Hinman	L. G. Camp's	190
5	Charlotte	Chittenden	Henry Thorp	Pavilion, 72	95
	Chelsea	Orange	Alvah W. Whitney	Union, 14	156
	Chester	Windsor	Nehemiah A. Edson	Bennett's	34
	Chittenden	Rutland	Charles R. Holden	E. S. Camp's	21
	Clarendon	"	Edwin Congdon	H. D. Hopkins'	60
	Colchester	Chittenden	Josiah O. Crampton	Pavilion	5
	Concord	Essex	Willard Chase	American, 47	138
	Corinth	Orange	Caleb C. Sargent	Bishop's, 10	149
	Cornwall	Addison	Anson W. Frost	Mrs. True's, 30	201
	Coventry	Orleans	Joseph S. Kidder	Huntington's	211
	Craftsbury	"	Willard W. Miles	Chas. Hathaway's	180
	Danby	Rutland	Edward J. Read	Mrs. Walling's	164
	Danville	Caledonia	George E. Eaton	Pavilion, 46	153
	Derby	Orleans	Benjamin Hinman	Pavilion, 67	218

Towns.	Counties.	Representatives.	Rooms.	No. of Seat.
Dorset	Bennington	Isaac Barrows	H. C. Hopkins'	62
Dover	Windham	Augustus Fitch, Jr.	Mrs. True's, 16	192
Dummerston	"	Horace R. Stoddard	A. S. Needham's	122
Duxbury	Washington	Lyman V. Turner	Union, 15	99
East Haven	Essex	Noah S. Powers	A. S. Needham's	182
East Montpelier	Washington	Austin Templeton	Riverside, 6	13
Eden	Lamoille	Bailey W. Fuller	Bishop's, 31	104
Elmore	"	Norman Camp	E. S. Camp's	6
Enosburgh	Franklin	John G. Jenne	American, 61	135
Essex	Chittenden	Marcellus A. Bingham	Bishop's 6	147
Fairfax	Franklin	Gardner G. Orton	Orrin Daley's	50
Fairfield	"	Thomas B. Kennedy	Bishop's, 28	170
Fair Haven	Rutland	George M. Fuller	L. G. Camp's	65
Fairlee	Orange	William H. Gilmore	Pavilion, 118	203

Fayston	Washington	Seth Boyce	Bishop's, 45	61
Ferrisburgh	Addison	Harvey C. Martin	A. Davis'	205
Fletcher	Franklin	Sidney B. Beardsley	American, 55	9
Franklin	"	Carmi L. Marsh	Pavilion, 121	136
Georgia	"	Ephraim Mills	Orrin Daley's	49
Glastenbury	Bennington	Obed Eddy	Bennett's	92
Glover	Orleans	Wilbur F. Templeton	P. P. Pitkin's	238
Goshen	Addison	Samuel F. Washburn	Bennett's	78
Grafton	Windham	Samuel Phelps	Mrs. True's, 20	134
Granby	Essex	Ethan P. Shores	Mrs. Newcomb's	33
Grand Isle	Grand Isle	William C. McGowan	J. L. Tuttle's	45
Granville	Addison	Not represented.		
Greensboro	Orleans	William W. Goss	E. S. Camp's	206
Groton	Caledonia	Not represented.		
Guildhall	Essex	William H. Hartshorn	Riverside, 23	1
Guilford	Windham	Charles E. Alexander	Mrs. True's, 29	124

Towns.	Counties.	Representatives.	Rooms.	No. of Seat.
Halifax	Windham	Joseph L. Harrington	Mrs. True's, 31	27
Hancock	Addison	Ehud Darling	A. S. Needham's	32
Hardwick	Caledonia	Alden E. Judevine	Riverside, 2	83
Hartford	Windsor	Noah B. Hazen	John Witt's	213
Hartland	"	Charles C. Thornton	Riverside	18
Highgate	Franklin	Owen E. Sheridan	Bishop's, 19	106
Hinesburgh	Chittenden	Frederick Mæck	Pavilion, 71	140
Holland	Orleans	Lemuel R. Tabor	Mrs. Walling's	158
Hubbardton	Rutland	Albert Bresee	Orrin Daley's	228
Huntington	Chittenden	Henry R. Norton	Bishop's 30	200
Hydepark	Lamoille	Samuel Cinnamon	Bennett's	204
Ira	Rutland	Eben B. Perry	Bennett's	115
Irasburgh	Orleans	Zuar E. Jameson	J. L. Tuttle's	71
Isle La Motte	Grand Isle	John D. Bowman	Mrs. True's, 18	105

Jamaica	Windham	William H. H. Holton	Mrs. Newcomb's	82
Jay	Orleans	Harrison C. Sisco	Graves'	111
Jericho	Chittenden	Jesse Gloyd	Bishop's, 24	139
Johnson	Lamoille	Heman A. Waterman	Bishop's, 31	185
Kirby	Caledonia	Merritt S. Parker	C. H. Farnsworth's	195
Landgrove	Bennington	Warren W. Wiley	Bennett's	31
Leicester	Addison	Frank Chandler	Mrs. Needham's	224
Lemington	Essex	William H. Sims	Riverside, 21	137
Lincoln	Addison	Milton J. Stearns	American, 52	127
Londonderry	Windham	James L. Martin	Pavilion, 108	Chair.
Lowell	Orleans	Don E. Curtis	L. G. Camp's	3
Ludlow	Windsor	Elwin A. Howe	L. G. Camp's	189
Lunenburgh	Essex	Chester Thomas	H. C. Hopkins'	214
Lyndon	Caledonia	Benjamin F. Lincoln	Riverside, 13	196
Maidstone	Essex	Freedom D. Beede	Riverside, 22	94
Manchester	Bennington	Theodore Swift	Pavilion, 12	52

Towns.	Counties.	Representatives.	Rooms.	No. of Seat.
Marlboro	Windham	Zenas H. Whitney	Mrs. True's, 17	239
Marshfield	Washington	Daniel M. Perkins	Bishop's, 11	74
Mendon	Rutland	Hiram Temple	Bennett's	98
Middlebury	Addison	George Hammond	Mrs. True's, 14	29
Middletown	Rutland	Miletus N. Paul	L. G. Camp's	38
Middlesex	Washington	Myron W. Miles	Bishop's	89
Milton	Chittenden	Eli T. Holbrook	Pavilion, 22	207
Monkton	Addison	Lewis L. Collins	Anson Davis'	132
Montgomery	Franklin	Albert T. Kingsley	Union, 10	221
Montpelier	Washington	Hiram A. Huse	At home	186
Moretown	"	George Howes	Bishop's, 36	37
Morgan	Orleans	Matthew Whitehill	J. F. Stone's	16
Morristown	Lamoille	Sylvester N. Palmer	Mrs. Walling's	19
Mount Holly	Rutland	Judson D. S. Packer	Bennett's	187

Mount Tabor	Rutland	James Dougan	Mrs. Walling's	161
Newark	Caledonia	Almon Smith	A. S. Needham's	54
Newbury	Orange	Levi L. Tucker	Mrs. Walling's	20
Newfane	Windham	John H. Merrifield	Mrs. True's, 28	240
New Haven	Addison	Dorastus W. Nash	Pavilion, 54	152
Newport	Orleans	David M. Camp	L. G. Camp's	210
Northfield	Washington	Not represented.		
North Hero	Grand Isle	David Dodds	Bennett's	174
Norwich	Windsor	William E. Lewis	Mrs. True's, 19	57
Orange	Orange	Homer D. Camp	American, 68	76
Orwell	Addison	Moses J. Clark	Bishop's, 3	217
Panton	"	Ichabod Sherman	H. S. Harwood's	198
Pawlet	Rutland	Fayette Potter	Mrs. Hibbard's	44
Peacham	Caledonia	Isaac N. Watts	H. S. Harwood's	113
Peru	Bennington	George K. Davis	Bishop's, 32	80
Pittsfield	Rutland	Loren B. Houghton	Mrs. True's, 27	159

Towns.	Counties.	Representatives.	Rooms.	No. of Seat.
Pittsford........	Rutland	Rollin S. Meacham	Riverside, 4...	35
Plainfield	Washington	Frank A. Dwinell......	Bishop's, 13	40
Plymouth.......	Windsor.........	Alonzo F. Hubbard.....	Bennett's....... ...	58
Pomfret.........	"	William C. Whipple....	Mrs. Langley's......	125
Poultney........	Rutland	Nelson C. Hyde........	Central House, 22...	90
Pownal...... ...	Bennington......	Ichabod F. Paddock....	American, 31........	77
Putney..........	Windham........	William Robertson.....	Pavilion, 63.	7
Randolph........	Orange..........	John Buswell...........	Mrs. Newcomb's....	110
Reading	Windsor	Not represented.		
Readsboro.......	Bennington	Merritt M. Houghton...	J. F. Stone's........	120
Richford.........	Franklin.........	William C. Brown......	Bishop's, 47.........	129
Richmond.......	Chittenden	George A. Edwards.....	Bishop's, 29.........	97
Ripton	Addison.........	Henry C. Powers.......	Riverside, 24..	146
Rochester.......	Windsor.........	Not represented.		

Rockingham....	Windham........	Henry C. Johnson......	Orrin Daley's.......	216
Roxbury........	Washington.....	William B. Orcutt......	American, 16	230
Royalton........	Windsor.........	Martin S. Adams.......	American, 45... ...	8
Rutland.........	Rutland.........	Lyman W. Redington..	Pavilion, 52.........	150
Rupert..........	Bennington.....	William Root..........	H. C. Hopkins's.....	63
Ryegate........	Caledonia	Henry McCole..........	J. F. Stone's........	48
Salem...........	Orleans..........	George W. Wilson......	Mrs. Walling's......	162
Salisbury......	Addison.........	Frank W. Atwood.....	Pavilion, 55.........	151
Sandgate........	Bennington......	John F. Barber	Riverside, 18.........	85
Searsburgh......	"	Allen E. Briggs........	Bennett's...........	142
Shaftsbury......	"	Joel Harrington.......	American, 32.......	176
Sharon..........	Windsor.........	Levi B. Steele..........	Mrs. Hibbard's......	69
Sheffield........	Caledonia........	Charles Ingalls.........	Riverside, 3.........	102
Shelburne.......	Chittenden......	Edgar Nash............	Pavilion, 113....	96
Sheldon.........	Franklin.........	John A. Potter.........	American, 61.	87
Sherburne......	Rutland.........	Richard D. Estabrook..	Mrs. True's, 27......	215

Towns.	Counties.	Representatives.	Rooms.	No. of Seat.
Shoreham	Addison	Harvey S. Brookins	Bishop's, 3	194
Shrewsbury	Rutland	Nathaniel J. Aldrich	Bennett's	212
Somerset	Windham	Not represented.		
So. Burlington	Chittenden	Chester H. Steele	E. R. Skinner's	26
South Hero	Grand Isle	Edward White	A. S. Needham's	10
Springfield	Windsor	Frederick W. Porter	S. P. Redfield's	178
Stamford	Bennington	Patrick Morrissey	J. F. Stone's	79
Stannard	Caledonia	Albion L. Weed	J. F. Stone's	117
Starksboro	Addison	Josiah G. Fuller	Bishop's, 30	199
St. Albans	Franklin	Edward G. Greene	Bishop's, 8	220
St. George	Chittenden	Mitchell W. Hinsdill	Mrs. True's, 15	81
St. Johnsbury	Caledonia	Luke P. Poland	Pavilion, 61	2
Stockbridge	Windsor	Nathan Davis	Orrin Daley's	56
Stowe	Lamoille	Richard R. Waite	Bishop's, 39.	231

Strafford	Orange	Benjamin F. Jefferson	Mrs. Hibbard's	70
Stratton	Windham	Andrew D. Knight	Mrs. True's, 25	101
Sudbury	Rutland	Nathaniel A. Bucklin	Bishop's 42	12
Sunderland	Bennington	Winfield S. Holt	Mrs. True's	51
Sutton	Caledonia	Albert H. Ball	Riverside, 15	148
Swanton	Franklin	Edgar N. Bullard	Mrs. True's, 23	219
Thetford	Orange	Cyrel H. Emerson	Orrin Daley's	163
Tinmouth	Rutland	Elias E. Clark	J. L. Tuttle's	24
Topsham	Orange	Not represented.		
Townshend	Windham	Oscar R. Garfield	Mrs. True's, 24	22
Troy	Orleans	John W. Currier	Pavilion, 37	225
Tunbridge	Orange	James L. Farnham	Union House, 13	171
Underhill	Chittenden	John J. Monahan	Bishop's, 33	43
Vergennes	Addison	Walter Scranton	Pavilion, 23	236
Vernon	Windham	Roswell S. Wood	Mrs. Walling's	23
Vershire	Orange	George N. Derby	Bishop's, 37	166

Towns.	Counties.	Representatives.	Rooms.	No. of Seat.
Victory	Essex	Charles Damon	Riverside, 55	53
Waitsfield	Washington	Lucius M. Tyler	Bishop's, 15	183
Walden	Caledonia	William H. H. Davis	J. F. Stone's	116
Wallingford	Rutland	Calvin N. Townshend	H. D. Hopkins'	59
Waltham	Addison	Russell Williams	Riverside,	223
Wardsboro	Windham	Avery J. Dexter	Mrs. True's, 25	103
Warren	Washington	Sylvester Bannister	Bishop's, 34	184
Washington	Orange	Warren Huntington	Bishop's, 17	160
Waterbury	Washington	Leander H. Haines	Bishop's, 21	222
Waterford	Caledonia	Charles Ross	Orrin Daley's	100
Waterville	Lamoille	Varnus P. Locke	Mrs. Langley's	145
Weathersfield	Windsor	Justus Dartt	Riverside, 17	177
Wells	Rutland	Hiram W. Lewis	E. R. Skinner's	81
West Fairlee	Orange	Ely Ely-Goddard	Pavilion, 34	157

West Haven	Rutland	Jacob W. Jakway	J. L. Tuttle's	91
West Windsor	Windsor	Eugene H. Spaulding	Bennett's	143
Westfield	Orleans	John H. Buck	Mrs. Walling's	181
Westford	Chittenden	John Allen	Mrs. True's, 27	4
Westminster	Windham	David C. Gorham	Mrs. True's, 24	237
Westmore	Orleans	Wendell Silsby	J. F. Stone's	227
Weston	Windsor	James M. Taylor	E. S. Camp's	68
Weybridge	Addison	Charles Sturtevant	H. C. Hopkins'	73
Wheelock	Caledonia	Charles Rogers	Luther Cree's	188
Whiting	Addison	David J. Brown	Bishop's, 3	42
Whitingham	Windham	Wells P. Jones	Mrs. True's, 31	191
Williamstown	Orange	Aaron S. Martin	Chas. Farnsworth's	112
Williston	Chittenden	Jonathan R. Talcott	Pavilion, 22	208
Wilmington	Windham	Not represented		
Windham	"	Samuel C. Woodburn	Mrs. True's, 20	133
Windsor	Windsor	James A. Pollard	Riverside, 17	234

Towns.	Counties.	Representatives.	Rooms.	No. of Seat.
Winhall	Bennington	Bainbridge C. Benson	H. C. Hopkins'	88
Wolcott	Lamoille	Asa M. Harriman	Hathaway's	84
Woodbury	Washington	Mark P. Goodell.	J. F. Stone's	114
Woodford	Bennington	Daniel W. Gibson	Bennett's	141
Woodstock	Windsor	Horace C. Lockwood	L. G. Camp's	173
Worcester	Washington	Augustus A. Bliss	Union House	41

OFFICERS OF THE HOUSE.

Names.	Towns.	Offices.	Rooms.
HENRY N. NEWELL,	Shelburne,	*Clerk,*	Pavilion, 109.
WILLIAM W. STICKNEY,	Ludlow,	*First Ass't Clerk,*	American, 28.
OLIN MERRILL,	Enosburgh,	*Second* " "	American, 28.
HAYNES P. CUSHING,	Burke,	*Chaplain,*	American, 27.

Hiram Skeels,	Highgate,	*Doorkeeper,*	Bishop's, 28.
William E. Bailey,	Albany,	*Ass't Doorkeeper,*	Albert Lane's.
Grant M. Sprague,	St. Albans,	*Page,*	H. D. Hopkins'.
Earnest A. Blodgett,	St. Johnsbury,	*Page,*	H. D. Hopkins'.
Charles W. Holton,	Jamaica,	*Page,*	Mrs. Newcomb's.
Jed. P. Ladd, Jr.,	Alburgh,	*Page,*	Pavilion, 59.

REPORTERS.

Andrew C. Brown,	Montpelier,	At Home.
Edward Dana,	Rutland,	American, 28

COMMITTEES.

JOINT STANDING COMMITTEES.

UNDER THE FOURTH JOINT RULE.

Of the Senate—Mr. Peck, of Chittenden,
Rann, of Rutland,
Paine, of Orleans.

Of the House—Mr. Sturtevant, of Weybridge,
Edwards, of Athens,
Temple, of Mendon.

ON JOINT RULES.

Of the Senate—Mr. Dillingham, of Washington,
Rice, of Rutland.

Of the House—Mr. Eaton, of Danville,
Camp, of Newport,
Waterman, of Johnson.

ON THE LIBRARY.

Of the Senate—Mr. Cushman, of Orleans,
Webster, of Windham.

Of the House—Mr. Rockwell, of Brattleboro,
Hazen, of Hartford,
Stearns, of Lincoln.

ON THE REFORM SCHOOL.

Of the Senate—Mr. Belden, of Caledonia,
Danforth, of Windsor.
Of the House—Mr. Smalley, of Burlington,
Garfield, of Townshend,
Bullard, of Swanton.

ON THE STATE WORK HOUSE.

Of the Senate—Mr. Rice, of Rutland,
Franklin, of Windham.
Of the House—Mr. Poland, of St. Johnsbury,
Steele, of Sharon,
Meacham, of Pittsford.

ON GAME AND FISHERIES.

Of the Senate—Mr. Deane, of Windsor,
Beardsley, of Grand Isle,
Dyer, of Rutland.
Of the House—Mr. Root, of Rupert,
Smith, of Bridgewater,
Woodburn, of Windham,
Powers of Ripton,
Damon, of Victory.

STANDING COMMITTEES OF THE SENATE.

On Rules.

Mr. Munson,
Battell,
King.

On Finance.

Mr. Dyer,
Thompson,
Gay.

On Judiciary.

Mr. Belden,
Deane,
Ormsbee,
Ballard,
Dillingham,
Powell,
Witters.

On Claims.

Mr. Powell,
Danforth,
Stearns,
Arnold,
Dunshee.

On Education.

Mr. Mead,
Rice,
Peck,
Franklin,
King.

On Agriculture.

Mr. Franklin,
Leach,
Dwinell.

On Manufactures.

Mr. Gay,
Paine,
Rann.

On Elections.

Mr. Danforth,
Arnold,
Sowles.

On Military Affairs.

Mr. Dunshee,
Stearns,
Leach.

On Railroads.

Mr. Parker,
Witters,
Thompson,
Webster,
Dillingham,
Battell,
Beardsley.

On Highways & Bridges

Mr. Paine,
Beardsley,
Mead.

On Banks.

Mr. Sowles,
Cushman,
Dyer.

On Land Taxes.

Mr. King,
Dwinell,
Rann.

On Printing.

Mr. Cushman,
Parker,
Rice.

General Committee.

Mr. Webster,
Sowles,
Belden.

On Federal Relations.

Mr. Deane,
Ballard,
Ormsbee.

On State Prison.

Mr. Ballard,
Stearns,
Thompson.

On Insane Asylum.

Mr. Ormsbee,
Witters,
Dillingham.

On Grand List.

Mr. Dwinell,
Peck,
Battell.

STANDING COMMITTEES OF THE HOUSE.

ON RULES.

Mr. Fuller, - - - - - *of Fair Haven,*
Bingham, - - - - *of Essex,*
Dartt, - - - - - *of Weathersfield.*

ON ELECTIONS.

Mr. Thornton, - - - - - *of Hartland,*
Derby, - - - - - *of Vershire,*
Wood, - - - - - *of Vernon,*
Clark, - - - - - *of Tinmouth,*
Sheridan, - - - - - *of Highgate,*
Kidder, - - - - - *of Coventry,*
Howes, - - - - - *of Moretown.*

ON FEDERAL RELATIONS.

Mr. Norton, - - - - *of Huntington,*
Potter, - - - - - *of Pawlet,*
Huntington, - - - - *of Washington,*
Edson, - - - - - *of Chester,*
Sherman, - - - - *of Panton,*
Barrows, - - - - - *of Dorset,*
Lewis, - - - - *of Wells.*

ON WAYS AND MEANS.

Mr. Sprague, - - - - - *of Brandon,*
Judevine, - - - - *of Hardwick,*
Pollard, - - - - - *of Windsor,*
Scranton, - - - - *of Vergennes,*
Talcott, - - - - - *of Williston,*
White, - - - - - *of Calais.*
Hinman, - - - - - *of Charleston,*
Bliss, - - - - - *of Bradford,*
Curtis, - - - - - *of Lowell.*

ON MILITARY AFFAIRS.

Mr. Holton, - - - - *of Jamaica,*
Howe, - - - - - *of Ludlow,*
Brookins, - - - - *of Shoreham,*
Gilmore, - - - - - *of Fairlee,*
Kennedy, - - - - *of Fairfield,*
Cramton, - - - - - *of Colchester,*
Ross, - - - - - *of Waterford.*

ON JUDICIARY.

Mr. Poland, - - - - *of St. Johnsbury,*
Huse, - - - - - *of Montpelier,*
Redington, - - - - *of Rutland,*
Potter, - - - - - *of Pawlet,*
Fuller, - - - - - *of Fair Haven,*
Bingham, - - - - - *of Essex,*
Hartshorn, - - - - *of Guildhall,*
Miles, - - - - - *of Craftsbury,*
Monahan, - - - - *of Underhill.*

ON EDUCATION.

Mr. Camp, - - - - - *of Newport,*
Eaton, - - - - - *of Danville,*
Howe, - - - - - *of Castleton,*

Mr. Dartt, - - - - - *of Weathersfield,*
Phelps, - - - - - *of Grafton,*
Swift, - - - - - *of Manchester,*
Nash, - - - - - *of Shelburne.*

ON CLAIMS.

Mr. Hammond, - - - - *of Middlebury,*
Camp, - - - - - *of Elmore,*
Collins, - - - - - *of Barton,*
Dexter, - - - - *of Wardsboro,*
Houghton, - - - - *of Readsboro,*
Mott, - - - - - *of Alburgh,*
Davis, - - - - - *of Stockbridge,*
Moren, - - - - *of Berskhire,*
Chase, - - - - - *of Concord.*

ON RAILROADS.

Mr. Rogers, - - - - *of Wheelock,*
Smalley, - - - - - *of Burlington,*
Jones, - - - - - *of Whitingham,*
Adams, - - - - - *of Royalton,*
Spear, - - - - - *of Braintree,*
Martin, - - - - - *of Ferrisburgh,*
Davis, - - - - - *of Peru,*
Cinnamon, - - - - *of Hydepark,*
Perkins, - - - - *of Marshfield.*

ON HIGHWAYS, BRIDGES AND FERRIES.

Mr. Lewis, - - - - - *of Norwich,*
Brown, - - - - - *of Benson,*
Benjamin, - - - - *of Berlin,*
Marsh, - - - - *of Franklin,*
Buck, - - - - - *of Westfield,*
Palmer, - - - - *of Morristown,*
Bowman, - - - - - *of Isle La Motte.*

ON BANKS.

Mr. Hyde, - - - - - *of Poultney,*
Rockwell, - - - - *of Brattleboro,*
Thorp, - - - - - *of Charlotte,*
Haines, - - - - - *of Waterbury,*
Peck, - - - - - *of Barnet,*
Porter, - - - - - *of Springfield,*
Ely-Goddard, - - - - *of West Fairlee.*

ON MANUFACTURES.

Mr. Spaulding, - - - - *of West Windsor,*
Bannister, - - - - *of Warren,*
Holbrook, - - - - *of Milton,*
Meader, - - - - - *of Bristol,*
Jefferson, - - - - *of Strafford,*
Aldrich, - - - - - - *of Shrewsbury,*
Robertson, - - - - *of Putney.*

ON AGRICULTURE.

Mr. Jameson, - - - - *of Irasburgh,*
Whipple, - - - - - *of Pomfret,*
Watts, - - - - - *of Peacham,*
Steele, - - - - - *of So. Burlington,*
Mills, - - - - - *of Georgia,*
Waite, - - - - - *of Stowe,*
Martin, - - - - - *of Williamstown,*
Clark, - - - - - - *of Orwell,*
McGowan, - - - - *of Grand Isle,*
Derrick, - - - - - *of Arlington,*
Thomas, - - - - *of Lunenburgh,*
Templeton, - - - - *of East Montpelier,*
Stoddard, - - - - *of Dummerston,*
Bucklin, - - - - - *of Sudbury.*

ON LAND TAXES.

Mr. Sims, - - - - *of Lemington,*
Emerson, - - - *of Thetford,*
Potter, - - - - *of Sheldon,*
Parker, - - - *of Kirby,*
Rowell, - - - - *of Albany,*
Barber, - - - *of Sandgate,*
Reade, - - - - *of Danby,*
Fitch, - - - - *of Dover,*
Locke, - - - - *of Waterville,*
Chandler, - - - *of Leicester,*
Sherwin, - - - - *of Baltimore,*
Boyce, - - - - *of Fayston,*
Dodds, - - - - *of North Hero,*
Hinsdill, - - - *of St. George.*

ON GRAND LIST.

Mr. Sargent, - - - *of Corinth,*
Alexander, - - - *of Guilford,*
Lockwood, - - - *of Woodstock,*
Darling, - - - - *of Hancock,*
Maeck, - - - - *of Hinesburgh,*
Goss, - - - - *of Greensboro,*
Congdon, - - - *of Clarendon,*
Orcutt, - - - - *of Roxbury,*
Townshend, - - - *of Burke,*
Jenne, - - - - *of Enosburgh,*
Benson, - - - - *of Winhall,*
Melendy, - - - - *of Cambridge,*
Dodds, - - - - *of North Hero,*
Beede, - - - - *of Maidstone.*

GENERAL COMMITTEE.

Mr. Waterman, - - - *of Johnson,*
Tyler, - - - - *of Waitsfield,*

Mr. Whitney, - - - - - of *Chelsea,*
Morrissey, - - - - of *Stamford,*
Frost, - - - - - - of *Cornwall,*
Johnson, - - - - of *Rockingham,*
Fletcher, - - - - - of *Cavendish,*
Edwards, - - - - of *Richmond,*
Cook, - - - - - of *Bloomfield,*
Hinman, - - - - of *Derby.*
Beals, - - - - - - of *Bakersfield,*
Packer, - - - - - of *Mount Holly,*
Ingalls, - - - . - of *Sheffield,*
McGowan, - - - - of *Grand Isle.*

DISTRIBUTING COMMITTEE.

Mr. Harrington, - - - - of *Shaftsbury,*
Orton, - - - - - of *Fairfax,*
Washburn, - - - - - of *Goshen,*
Smith, - - - - - of *Newark,*
Gloyd, - - - - - of *Jericho,*
Powers, - - - - - of *East Haven,*
Bowman, - - - - of *Isle La Motte,*
Winthrop, - - - of *Belvidere,*
Camp, - - - - - of *Orange,*
Tabor, - - - - - of *Holland,*
Perry, - - - - - of *Ira,*
Miles, - - - of *Middlesex,*
Knight, - - - - of *Stratton,*
Black, - - - - - of *Barnard.*

ON STATE PRISON.

Mr. Nash, - - - - - of *New Haven,*
Currier, - - - - of *Troy,*
Merrifield, - - - - of *Newfane,*
Lincoln, - - - - of *Lyndon,*

Mr. Brown, - - - - - *of Richford,*
Shores, - - - - - *of Granby,*
Wiley, - - - - - *of Landgrove.*

ON CORPORATIONS.

Mr. Morgan, - - - - *of Bennington,*
Porter, - - - - - *of Springfield,*
Greene, - - - - *of St. Albans,*
Allen, - - - - - *of Westford,*
Williams, - - - - *of Bridport,*
Gorham, - - - - - *of Westminster,*
Townshend, - - - - *of Wallingford.*

ON TOWN LINES.

Mr. Buswell, - - - - *of Randolph,*
Kingsley, - - - - *of Montgomery,*
Moody, - - - - - *of Bethel,*
Bresee, - - - - - *of Hubbardton,*
Town, - - - - - *of Cabot,*
Higgins, - - - - - *of Brookline,*
Gilkey, - - - - - *of Brunswick.*

ON MILEAGE AND DEBENTURES.

Mr. Beardsley, - - - - *of Fletcher,*
Hayward, - - - - *of Addison,*
Briggs, - - - - - *of Searsburgh,*
Davis, - - - - - *of Walden,*
White, - - - - - *of Bolton,*
Garland, - - - - *of Brighton,*
Taylor, - - - - - *of Weston,*
Harriman, - - - - *of Wolcott,*
Tucker, - - - - - *of Newbury,*
Gross, - - - - - *of Brownington,*
Holden, - - - - - *of Chittenden,*
Turner, - - - - *of Duxbury,*
Whitney, - - - - - *of Marlboro,*
White, - - - - *of South Hero.*

ON PUBLIC BUILDINGS.

Mr. Jackson, - - - - *of Barre,*
Fuller, - - - - - *of Eden,*
Farnham, - - - - *of Tunbridge,*
Way, - - - - - *of Andover,*
Paul, - - - - - *of Middletown,*
Holt, - - - - - *of Sunderland,*
Fuller, - - - - - *of Starksboro.*

ON THE INSANE.

Mr. Templeton, - - - *of Glover,*
Harrington, - - - - *of Halifax,*
Dwinell, - - - - - *of Plainfield,*
Hubbard, - - - - *of Plymouth,*
Paddock, - - - - - *of Pownal.*

BIOGRAPHICAL NOTES.

BIOGRAPHICAL AND POLITICAL NOTES

OF THE

FEDERAL OFFICERS, CONGRESSIONAL DELEGATION, JUDICIARY, MEMBERS OF THE EXECUTIVE DEPARTMENT, SENATE AND HOUSE OF REPRESENTATIVES, CONSTITUTING THE CIVIL GOVERNMENT OF VERMONT.

FEDERAL OFFICERS.

Hon. Hoyt H. Wheeler, of Jamaica, district judge, was born in Chesterfield, N. H., August 30, 1833; received an academical education at Chesterfield Academy and Newfane, Vt.; read law with the Hon. Charles K. Field, then of Newfane, and with Bradley & Kellogg, of Brattleboro; was admitted to the bar of Windham county in 1859, and located in Jamaica the same year. Judge Wheeler represented Jamaica in 1867, and was a senator from Windham county in 1868–69. In the latter year he was elected a judge of the supreme court, which position he continuously occupied until March 31, 1877, when he resigned, having been appointed by President Hayes, judge for the district of Vermont. Religious preference, Congregationalist, and in politics is a republican.

Hon. Benjamin F. Fifield, of Montpelier, district attorney, was born in Orange, Vt., Nov. 18, 1832; graduated at the University of Vermont, class of 1855; studied law with Peck & Colby, succeeding to their business after his admission to the bar of Washington county, which took place in

1859, and from that time Montpelier has been his permanent residence. In 1869 he was appointed by President Grant, district attorney, which office he has continuously held since. Religious preference, Episcopalian, and in politics is a republican.

Hon. BRADLEY B. SMALLEY, of Burlington, clerk of the district of Vermont, was born in Jericho, Vt., Nov. 26, 1836, and removed to Burlington in 1839. Mr. Smalley received a common school and academic education; studied law with his father, the late Hon. DAVID A. SMALLEY; was appointed district clerk in 1861, and admitted to the bar of Chittenden county in 1863, He represented the city of Burlington in the legislature of 1874, and has held various municipal offices in his adopted city. Religious preference, Episcopalian, and in politics is a democrat.

Gen. GEORGE P. FOSTER, of Burlington, marshal, was born in Walden, Vt, Oct. 3, 1835; received an academical education, and located in Burlington in 1870. Gen. Foster was commissioned as captain of Co. —, 4th Vt. Vols., promoted successively to the positions of major, lieutenant colonel, colonel, and for gallant services on the field was made brigadier general by brevet. In 1868 and '69 he represented the town of Wolcott in the legislature, and was appointed by President Grant marshal of the district of Vermont in 1870. Religious preference, Congregationalist, and in politics is a republican.

General WILLIAM WELLS, of Burlington, collector of customs, was born in Waterbury, Vt., Dec. 14, 1837; received an academical education at Barre, Vt., and Kimball Union Academy, of Meriden, N. H., and engaged in the mercantile life. Early in the war of the rebellion he enlisted as a private in Co. C, First Vt. Cav., receiving successive promotions as first lieutenant, captain, major, colonel, brevet brigadier, brigadier and brevet major general of volunteers. In 1865 and '66 he represented his native town in the legislature. In 1866 he was elected adjutant and inspector general, which position he held by successive elections till May, 1872, when he was appointed by President Grant collector of customs, and the same year located in Burlington. Religious preference, Episcopalian, and in politics is a republican.

Hon. CHARLES S. DANA, of St. Johnsbury, was born in Danville, Vt., Nov. 18, 1815; was a graduate of Dartmouth College, class of 1837; studied law and graduated at the Harvard Law School in 1840. He was judge of probate for the district of Caledonia from 1846 to 1854; removed to St. Johnsbury in 1856, and was appointed clerk of the county, which position he occupied for eight years; was a member of the house in 1862 and '63, and senator from Caledonia county in 1864. In 1864 Judge Dana was appointed collector of internal revenue by President Lincoln, which office he has since held. Religious preference, Episcopalian, and in politics is a republican.

CONGRESSIONAL DELEGATION.

Hon. GEORGE F. EDMUNDS, of Burlington, senator, was born at Richmond, Vt., Feb. 1, 1828; received a common school education and the instruction of a private tutor; studied law with A. B. Maynard, Esq., of Richmond, in 1846 and '47,—with Messrs. Smalley & Phelps, of Burlington, in 1848 and '49; was admitted to the bar of Chittenden county in 1849; practiced law in Richmond till November, 1851, when he located in Burlington. In 1854, '55, '57, '58 and '59 he was a representative in the legislature, serving as speaker of the house in '57, '58 and '59; was a member and president *pro tempore* of the senate in 1861 and '62. He was appointed United States senator, to fill the vacancy occasioned by the death of the Hon. Solomon Foot, and took his seat April 5, 1866, was elected for the remainder of the term ending March 4, 1869, and has received two successive elections since; his present term will expire in 1881. He was a member of the electoral commission in 1876, is chairman of the senate judiciary committee, and is the acknowledged leader of the United States senate. Religious preference, Episcopalian, and in politics is a republican.

Hon. JUSTIN S. MORRILL, of Strafford, was born at Strafford, Vt., April 14, 1810; received an academic education; was a merchant, and afterwards engaged in agricultural pursuits; was a representative in the 34th, 35th, 36th, 37th, 38th and 39th congresses. In 1866 he was elected to succeed the Hon. Luke P. Poland in the United States senate, took his seat March 4, 1867, and was re-elected in 1872, his present term ending March 3, 1879. Religious preference, Congregationalist, and in politics is a republican.

REPRESENTATIVES.

FIRST DISTRICT.

Counties—Addison, Bennington, Rutland, and Washington.

Hon. CHARLES H. JOYCE, of Rutland, was born near Andover, England, Jan. 30, 1830, and emigrated to this country when a mere lad. He received an academical education, and commenced the study of law with John L. Buck, Esq., of Northfield, about the year 1850, reading also in the offices of F. V. Randall, Esq., and Hon. Ferrand F. Merrill, of Montpelier; was admitted to the bar of Washington county in 1852, and located in Northfield. In 1853 and '54 he held the office of state librarian. In 1856 he was elected state's attorney of Washington county, and re-elected in 1857. In 1861 he was commissioned major of the 2d reg't Vt. Vols., and was promoted to the rank of lieutenant colonel in 1862. In 1863 he removed to Rutland, which town he represented in 1870, serving as speaker the same year. Col. Joyce was elected, from the first district of Vermont, to the 44th and 45th congresses, and re-elected to the 46th, as a republican, receiving 12,600 votes against 5,897 votes for Jean J. R. Randall, democrat; scattering, 17.

—

SECOND DISTRICT.

Counties—Caledonia, Orange, Windsor, and Windham.

Hon. DUDLEY CHASE DENISON, of Royalton, was born at Royalton, Vt., Sept. 13, 1818; received a classical education, graduating at the University of Vermont in 1840; studied law, was admitted to the bar in 1844, and has practised since; was a member of the senate in 1853 and '54, and of the house of representatives in 1861, '62, and '63; was state's attorney in 1858–'60; was United States district attorney for the district of Vermont; was elected to the 44th congress, and was re-elected to the 45th congress, as a republican, receiving 14,430 votes against 5,739 votes for A. M. Dickey, democrat. His term of office will expire March 4th, 1879.

Hon. JAMES M. TYLER, of Brattleboro, representative elect from the second district, was born in Wilmington, Vt., April 27, 1835; received an academical education; studied law with Messrs. Keyes & Howe, of Brattleboro; was one year in the law department of the University of Albany, N. Y., and was admitted to the bar in 1860; practiced law in his native town till 1864, when he located in Brattleboro. Mr. Tyler has never mingled in political life, but has strictly and successfully devoted himself to the pursuits of his profession, never holding any office except that of trustee of the Vermont asylum for the insane. He was elected to the 46th congress as a republican, receiving 12,281 votes against 4,790 votes for Asa M. Dickey, democrat, and 45 votes scattering.

—

THIRD DISTRICT.

Counties—Chittenden, Essex, Franklin, Grand Isle, Lamoille and Orleans.

Hon. GEORGE WHITMAN HENDEE, of Morrisville, was born at Stowe, Vt., Nov. 30, 1832; received an academic education; studied law, was admitted to the bar, and has been in practice since; was state's attorney in 1858–'59; was a member of the house of representatives in 1861 and '62; was a member of the senate in 1866, '67, and '68, and president *pro tempore* the last year; was lieutenant governor in 1869; was governor in 1870; was elected to the 43d and 44th congresses, and was re-elected to the 45th congress, as a republican, receiving 11,974 votes against 5,367 votes for John L. Edwards, democrat. His term of office will expire March 4, 1879.

JUDICIARY.

Hon. JOHN PIERPOINT, of Vergennes, chief justice, republican, was born in Litchfield, Conn., Sept. 10, 1806. He read law, graduating at Judge Gould's law school, and located in Vergennes in 1832. Was educated at the public schools and academies. Was a member of the house in 1841, and of the senate from Addison county in 1855, '56, and '57. In 1857 he was elected fourth assistant justice, and in 1865 succeeded to the chief justiceship of the supreme court of Vermont. Religious preference, Congregationalist.

Hon. JAMES BARRETT, of Woodstock, first associate justice, republican, was born in Strafford, Vt., May 31, 1814. He is a lawyer by profession, and located in Woodstock in 1839. Previous to 1832, when he entered Orange Co. Grammar School preparatory for college, Judge Barrett worked in a wool carding and clothing mill. He entered college in 1833—but was obliged to suspend his studies one year for want of means—and graduated at Dartmouth in 1838. He was a senator from Windsor county in 1844 and '45, serving as president *pro tempore* the latter year; was state's attorney in 1854 and '55, and was elected a judge of the supreme court in 1857, and has occupied a seat upon the bench through successive elections since that time. Religious preference, Congregationalist.

Hon. HOMER E. ROYCE, of St. Albans, second associate justice, republican, was born in Berkshire, Vt., in 1819. He is a lawyer by profession, and located in St. Albans in 1869. Was educated at the common schools. Was a member of the house from Berkshire in 1846, '47, and in 1861, and was a senator from Franklin county in 1849, '50 and '51. Held the office of state's attorney in 1846 and '47. Was elected a member of congress from the third district in 1856, '58, and '60, and elected a judge of the supreme court in 1870, and has received continuous elections since. Has held a number of town offices in Berkshire. Religious preference, Episcopalian.

Hon. TIMOTHY P. REDFIELD, of Montpelier, third associate justice, was born in Coventry, Vt., Nov. 3, 1812. He graduated at Dartmouth College, class of 1836; read law with his brother, the late Hon. ISAAC F. REDFIELD, formerly chief justice of the supreme court, and was admitted to the bar of Orleans county in 1839, settled in Irasburgh, and practiced his profession till 1848, when he removed to Montpelier. In 1848 he was a senator from Orleans county. In 1870 was elected a judge of the supreme court, and has received successive elections since. In politics Judge Redfield adheres to the "Constitution and the Law." Religious preference, Episcopalian.

Hon. JONATHAN ROSS, of St. Johnsbury, fourth associate justice, republican, was born in Waterford, Vt., April 30, 1826. He is a lawyer, having read for that profession in the office of the late Hon. Wm. Hebard, and located in town in 1856. Was a graduate of Dartmouth College. Was a member of the house in 1865, '66, and '67, and a senator from the county of Caledonia in 1870. Was a member of the state board of education from 1866 to 1870. Was one of the council of censors in 1869, and was elected as associate justice of the supreme court in 1870, and has received successive elections since. Religious preference, Congregationalist.

Hon. H. HENRY POWERS, of Morristown, fifth associate justice, republican, was born in Morristown, Vt., May 29, 1835. Was a graduate of the University of Vermont, class of 1855. Read law with the late Hon. Thomas Gleed, of

Morristown; was admitted to the bar of Lamoille county in 1858; commenced the practice of his profession in Hydepark, and represented that town in the general assembly of 1858. In 1874 he was representative from Morristown, serving that year as speaker of the house. He was state's attorney of Lamoille county in 1861 and '62; was a member of the council of censors in 1869, and of the constitutional convention in 1870. In 1872 he was a senator from Lamoille county; was elected to the supreme bench in 1874, and re-elected in 1876. Religious preference, Liberal. P. O. address, Morrisville.

Hon. WALTER C. DUNTON, of Rutland, sixth associate justice, republican, was born in Bristol, Vt., Nov. 59, 1830. He is a lawyer by profession, and located in Rutland in 1861. Was educated at Malone Academy, and graduated at Middlebury College in 1857. Read law with Messrs. Dillingham & Durant, of Waterbury, and Linsley & Prout, of Rutland, and was admitted to the bar of Rutland county in 1858. He was commissioned and served as captain of Co. H, 14th reg't Vt. Vols. Judge Dunton resided for six years in Kansas prior to its admission as a state, and was a member of the last territorial legislature in 1861. He was a member of the constitutional convention in 1870. Was elected judge of probate for the district of Rutland in 1865, and held that office by continuous elections till April 14, 1877, when he was appointed by Gov. Fairbanks, judge of the supreme court, to fill the vacancy occasioned by the appointment of Hon. Hoyt H. Wheeler as judge for the district of Vermont. Religious preference, Congregationalist.

—

Hon. JOHN W. ROWELL, of Randolph, reporter, republican, was born in Lebanon, N. H., June 9, 1835. He is a lawyer by profession, and located in town in 1856. Was educated at West Randolph Academy. Was state's attorney of Orange county in 1862 and '63, representing the town of Randolph in 1861 and '62, and was senator from that county in 1874. Has held the office of director of the Northfield National bank, is now director and vice president of the Randolph National bank, and was elected reporter of the decisions of the supreme court in 1872. Religious preference, Christian. P. O. address, West Randolph.

EXECUTIVE DEPARTMENT.

GOVERNOR.

His Excellency, REDFIELD PROCTOR,

of Rutland, was born in Cavendish (Proctorsville), June 1st, 1831. He is a son of the Hon. Jabez Proctor, deceased, who was a member of the Governor's Council from 1822 to 1827, and was twice a Presidential Elector, in 1824 and in 1836. He was educated at Dartmouth College, graduating in the class of 1851. After leaving college, and until 1861, he devoted his attention to agricultural pursuits in his native town, in the meantime studying law and graduating at the Law Department of the University of Albany, N. Y., but did not enter upon the practice of his profession. At the breaking out of the rebellion in 1861, he was appointed quartermaster of the 3d reg't Vt. Vols., and upon the organization of the nine months' regiments was elected colonel of the 15th Vt. Vols. At the expiration of his term of service in 1863, he removed to Rutland, and for a short time was the senior member of the law firm of Proctor & Veazey; he soon resumed the care of his farm at Rutland, and continued in the pursuit of his favorite occupation till 1869, when he entered into the marble business at Sutherland Falls, in which he is now extensively engaged. He was selectman of Rutland in 1865–66. Representative of that town in 1867–68; was a member of the senate from Rutland county in 1874, and was elected president *pro tempore* of that body. In 1876 he was elected lieutenant governor of the State by a majority of 23,825 votes. Religious preference, Methodist. He was elected, as a republican, governor, receiving 37,312 votes against 17,247 votes for Wm. H. H. Bingham, democrat, and 2,635 votes for Carlos C. Martin, greenback, 730 votes for C. W. Willard, reform, and 32 votes scattering.

HARRY P. STIMSON, Rutland, Secretary of Civil and Military Affairs, republican, was born in Ludlow, October 20, 1855. He is engaged in the marble business, and located in town in 1878. Was educated at Middlebury College, graduating in the class of 1877. Religious preference, Congregationalist. P. O. address, Sutherland Falls.

FRANKLIN G. BUTTERFIELD, Clerk in the Executive Department, republican, was born in Rockingham, May 11, 1842. He is a law student. Entered Middlebury College, class of 1863, but left in his junior year. Was second lieutenant in the 6th regiment Vt. vols., and was successively promoted to first lieutenant, captain, and lieutenant-colonel of said regiment. Has been justice of the peace for the last seven years, and was elected high bailiff of Windham county in 1878. Religious preference, Congregationalist. P. O. address, Saxtons River.

FRANK C. PARTRIDGE, Middlebury, Messenger for the Governor, was born in Middlebury, May 7, 1861. He is student in Amherst College, class of '82. Was page in the Senate, 1876. P. O. address, East Middlebury.

LIEUTENANT GOVERNOR.

His Honor, EBEN POMEROY COLTON, of Irasburgh, was born in West Fairlee. Vt., Feb. 11, 1828, and removed to Irasburgh in 1841. He is a farmer, taking a prominent part in the development of the agricultural interests of Vermont. For a number of years he was master of the State Grange, and did much in extending and perpetuating the benefits of the order. In 1859, 1860 and 1876 he represented Irasburgh, and was a senator from Orleans county in 1870 and '72. Religious preference, Methodist. He was elected as a republican, lieutenant governor, receiving 37,592 votes against 17,905 votes for Pierce, democrat, and Jerome W. Rice, 87; 2,648 votes for John W. Currier, greenback; scattering, 16.

TREASURER.

Hon. JOHN A. PAGE, of Montpelier, was born in Haverhill, N. H., June 17, 1814. He is son of the late Hon. John Page, governor of New Hampshire in 1839, '40 and '41, and received his education at the common schools and Haverhill Academy. In September, 1837, he was appointed cashier of the Grafton bank in Haverhill, which institution was closed in 1844, when he removed to Danville, and was there engaged as cashier of the Caledonia County bank till November, 1848. In April, 1849, he removed to Montpelier, and became cashier of the Vermont bank. At the organization of the First National bank of Montpelier in 1865, he was elected president, which office he has held to the present time. He was repeatedly elected treasurer of Danville, and represented that town in the legislature of 1848. He was treasurer of Montpelier for many years. In 1853 he was elected state treasurer, and again in 1866, since which time he has held that office continuously. Religious preference, Congregationalist. He was elected as a republican, treasurer, receiving 37,651 votes against 17,809 votes for Geo. E. Royce, democrat, and 2,818 votes for Fletcher Tarble, greenback; scattering, 3.

INSPECTOR OF FINANCE.

Hon. WILLIAM H. DUBOIS, of Randolph, republican, was born in Randolph, March 24, 1835. Received an academical education. Was representative from Randolph in 1876, and was appointed Inspector of Finance the same year. He is president of the Randolph National Bank. Religious preference, Baptist. P. O. address, West Randolph.

SECRETARY OF STATE.

Hon. GEORGE NICHOLS, of Northfield, republican, was born in that town, April 17, 1827. Graduated as a physician and surgeon at the Vermont Medical College (Woodstock) in 1851. He was surgeon of the 13th regiment Vermont Volunteer Militia. He has repeatedly held the usual town offices. In 1868 he was elected director, and in 1874 president, of the Northfield National bank. In 1848 he was appointed state librarian by Gov. Coolidge, and received successive annual elections till 1853. In 1870 he was president of the constitutional convention. He was delegate to the National republican convention of 1872, and member of the National republican committee, and has been a member and secretary of the Republican state committee since that year. Dr. Nichols was appointed secretary of state by Gov. Smith, to fill the vacancy occasioned by the death of Hon. George W. Bailey, Jr., in 1865. Religious preference, Episcopalian.

CHARLES W. PORTER, of Montpelier, Deputy Secretary of State, republican, was born in Hartford, July 11, 1849. He is a lawyer, and located in town in 1872. Has been deputy since 1872, and was admitted to the bar in 1874. Religious preference, Congregationalist.

EUGENE W. J. HAWKINS, Starksboro, Engrossing Clerk, republican, was born in Starksboro, July 28, 1851. He is a lawyer, having been admitted to the bar of Addison county in 1873. Has held the offices of superintendent, agent, notary, and has been reporter for the Addison county court. Religious preference, Methodist.

FREDERICK A. WOODBRIDGE, of Vergennes, Messenger, republican, was born in Vergennes, July 26, 1857. He is a student, and was first appointed to his present position in 1876. Religious preference, Congregationalist.

AUDITOR OF ACCOUNTS.

Hon. JED. P. LADD, of Alburgh, republican, was born in North Hero, Sept. 28, 1828. He is an attorney, and located in town in 1863. He was senator from Grand Isle county in 1868-69. Was representative from Alburgh in 1874 and '76. Has held various town and county offices. Was deputy collector of customs in 1863-4. Is county auditor, and was elected auditor of accounts in 1876. P. O. address, Alburgh Springs.

SERGEANT-AT-ARMS.

Hon. TRUMAN C. PHINNEY, of Montpelier, republican, was born in Middlesex, April 11, 1827, and removed to Montpelier in 1849, where he is successfully engaged as a bookseller and stationer. He was elected to the office of sergeant-at-arms in 1870. Religious preference, Episcop'n.

ERASTUS S. CAMP, of Montpelier, Assistant Sergeant-at-Arms, republican, was born in Stanstead, P. Q., April 30, 1812. He is a farmer and lumber manufacturer, and located in town in 1834. He has been sergeant-at-arms, deputy sheriff, etc. Religious preference, Unitarian.

BURLEIGH F. SPAULDING, Glover, Clerk, republican, was born in Craftsbury, December, 1853. He is a law student, and located in town in 1865. Was educated at Norwich University, class of 1877. Religious preference, Liberal. P. O. address, Montpelier.

GEORGE R. MINER, Manchester, Messenger, was born in Manchester, August 17, 1862. He is a student. Religious preference, Episcopalian.

JOHN F. MEAD, Randolph, Messenger, was born in Randolph, August 16, 1861. He is a student. Religious preference, Congregationalist.

GEORGE D. TUTTLE, Rutland, Messenger, was born in Jersey City, N. Y., October 22, 1862. He is a student. Religious preference, Baptist.

HERMAN D. HOPKINS, Jr., Montpelier, Messenger, was born in Montpelier, July 24, 1864. He is a student. Was messenger in 1876. Religious preference, Congregationalist.

EDWARD L. SMITH, Montpelier, Messenger, was born in Montpelier, April 6, 1865. He is a student. Religious preference, Congregationalist.

ADJUTANT AND INSPECTOR GENERAL.

Gen. JAMES S. PECK, of Montpelier, republican, was born in that town, December, 1839, and graduated at the University of Vermont in 1860. He studied law, and was admitted to the bar in 1866. He was lieutenant and adjutant of the 13th, adjutant and major of the 17th regiment Vt. Vols. He was elected to the office of adjutant and inspector general in 1872. Religious preference, Episcopalian.

—

QUARTERMASTER GENERAL.

Gen. LEVI G. KINGSLEY, of Rutland, republican, was born in Shrewsbury, May 21, 1832, and is an alumnus of Norwich University, class of 1853. He removed to Rutland in 1857, and has since been engaged in mercantile business in that town. He was second lieutenant in the 1st, and captain and major in the 12th reg't Vt. Vols.; was made colonel of the Vermont state militia in 1864, and elected quartermaster general in 1874. Religious preference, Episcopalian.

—

STATE LIBRARIAN.

Hon. HIRAM A. HUSE, of Montpelier, republican, was born in Randolph, Jan. 17, 1843. He is a lawyer, and located in town in 1872. Was educated at Dartmouth College, graduating in the class of 1865. Was a resident of Wisconsin from 1845 to 1868. In 1862 he enlisted as a private in Co. F, 12th reg't Vt. Vols. In 1873 he was appointed state librarian to fill the vacancy occasioned by the death of the Hon. Charles Reed. Religious preference, Episcopalian.

JAMES W. FARGO, of Randolph, Assistant Librarian, republican, was born in Warren, December 21, 1844. He is a merchant, and located in town in 1849. Is town treasurer, and has been assistant in the library since 1870. Religious preference, Episcopalian.

THOMAS L. WOOD, of Randolph, Assistant Librarian, republican, was born in Randolph, August 1, 1839. He is a clerk, and was a member of the 10th regiment Vermont Volunteers. Was messenger in the library in 1876. Religious preference, Methodist.

EDWIN H. JOHNSON, Burlington, Messenger, republican, was born in Chicago, Ill., January 20, 1861. He is a student, and located in town in 1863. Was a messenger of the Senate in 1874. Religious preference, Episcopalian.

GEOLOGIST, AND CURATOR.

Hon. HIRAM A. CUTTING, of Lunenburgh, republican, was born in Concord, Dec. 23, 1832. He is a merchant, and located in Lunenburgh in 1854. He graduated in medicine at Dartmouth College, and received the honorary degree of Master of Arts at Norwich University. He was appointed state geologist and curator of the state cabinet in 1871. Religious preference, Methodist.

THE SENATE.

ADDISON COUNTY.

Hon. NOBLE F. DUNSHEE, of Bristol, republican, was born in Bristol, Vt., April 4, 1833. He is a merchant. Was educated at the common schools and academy. Was captain of Co. G, 14th reg't Vt. Vols., and represented his native town in the legislature of 1863 and '64.

Hon. JOSEPH BATTELL, of Ripton, republican. He is a hotel keeper, and was a member of the general assembly from Ripton in 1872 and '76. P. O. address, Bread Loaf.

BENNINGTON COUNTY.

Hon. LOVELAND MUNSON, of Manchester, republican, was born in Manchester, Vt., July 21, 1843. He is a lawyer. Was educated at the Burr & Burton Seminary. Was a member of the constitutional convention in 1870, and of the house in 1872 and '74. Religious preference, Congregationalist.

Hon. WILLIAM B. ARNOLD, of Pownal, republican, was born in Pownal, Vt., Nov. 28, 1827. He is a farmer. Was educated at the common schools. Was a member of the house in 1864, serving on the general committee. Has held the various town offices, and is town agent. Religious preference, Congregationalist. P. O. address, Bennington.

CALEDONIA COUNTY.

Hon. SUMNER SHAW THOMPSON, of Lyndon, republican, was born in Halifax, Mass., April 12, 1823. He settled in Lyndon in 1856, where he is engaged in an extensive business as railway contractor, and also as a lumber, grain and flour dealer. Was town representative from Lyndon in 1866–67. Was selectman for five years, and has held other town offices. Mr. Thompson was a senator from Caledonia county in 1876.

Hon. HENRY C. BELDEN, of St. Johnsbury, republican, was born in Burke, August 20, 1841. He is a lawyer, and located in St. Johnsbury in December, 1870, where he has pursued his profession with success. He was state's attorney for Caledonia county in 1868–9, and was a member of the senate from that county in 1876. Religious preference, Unitarian.

CHITTENDEN COUNTY.

Hon. HENRY BALLARD, of Burlington, republican, was born in Tinmouth, Vt., April 20, 1839. He is a lawyer, and located in town in 1863. Fitted for college at Castleton Seminary, graduated at the University of Vermont in 1861, and at the law department of the University of Albany in 1863. Enlisted as a private in August, 1861, and mustered as second lieutenant of Co. I, in the 5th reg't of Vt. Vols., and served in that capacity till compelled to resign in 1862 on account of ill health. Religious preference, Congregationalist.

Hon. CHESTER W. WITTERS, of Milton, republican, was born in Milton, Vt., June 10, 1836. He is a lawyer, and has always lived in town, except two years (1857–'58) in the west. Was educated at the common schools and Georgia (Vt.) Academy. Religious preference, Congregationalist.

Hon. CICERO G. PECK, of Hinesburgh, republican, was born in Hinesburgh, Vt., Feb. 17, 1828. He is a farmer. Fitted for college at Hinesburgh Academy, but never entered, being compelled to abandon his studies by reason of ill health. Has held the office of selectman for seven years. Has been honored with many and various positions of trust, and employs his time mostly in these latter duties. Is town superintendent and chairman of the board of school directors. Religious preference, Methodist.

ESSEX COUNTY.

Hon. CHARLES W. KING. of Lunenburgh, republican, was born in Lunenburgh, Vt., Nov. 9, 1832. He is a farmer. Was educated at the common schools. Was a member of the house from Lunenburgh in 1874. Has held the office of selectman, lister, overseer, justice of the peace, notary public, town agent, and was superintendent of schools fourteen years. Religious preference, Congregationalist.

FRANKLIN COUNTY.

Hon. ALBERT SOWLES, of St. Albans, republican, was born in Alburgh, Vt., October 5, 1833, and graduated at the Chambly College, in the class of 1850. In 1855-6, while at Swanton, he edited the *Swanton Journal*. Mr. Sowles was secretary of the first republican district convention held at St. Albans in June, 1856. In 1857 he settled in St. Albans and engaged in the business of banking—first in the Franklin County bank, and afterwards, in 1864, organized the First National bank of St. Albans. He outlived the memorable raid upon the banks in October, 1864, and is now cashier and manager of the same bank. He was elected first selectman of St. Albans in 1877 and '78. Religious preference, Episcopalian.

Hon. E. HENRY POWELL, of Richford, republican, was born in Richford, Vt., Sept. 3, 1839. He read law, and was admitted to the bar in 1866. Was educated at Potsdam (N. Y.) and Fairfax Academies. He held the office of inspector of customs in 1866, '67, and '68, and was state's attorney for Franklin county in 1872 and '73. In 1874, he was a member of the house from the town of Richford. Religious preference, Baptist.

Hon. CHESTER K. LEACH, of Fletcher, republican, was born in Fairfield, Vt., Jan. 17, 1830. He is a farmer, and located in town in 1850. Was educated at the common schools. Was successively second and first lieutenant of Co. H, 2d reg't Vt. Vols., and was commissioned captain, but declined to be mustered as such. Has held the usual town offices, and has been constable and collector since 1870. Religious preference, Universalist.

GRAND ISLE COUNTY.

Hon. GEORGE W. BEARDSLEY, of Alburgh, democrat, was born in Alburgh, Vt., March 21, 1825. He is a merchant and farmer. Received a common school and academical education. Has held several important town offices, and at different times has held agencies and responsible trusts. Religious preference, Independent. P. O. address, Alburgh Springs.

LAMOILLE COUNTY.

Hon. RICHARD F. PARKER, of Wolcott, republican, was born in Lyman, N. H., Oct. 24, 1826. He is a lawyer, and located in Wolcott in 1860. Was educated at the academy at Johnson. Was a member of the house in 1865, '66, and

'67. Was state's attorney in 1865–66, and railroad commissioner from 1869 to 1872. Has held a number of town offices. Religious preference, Universalist.

ORANGE COUNTY.

Hon. JOHN B. MEAD, of Randolph, republican, was born in Stratham, N. H., March 15, 1831. He is a farmer, and located in Randolph in 1841. Was educated at the Orange County Grammar School and the academy in Orford, N. H. Col. Mead was commissioned as second lieutenant of Co. G, 8th reg't Vt. Vols., and successively promoted to first lieutenant and captain of said company, to major, lieutenant colonel and colonel of the regiment. He was a member of the house in 1867. Religious preference, Congregationalist.

Hon. JOHN C. STEARNS, of Bradford, republican, was born in Chelsea, Vt., Feb. 11, 1831. He is a farmer, and located in Bradford in 1844, Was educated at the common schools and Bradford Academy. Was a private and sergeant major of the 1st and adjutant of the 9th reg't of Vt. Vols. He was United States assessor of internal revenue for the 2d district of Vt. from 1870 to 1873. Religious preference, Congregationalist.

ORLEANS COUNTY.

Hon. ISAAC N. CUSHMAN, of Irasburgh, republican, was born in Woodstock, Vt., March 21, 1821. He is an alumnus of Norwich University, and located in Irasburgh in 1849. He read law with his father and the Hon. T. P. Redfield, and was admitted to the bar of Orleans county in 1846. He was a member of the house from Glover in 1849, and from Irasburgh in 1861 and '62; was judge of probate from 1849 to 1853, cashier of the Bank of Irasburgh from 1853 to 1861, and court auditor at the same time. In 1853 was also appointed county treasurer, and in 1861 clerk of the county, which positions he now occupies. Religious preference, Episcopalian.

Hon. BENJAMIN F. PAINE, of Jay, republican, was born Lowell, Vt., Oct. 29, 1838. He is a manufacturer and dealer in lumber, and located in town in 1870. Was educated at the "Peoples' Academy," at Morrisville. Was a member of the house from Lowell in 1863 and '64. Has held the office of selectman and lister in Lowell, also in Jay, and has been superintendent of schools in the latter town. Religious preference, Congregationalist.

RUTLAND COUNTY.

Hon. HORACE H. DYER, of Rutland, republican, was born in Rutland, Vt., April, 1820. He is a farmer. Received an academical education. Has held the office of selectman for the last three years, and is president of the Rutland county agricultural society. Religious preference, Episcopalian.

Hon. EBENEZER J. ORMSBEE, of Brandon, republican, was born in Shoreham, Vt., June 8, 1834. Read law in the office of Briggs & Nicholson, of Brandon, was admitted to the bar of Rutland county, and located in town in 1861. Received an academical education. Was second lieutenant of Co. G, 1st reg't, and captain of Co. G, 12th reg't, Vt. Vols. Was a representative from the town of Brandon in 1872, serving on the judiciary committee. Has been justice of the peace, notary, and was assistant assessor, internal revenue department, from 1867 till 1870, and is a member of the republican state committee. Religious preference, Episcopalian.

Hon. LEVI RICE, of Tinmouth, republican, was born in Tinmouth, Vt., in 1826. He is a merchant and farmer. Received a common school and academical education. Was a member of the house in 1853 and '54. Has held the offices of town clerk, constable, treasurer, superintendent and justice of the peace. Religious preference, Orthodox.

Hon. CHARLES A. RANN, of Poultney, republican, was born in Poultney, Vt., May 23, 1823. He is a farmer and dealer in produce. Was educated at the district school. Was second lieutenant of Co. F, 14th reg't Vt. Vols. Has held the office of constable, lister, overseer, and has been a justice of the peace for twelve years. Religious preference, Congregationalist. P. O. address, East Poultney.

WASHINGTON COUNTY.

Hon. WILLIAM PAUL DILLINGHAM, of Waterbury, republican, was born in Waterbury, December 12, 1843. He read law in the office of his father, the Hon. Paul Dillingham, and was admitted to the bar of Washington county in 1867. Was educated at the common schools and academy. Was appointed secretary of civil and military affairs in 1866, to fill a vacancy occasioned by the resignation of Charles M. Gay, Esq., and again in 1874. He was elected state's attorney for Washington county in '72 and '74, and was a member of the house from Waterbury in 1876. Religious preference, Methodist.

Hon. ALBERT DWINELL, of Calais, republican, was born in Calais, Vt., January 15, 1823. He is a farmer. Was educated at the common schools and academies. Was a member of the general assembly from Calais in 1860 and '61. Has held various town offices, and was a member of the first state board of equalization in 1874. Religious preference, Congregationalist. P. O. address, East Calais.

WINDHAM COUNTY.

Hon. ALVIN B. FRANKLIN, of Newfane, republican, was born in Newfane, Aug. 17, 1838. He is a farmer. Was a member of the 8th reg't Vt. Vols., first lieutenant from 1862 to 1863, captain from 1863 to 1865, and lieutenant colonel in 1865. Was a member of the general assembly from Newfane in 1874 and '76. Has been selectman. Religious preference, Congregationalist. P. O. address, Townshend.

Hon. DAN P. WEBSTER, of Putney, republican, was born in Northfield, Vt., Dec. 7, 1845. He is a physician, having read medicine with Dr. Buchanan, of Philadelphia, and graduated at the medical department, U. V. M., and located in town in 1867. Was educated at Newbury (Vt.) Seminary. Was a member of the house in 1872 and '74, was surgeon general on the staff of Gov. Peck in 1874–'76, and is deputy grand master of the grand lodge (F. & A. M.) of Vermont. Religious preference, Methodist.

WINDSOR COUNTY.

Hon. JOHN F. DEANE, of Cavendish, republican, was born in Weathersfield, Vt., June 29, 1817. He is a lawyer, and located in Cavendish in 1840. Was educated at the University of Vermont, graduating in the class of 1838. Was a member of the house of representatives in 1847, '48, '49, '52, '54, '57, '58, '63, and '64. Was a member of the constitutional convention in 1850, and was for a number of years reporter of the decisions of the supreme court. Religious preference, Episcopalian.

Hon. NELSON GAY, of Stockbridge, republican, was born in Stockbridge, Feb. 22, 1832. He is an extensive manufacturer. Was educated at the common schools. Was a member of the general assembly in 1862 and '63, and again in 1868 and '69. Has held the office of clerk and treasurer of his town for the last twenty years ; has been justice of the peace for the last twelve years, and is president of the White River National bank at Bethel. Religious preference, Universalist. P. O. address, Gaysville.

Hon. WILLIAM C. DANFORTH, of Barnard, republican, was born in Barnard, Vt., Feb. 9, 1828. He is engaged in mercantile and agricultural pursuits. Was educated at the common schools, and for a short time was a member of Norwich University, under Capt. Alden Partridge. Was a representative from Barnard in 1861, '62, and in 1874. Has been selectman for ten years. Was president of the White River agricultural society in 1876 and '77, and is a justice of the peace. Religious preference, Congregation't.

OFFICERS OF THE SENATE.

FREDERICK W. BALDWIN, Barton, Secretary, republican, was born in Lowell, Sept. 29, 1848. He is a lawyer, and located in town in 1872. Was assistant secretary of the Senate in 1872, and has been secretary since 1874. Has been superintendent of schools. Religious preference, Universalist.

CHAUNCEY W. BROWNELL, Jr., Burlington, Assistant Secretary, republican, was born in Williston, Oct. 7, 1847. He is a lawyer, and located in Burlington in 1873. Is a graduate of the University of Vermont, class of 1870, and of the Law University of Albany in 1872. Has been assistant secretary of the Senate since 1874. Religious preference, Congregationalist.

LEWIS BAKER HIBBARD, Cavendish, Chaplain, republican, was born in St. Armand, P. Q., Nov. 20, 1834. He is a clergyman, and located in town in 1877. Was educated at Fairfax and Newton Theological Seminaries. Has held several town offices. Religious preference, Baptist.

ELBRIDGE M. BUCK, Cavendish, Door-Keeper, republican, was born in Cavendish, April 10, 1852. He is a student. Was assistant door-keeper of the House in 1876. Religious preference, Universalist.

ALVIN D. WHITE, Huntington, Assistant Door-Keeper, republican, was born in Huntington in 1841. He is a farmer. Was a member of Co. F, 13th reg't Vt. Vols. Religious preference, Universalist.

CHARLES A. DINSMORE, Woodstock, Page, was born in New York City, Aug. 4, 1860. He is a student, and located in Woodstock in 1867. Religious preference, Congregation't.

EVERETT C. BENTON, Guildhall, Page, was born in Guildhall, Sept. 25, 1862. He is a student. Religious preference, Methodist.

ROBERT ROBERTS, of Burlington, Reporter, republican, was born in Manchester, January 1, 1848. He is a lawyer, and located in Burlington in 1857. Graduated at the University of Vermont, Class of '69. Held the office of Reporter for the Senate in 1874. Religious preference, Congregationalist.

RECAPITULATION.

The Senate is composed of twenty-nine Republicans and one Democrat. Messrs. Thompson and Belden, of Caledonia county, were members in 1876, and are the only two who have been members before. Eighteen have been members of the House, and ten are new members.

The oldest Senator is the Hon. JOHN F. DEANE, of Windsor county, and the youngest is the Hon. DAN P. WEBSTER, of Windham county.

Fifteen reside in the town where they were born.

The following table exhibits the place of birth, occupation, and religious preference.

PLACE OF BIRTH.

Vermont	27	Massachusetts	1
New Hampshire	2		

OCCUPATION.

Lawyers	10	Physician	1
Farmers	10	R. R. Contractor	1
Merchants and Farmers	3	Banker	1
Manufacturers	2	Hotel Keeper	1
Merchant	1		—
Total			30

RELIGIOUS PREFERENCE.

Congregationalist	13	Baptist	1
Episcopalian	5	Unitarian	1
Methodist	3	No preference	4
Universalist	3		—
Total			30

HOUSE OF REPRESENTATIVES.

ADDISON COUNTY.

BENJAMIN CLEMENT HAYWARD, *Addison*, republican, was born in Addison, Sept. 13, 1837. He is a farmer. Received an academical education, and has held a few town offices. Religious preference, Baptist.

FRANK A. WILLIAMS, *Bridport*, republican, was born in Bridport in 1831. He is a farmer. Was educated at the Vergennes High School. Has held the office of lister and selectman, and is now first selectman. Religious preference, Congregationalist.

GEORGE F. MEADER, *Bristol*, republican, was born in Lincoln, Feb. 8, 1834. He is a farmer, and located in town in 1866. Was educated at the common schools. Has held the office of selectman and superintendent of common schools. Religious preference, Friends.

ANSON W. FROST, *Cornwall*, republican, was born in Cornwall, Sept. 22, 1822. He is a farmer. Was educated at the common school. Has held the office of constable and collector since 1865. Religious preference, Congregation't.

HARVEY C. MARTIN, *Ferrisburgh*, republican, was born in Ferrisburgh, April 11, 1835. He is a farmer. Was educated at the common school and academy. Has held the office of constable and collector since 1875. Religious preference, Methodist. P. O. address, No. Ferrisburgh.

SAMUEL FULLER WASHBURN, *Goshen*, republican, was born in Bridgewater, June 1, 1810. He is a farmer, and located in town in 1822. Was educated at the common schools. Has held the usual town offices. Religious preference, Methodist. P. O. address, Forestdale.

GRANVILLE—not represented.

EHUD DARLING, *Hancock*, republican, was born in Hancock, March 16, 1804. He is farmer and merchant. Was educated at the district school. Was a member of the general assembly from Hancock in 1856 and '57. Has held the office of justice of the peace for more than thirty years, is town clerk, and has been repeatedly honored with the offices of selectman, lister, constable, etc. Religious preference, Universalist.

Frank Chandler, *Leicester*, republican, was born in Coleraine, Mass., June 13, 1838. He is a farmer and hotel keeper, and located in town in 1863. Was educated at the common schools and academy. Has held a number of town offices. Religious preference, Methodist.

Milton James Stearns, *Lincoln*, republican, was born in Lincoln, Jan. 27, 1848. He is engaged in mercantile pursuits. Was educated at the common schools and Bristol academy. Was superintendent from 1872 to '75, and is notary and postmaster. Religious preference, Methodist. P. O. address, West Lincoln.

George Hammond, *Middlebury*, republican, was born in Middlebury, May 31, 1836. He is a farmer. Received an academical education. Has held the office of lister and selectman, and has been first selectman for the last three years. Religious preference, Congregationalist.

Lewis L. Collins, *Monkton*, republican, was born in Monkton, July 27, 1832. He is a farmer. Was educated at the common schools. Held the office of selectman in 1875, '76 and '77. Religious preference, Friends. P. O. address, Monkton Ridge.

Dorastus W. Nash, *New Haven*, republican, was born in New Haven, April 17, 1833. He is a farmer. Was educated at the public schools. Has held the office of selectman, lister and minor town offices.

Moses J. Clark, *Orwell*, republican, was born in Orwell, in 1815. He is a farmer. Was educated at the common schools. Religious preference, Congregationalist.

Ichabod Sherman, *Panton*, republican, was born in Monkton, Nov. 12, 1823. He is a farmer and banker, and located in town in 1856. Was educated at the common schools. Has held a number of town offices, both in Monkton and Panton. P. O. address, Vergennes.

Henry C. Powers, *Ripton*, republican, was born in Rochester, Dec. 17, 1834. Was formerly a member of the clerical profession, but latterly has devoted his entire time to the practice of medicine, and located in town in 1870. Was educated at the common schools and academy. Was a corporal in Co. G, 14th reg't Vt. Vols.. re-enlisted into Co. B, 11th reg't Vt. Vols., and during the last part of his service was acting hospital steward in Harwood General Hospital, Washington, D. C. Religious preference, Methodist.

Frank W. Atwood, *Salisbury*, republican, was born in Brandon, in 1837. He is a merchant and farmer, and located in town in 1860. Was educated at the common schools. P. O. address, West Salisbury.

HARVEY S. BROOKINS, *Shoreham*, republican, was born in Shoreham, Jan. 25, 1835. He is a farmer. He was captain of Co. E, 8th reg't Minnesota Vols., has been clerk in the treasury department at Washington, and held the office of sheriff in Wright county, Minn., in 1861. Has been constable seven years. Mr. Brookins was a member of the house in 1876, serving on the committee on agriculture. Religious preference, Universalist.

JOSIAH G. FULLER, *Starksboro*, republican, was born in Starksboro, Aug. 2, 1839. He is a farmer. Was educated at the common schools. Religious preference, Freewill Baptist. P. O. address, Huntington Centre.

WALTER SCRANTON, *Vergennes*, republican, was born in Scranton, Pa., Aug. 12, 1849. He is not engaged in any business at present. Mr. Scranton located in Vergennes in 1875. Was educated at Stockbridge, Mass. Religious preference, Presbyterian.

RUSSELL WILLIAMS, *Waltham*, republican, was born in New Haven, Jan. 27, 1824. He is a farmer, and located in town in 1868. Was educated at the common schools. Is justice of the peace and selectman. P. O. address, Vergennes.

CHARLES STURTEVANT, *Weybridge*, republican, was born in Weybridge, May 27, 1817. He is a farmer, and was educated at the common schools. Has held the office of selectman. Religious preference, Methodist.

DAVID J. BROWN, *Whiting*, republican, was born in Orwell, Dec. 17, 1836. He is a farmer, and located in town in 1872. Was educated at the common schools. Was a sergeant in the war of the rebellion. Has been selectman for the last two years. Religious preference, Universalist.

BENNINGTON COUNTY.

CHARLES A. DERRICK, *Arlington*, democrat, was born in Rensselaer county N. Y., in 1818. He is a farmer, and located in town in 1865. Was educated at the district schools, and held the office of selectman in 1871. P. O. address, West Arlington.

BENJAMIN F. MORGAN, *Bennington*, republican, was born in Pownal, Sept. 30, 1799. He is a physician, and located in town in 1856. Was educated at Bennington and Williamstown, Mass., and graduated at the Vermont Academy of Medicine, in connection with Middlebury College, in 1825. Served as surgeon on detached duty in the civil war. Was a representative from the town of Pownal in 1831, and senator from Bennington county in 1843 '44. Has been justice of the peace for several years. Religious preference, Congregationalist. P. O. address, Bennington Centre.

ISAAC BARROWS, *Dorset*, republican, was born in Dorset, April 21, 1820. He is a farmer. Has held the office of lister for many years, has been first constable since 1867, and is deputy sheriff. Religious preference, Congregationalist.

OBED EDDY, *Glastenbury*, democrat, was born in Woodford, Nov. 18, 1826. He is a lumberman, and located in town in 1870. Was a member of the general assembly in 1864. Has held the office of selectman in Glastenbury. P. O. address, South Shaftsbury.

WARREN W. WILEY, *Landgrove*, republican, was born in Landgrove, Oct. 17, 1833. He is a farmer. Was educated at the district school. Was a member of the house in 1866 and '67. Has held the various town offices, and is postmaster. Religious preference, Independent.

THEODORE SWIFT, *Manchester*, republican, was born in Manchester, Dec. 29, 1839. He is a merchant. Was educated at Burr & Burton Seminary. Religious preference, Congregationalist.

GEORGE K. DAVIS, *Peru*, democrat, was born in Manchester, Aug. 12, 1830. He is a hotel keeper, and located in town in 1833. Was educated at the common schools. Has held the offices of constable, selectman, agent, and grand juror at different times, and is postmaster. Religious preference, Congregationalist.

ICHABOD F. PADDOCK, *Pownal*, republican, was born in Bennington in 1824. He is a farmer, and located in town in 1844. Was educated at the district school. Was a member of the house in 1874. Has held a number of town offices. P. O. address, North Pownal.

MERRITT M. HOUGHTON, *Readsboro*, liberal democrat, was born in Readsboro, April 15, 1832. He is a merchant. Has been town clerk and treasurer, for the last seventeen years, and post-master for the last twenty years, and was a member of the house in 1874, '76, serving on the land tax committee. Religious preference, Univ.

WILLIAM ROOT, *Rupert*, republican, was born in Hebron, Washington county, N. Y., in 1818. He is a farmer, and located in town in 1850. Was educated at Granville (N.Y.) Academy. P. O. address, East Rupert.

JOHN F. BARBER, *Sandgate*, republican, was born in Sandgate, March 2, 1842. He is a farmer and manufacturer of lumber. Was educated at the common schools. Has held a number of town offices. Religious preference, Methodist.

ALLEN E. BRIGGS, *Searsburgh*, democrat, was born in Stamford, July 27, 1836. He is a farmer and lumberman, and located in town in 1852. Was educated at the common schools. Was a member of Co. F, 16th reg't Vt. Vols., and of the constitutional convention in 1870. Has held the office of selectman for six years. Religious preference, Universalist.

JOEL HARRINGTON, *Shaftsbury*, republican, was born in Shaftsbury in 1823. He is a farmer. Was selectman in 1868.

PATRICK MORRISSEY, *Stamford*, democrat, was born in Ireland, March 17, 1839. He is a farmer, and located in town in 1861. Was a member of the first Vt. Cav. Has held the usual town offices. Was a member of the house in 1876, and is deputy sheriff. Religious preference, Roman Catholic.

WINFIELD S. HOLT, *Sunderland*, republican, was born in Sunderland in 1852. He is a farmer and lumberman. Was educated at the common schools.

BAINBRIDGE C. BENSON, *Winhall*, republican, was born in Winhall, April, 1836. He is a farmer. Was educated at the common schools. Has held the office of lister several times, and is constable and collector. Religious preference, Universalist. P. O. address, Bondville.

DANIEL W. GLEASON, *Woodford*, democrat, was born in Whitingham, Jan. 19, 1832. He is an accountant, and located in town in 1833. Was educated at the common schools. Has held the office of constable and collector several years. Religious preference, Universalist.

CALEDONIA COUNTY.

WILLIAM E. PECK, *Barnet*, democrat, was born in Barnet, March 24, 1833. He is a farmer. Was educated at St. Johnsbury academy. Has been repeatedly elected to the more responsible town offices, but has always declined their acceptance. Has held the office of postmaster seven years. Religious preference, Baptist. P. O. address, Passumpsic.

DANIEL S. TOWNSHEND, *Burke*, republican, was born in Reading, Nov. 19, 1814. He is a merchant, and manufacturer of starch, and located in town in 1844. Was educated at the common schools. Has held the office of lister some six or eight years, and is one of the selectmen. Religious preference, Methodist. P. O. address, West Burke.

GEORGE E. EATON, *Danville*, democrat, was born in Danville, April 5, 1846. He is a newpaper publisher, and represented the town in 1876, serving on the committee on education.

GROTON—not represented.

ALDEN EDSON JUDEVINE, *Hardwick*, republican, was born in Concord, Aug. 4, 1811. He is a merchant, and farmer, and located in town in 1839. Received a liberal academical education. Was a member of the constitutional conventions of 1850, 1857, and 1870; represented Hardwick in the general assembly of 1853 and '54; was a senator from Caledonia county in 1860 and '61. Held the office of deputy sheriff and constable in Concord. Was elected assistant judge of the county court of Caledonia county in 1850 and '51; county commissioner in 1854. Has been repeatedly honored by election to the various town offices, holding the more important ones for a term of years, and has held the office of postmaster for twenty-three years. Religious preference, Liberal.

MERRITT S. PARKER, *Kirby*, republican, was born in Lyman, N. H., July 21, 1842. He is a farmer, and located in town in 1844. Was educated at the common schools. Was a sergeant of Co. A, 10th reg't Vt. Vols., and was detailed as color bearer. P. O. address, East St. Johnsbury.

BENJAMIN FRANKLIN LINCOLN, *Lyndon*, republican, was born in Wareham, Mass., Sept. 4, 1831. He is treasurer of the Lyndon Mill Co., and located in town in 1862. He has held various town offices, and was a member of the house in 1876, serving on the committee on the state prison. Religious preference, Congregationalist.

ALMON SMITH, *Newark*, democrat, was born in Hinsdale, N. H., June 21, 1808. In early life was a successful teacher of vocal music, but is now a farmer, and located in town in 1875. Was educated at the common schools. Has held a great variety of town offices, both in Brighton and Newark. P. O. address, East Newark.

ISAAC N. WATTS, *Peacham*, republican, was born in Peacham, Aug. 16, 1842. He is a farmer. Was sergeant of Co. M, of the 11th reg't Vt. Vols. He has held the usual town offices, and was a member of the house in 1876, serving on the committee on agriculture. Religious preference, Congregationalist.

HENRY MCCOLE, *Ryegate*, republican, was born in Ryegate, Dec. 26, 1842. He is a farmer. Was sergeant of Co. H, 4th reg't Vt. Vols. P. O. address, McIndoes Falls.

CHARLES INGALLS, *Sheffield*, democrat, was born in Sheffield in 1834. He is a farmer. Was educated at the common schools. Has held the office of selectman for a number of years, and has held a number of other town offices. Religious preference, Baptist.

LUKE POTTER POLAND, *St. Johnsbury*, republican, was born in Westford, Nov. 1, 1815. Judge Poland acquired his early education at the common schools mostly, never attending an academy but one term and part of another in his life. He read law, and at the age of twenty-one was admitted to the bar of Lamoille county on the first day the court was ever held in that county. He located and commenced the practice of law in Morrisville, held various town and county offices; was elected fifth associate justice of the supreme court in 1848, and with the establishment of a circuit court in 1850 was elected one of the judges thereof, which position he occupied continuously till the re-establishment of the supreme court in 1857, when he was elected second associate justice, and in 1860 succeeded to the chief justiceship of that court, which position he occupied till 1865, when he was appointed by Gov. Dillingham an United States senator, to fill the vacancy occasioned by the death of the Hon. Jacob Collamer. At the session of the legislature in 1866, he was elected to serve the remainder of that term, which ended March 4, 1867. He was elected to the 40th, 41st, 42d and 43d congresses from the second district of Vermont. In 1850 he removed from Morrisville to St. Johnsbury, and since his retirement from congress has resumed an extensive practice of law, combining with it the duties of president of the First National Bank in that place. Religious preference, Congregationalist.

ALBION L. WEED, *Stannard*, republican, was born in Stannard, July, 1848. He is a farmer. Was educated at the common schools. Has held the office of selectman, constable, overseer and lister since 1870.

ALBERT HOUGHTON BALL, *Sutton*, republican, was born in Sutton, Dec. 9, 1835. He is a farmer. Was educated at the district school. Has held the office of selectman since 1871. Religious preference, Freewill Baptist.

WILLIAM HENRY HARRISON DAVIS, *Walden*, republican, was born in Montpelier, Dec. 20, 1839. He is a farmer, and located in town in 1869. He was a member of the 6th Mass. Vols., and represented Walden in 1876.

CHARLES ROSS, *Waterford*, republican, was born in Waterford, Sept. 3, 1838. He is a farmer. Was educated at

St. Johnsbury Academy. Was a corporal of Co. A, 11th reg't Vt. Vols., promoted sergeant 1864, and commissioned as second lieutenant May 23, 1865. Has been lister and superintendent. Religious preference, Congregationalist. P. O. address, Lower Waterford.

CHARLES ROGERS, *Wheelock*, republican, was born in Alton, N. H., Aug. 28, 1823. He is a farmer, and located in town in 1829. Was a member of the general assembly from Wheelock in 1852, '54, '61, '62, and a senator from Caledonia county in 1872 and '74. Was assistant judge of the county court in 1868 and '69; has held the usual town offices for many years, and is one of the trustees of the Vt. reform school, having been elected to that office in 1874. Religious preference, Methodist.

CHITTENDEN COUNTY.

WALTER H. WHITE, *Bolton*, democrat, was born in Wallingford, March 8, 1823. He is a farmer, and located in town in 1860. Was educated at the public schools. Has held the office of selectman and overseer. P. O. address, North Duxbury.

BRADLEY B. SMALLEY, *Burlington*, democrat, (see biography with federal officers.)

HENRY THORP, *Charlotte*, republican, was born in Charlotte, Dec. 20, 1825. He is a farmer. Was educated at the district school. Held the office of selectman in 1869 and '70. P. O. address, West Charlotte.

JOSIAH O. CRAMTON, *Colchester*, democrat, was born in Berkshire, July 7, 1839. He is a physician, and located in town in 1870. Was educated at Fairfax Institute, and graduated in medicine at the Bellevue Medical College, New York city, in 1862. Dr. Cramton represented the town of Fairfield in the legislature of 1865 and '66. Has been town superintendent for five years. Religious preference, Episcopalian. P. O. address, Winooski.

MARCELLUS A. BINGHAM, *Essex*, republican, was born in Fletcher, Feb. 21, 1846. He read law; was admitted to the bar of Lamoille county in 1868, practiced his profession at Cambridge and Hydepark till August, 1873, when he located in Essex. He held the office of state's attorney of Lamoille county in 1869, '70 and '71. P. O. address, Essex Junction.

FREDERICK MAECK, *Hinesburgh*, republican, was born in Shelburne, Feb. 14, 1840. He is a farmer, and located in town in 1859. Was educated at the common schools. Has held the office of lister, auditor, and is selectman. Religious preference, Congregationalist.

HENRY R. NORTON, *Huntington*, republican, was born in Huntington, Dec. 21, 1834. He is a farmer. Was educated at the common schools. Has held the office of justice of the peace since 1868. Has held a number of minor offices. Religious preference, Freewill Baptist. P. O. address, Huntington Centre.

JESSE GLOYD, *Jericho*, republican, was born in Jericho, July 21, 1832. He is a farmer. Was educated at the common schools. Religious preference, Universalist. P. O. address, Jericho Centre.

ELI T. HOLBROOK, *Milton*, republican, was born in Milton, Oct. 16, 1832. He is a mechanic and farmer. Received a liberal academical education. Was a member of the Constitutional convention in 1870, and held the office of assistant assessor of internal revenue in 1864, '65 and '66. Has held a number of town offices.

GEORGE A. EDWARDS, *Richmond*, republican, was born in Richmond, June 25, 1844. He is a farmer, and was educated at the common schools and Williston Academy. Was a private of Co. A, 1st Vt. Cav., promoted successively to corporal and sergeant, serving three years. Religious preference, Universalist.

EDGAR NASH, *Shelburne*, republican, was born in Shelburne, March 31, 1831. He is a farmer. Was educated at the common schools. Was a private in Co. C, 12th reg't Vt. Vols. Has held town offices from highway surveyor to selectman during the last twenty years. Religious preference, Unitarian.

CHESTER H. STEELE, *South Burlington*, republican, was born in Hinesburgh in 1830. He is a farmer, and located in town in 1866. Was educated at the Hinesburgh Academy. Has held the office of lister in So. Burlington. Religious preference, Congregationalist. P. O. address, Burlington.

MITCHELL W. HINSDILL, *St. George*, republican, was born in St. George, April, 1845. He is a farmer. Was a member of Co. K, 17th reg't Vt. Vols. Has held the office of constable and collector since March, 1877.

JOHN J. MONAHAN, *Underhill*, democrat, was born in Rutland, May 6, 1843. He is a lawyer, and located in town in 1873. Was educated at the common school, Rutland, and Barre Academy. Has held offices of trust in Burlington and Underhill, and is town clerk. Religious preference, Roman Catholic.

JOHN ALLEN, *Westford*, republican, was born in Westford, Oct. 15, 1840. He is a farmer. Was educated at the district schools. Was elected selectman in 1876, '77 and '78. Religious preference, Congregationalist.

JONATHAN R. TALCOTT, *Williston*, republican, was born in Williston, May 3, 1844. He is a merchant. Was educated at the common schools and academy, and is postmaster. Religious preference, Universalist. P. O. address, North Williston.

ESSEX COUNTY.

MILTON COOK, *Bloomfield*, republican, was born in Compton, N. H., March 4, 1822. He is a farmer, and located in town in 1843. Was educated at the district schools. Has held the office of assistant judge of Essex county; justice of the peace for the last ten years; was town treasurer from 1861 to 1869, from 1870 to 1874, and from 1876 to the present time, and is one of the selectmen. Religious preference, Methodist.

ASA B. GARLAND, *Brighton*, republican, was born in Newfield, Me., Feb. 11, 1823. He is a railroad conductor, and located in town in 1853. Religious preference, Congregationalist. P. O. address, Island Pond.

JAMES M. GILKEY, *Brunswick*, democrat, was born in Columbia, N. H., in 1845. He is a farmer and dealer in lumber, and located in town in 1871. Was educated at the common schools. Has held the office of treasurer and surveyor and is selectman. P. O. address, North Stratford, N. H.

GEORGE HILLIARD, *Canaan*, democrat, was born in Colebrook, N. H., in 1844. He is a lumberman, farmer and broker, and located in town in 1876. Was educated at the common schools. Religious preference, Spiritualist.

WILLARD CHASE, *Concord*, republican, was born in Landgrove, March 10, 1840. He is a farmer, and located in town in 1842. Was educated at the common schools. Was a lieutenant of Co. C. Third reg't, Vt. Vols. Has held the office of selectman, lister, overseer, and has been repeatedly honored wifh various offices of trust. Religious preference, Universalist. P. O. address, West Concord.

NOAH S. POWERS, *East Haven*, republican, was born in Athens, in 1831. He is a farmer, and located in town in 1846. Was educated at the common schools. Was a member of Co. A. Tenth reg't Vt. Vols. Is justice of the peace and selectman. Religious preference, Freewill Baptist.

ETHAN P. SHORES, *Granby*, republican, was born in Victory, Feb. 7, 1842. He is a lumber manufacturer, and located in town in 1851. Was a member of the 8th reg't Vt. Vols. He has been selectman, and in 1876 was a member of the house, serving on the committee on manufactures. Religious preference, Congregationalist.

WILLIAM H. HARTSHORN, *Guildhall*, republican, was born in Lunenburgh, Feb. 10, 1819. He read law and was admitted to the bar, but by reason of other business, never practised his profession. Was educated at the common schools and academy, and located in Guildhall in 1842. Was an officer of the house in 1846, '47 and 48; was a senator from Essex county in '54 and '55; assistant clerk of the house in 1857, and a member from Guildhall in 1858 and '59. Was county clerk from 1848 to '63. Was elected town clerk in 1863, which office he now holds; was appointed postmaster in 1862, a member of the constitutional convention of 1870. Has been honored with various town and county offices, and has been judge of probate for the district of Essex since 1866. Religious preference, Congregation't.

WILLIAM H. SIMS, *Lemington*, republican, was born in Lemington, Oct. 20, 1822. He is a farmer. Was educated at the common schools. Was a member of the general assembly from Lemington in 1864 and '65. Religious preference, Methodist. P. O. address, Columbia, N. H.

CHESTER THOMAS, *Lunenburgh*, republican, was born in Lunenburgh, Aug. 5, 1824. He is a farmer. Was educated at the common schools and one term in academy. Has held the office of justice of the peace. Religious preference, Baptist.

FREEDOM D. BEEDE, *Maidstone*, democrat, was born in Lyndon, Feb. 20, 1829. He is a farmer, and located in town in 1873. Was educated at the common schools and Lyndon Academy. Was a member of the police department (chief) of Lancaster, N. H., from 1867 to 1873. Was selectman in Maidstone in 1876 and '77. Religious preference, Methodist. P. O. address, Guildhall.

CHARLES DAMON, *Victory*, independent, was born in Kirby, Jan. 9, 1824. He is a farmer, and located in town in 1874. Was educated at the public schools. Has held offices of honor and trust both in Canada and the States.

FRANKLIN COUNTY.

ELISHA H. BEALS, *Bakersfield*, democrat, was born in Fairfield, Jan. 20, 1824. He is a hotel keeper, and located in town in 1854. Was educated at the common schools.

Has held many offices of position and trust at the hands of his fellow townsmen. Religious preference, Universalist.

DANIEL MOREN, *Berkshire*, democrat, was born in Ireland, June 15, 1825. He is a merchant, and located in town in 1831. Was educated at the common schools. Has held the office of constable, selectman, lister, and justice of the peace. P. O. address, East Berkshire.

JOHN G. JENNE, *Enosburgh*, National Greenback Labor, was born in Berkshire, July 14, 1833. He is a hardware merchant, and located in town in 1867. Was educated at the common schools. Has held the office of selectman, and is justice of the peace. Religious preference, Universalist. P. O. address, Enosburgh Falls.

GARDNER G. ORTON, *Fairfax*, republican, was born in Fairfax, Dec. 14, 1840. He is a farmer, and was educated at the common schools. Religious preference, Baptist. P. O. address, No. Fairfax.

THOMAS B. KENNEDY, *Fairfield*, democrat, was born in Milton, Aug. 2, 1840. He located in town in 1869, commencing business as a merchant, but for the last few years has devoted his time to agricultural pursuits. Was educated at the common schools and academy. Was captain of Co. K, 6th reg't Vt. Vols. Was a member of the general assembly from Fairfield in 1874; has held the offices of selectman, constable and collector, and superintendent of schools. Religious preference, Roman Catholic.

SIDNEY B. BEARDSLEY, *Fletcher*, democrat, was born in China, N. Y., May 28, 1836. He is a farmer, and located in town in 1846. Was educated at the public schools in Fletcher. Religious preference, Universalist. P. O. address, Fairfax.

CARMI L. MARSH, *Franklin*, republican, was born in Franklin, Aug. 4, 1842. He is a farmer. Was educated at the common schools and academy. Was second lieutenant of Co. K, 13th reg't Vt. Vols. P. O. address, E. Franklin.

EPHRAIM MILLS, *Georgia*, republican, was born in Essex, July 2, 1826. He is a farmer, and located in town in 1855. Was educated at the district schools. Has held the office of lister, and is a justice of the peace and selectman. Religious preference, Methodist. P. O. address, Georgia Plains.

OWEN E. SHERIDAN, *Highgate*, democrat, was born in Highgate in 1832. He is engaged in the foundry business. Was educated at the common schools. Has held the office of selectman, and is constable and collector, and town agent. Religious preference, liberal. P. O. address, Highgate Centre.

ALBERT T. KINGSLEY, *Montgomery*, republican, was born in Montgomery, March 14, 1841. He is a farmer. Was educated at the district schools. Was sergeant of Co. G, 13th reg't Vt. Vols. Has held the office of justice of the peace.

WILLIAM C. BROWN, *Richford*, democrat, was born in Richford, May 26, 1825. He is a farmer. Was educated at the common schools. Was a member of the general assembly from Richford in 1869 and '70. Has been lister, overseer, and is selectman. Religious preference, Methodist.

JOHN A. POTTER, *Sheldon*, republican, was born in Sheldon, April 7, 1829. He is a farmer. Was educated at the common schools and Bakersfield Academy. Is selectman. Religious preference, Methodist. P. O. address, North Sheldon.

EDWARD G. GREENE, *St. Albans*, democrat, was born in St. Albans, May 10, 1834. He is a merchant. Was educated in the schools of St. Albans. Has held the office of selectman since 1877. Religious preference, Liberal.

EDGAR NELSON BULLARD, *Swanton*, democrat, was born in Swanton, March 8, 1837. He is a farmer. Was educated at Swanton Academy. Was commissioned captain of Co. F, 7th reg't Vt. Vols., and promoted major of the regiment, June 29, 1865. Religious preference, Episcopalian.

GRAND ISLE COUNTY.

HENRY MOTT, *Alburgh*, republican, was born in Alburgh, June 7, 1837. He is a farmer and speculator. Was educated at the public schools. Religious preference, Protestant.

WILLIAM C. MCGOWAN, *Grand Isle*, independent, was born in Grand Isle, May 12, 1825. He is a farmer.

JOHN D. BOWMAN, *Isle La Motte*, democrat, was born in Isle La Motte, Sept. 3, 1837. He is a farmer. Was educated at the district schools. Was a sergeant of Co. H. 3d reg't Vt. Vols. Has held the office of selectman, constable, and minor town offices and is justice of the peace. Religious preference, Liberal.

DAVID DODDS, *North Hero*, democrat, was born in Renfrewshire, Scotland, in 1828. He is a farmer, and located in town in 1848. Was educated at the public schools in Paisley, Scotland. Was constable and collector from 1870 to 1876. Religious preference, Presbyterian.

EDWARD WHITE, *South Hero*, democrat, was born in St. Luke, Canada, in 1835. He is a farmer and mechanic, and located in town in 1850. Was educated at the common schools. Religious preference, Roman Catholic.

LAMOILLE COUNTY.

WILLIAM WINTHROP, *Belvidere*, democrat and greenback, was born in Carrickfergus, County Antrim, Ireland. He is a farmer, and located in town in 1848. Was educated at the common schools. Has held the office of overseer, and is first selectman. Religious preference, Presbyterian.

WILLIAM MELENDY, *Cambridge*, greenback, was born in Sterling, Dec. 29, 1819. He is a farmer, and located in town in 1845. Was educated at the common schools. Has held the office of selectman and justice of the peace. In religious tenets, Mr. Melendy holds to the precepts and practice of the Good Samaritan. P. O. address, Jeffersonville.

BAILEY WILLARD FULLER, *Eden*, greenback, was born in Cambridge, Jan. 21, 1845. He is a farmer, and located in town in 1864. Is selectman, and was a member of the general assembly from Eden in 1876, serving on the committee on mileage and debentures.

NORMAN CAMP, *Elmore*, republican, was born in Elmore, Dec. 28, 1830. He is a harness maker. Held the office of sheriff of Lamoille county from 1872 to 1874. Was elected town clerk in 1868, and treasurer in 1869, and still holds those offices. Religious preference, Methodist.

SAMUEL CINNAMON, *Hydepark*, republican, was born in Armagh, Ireland, Nov. 20, 1825. He is a farmer, and located in town in 1858. Was educated at the common schools in Fairfax and Westford. Has held the office of first constable, lister, justice of the peace, and other minor offices. Religious preference, Congregationalist. P. O. address, No. Hydepark.

HEMAN ALLEN WATERMAN, *Johnson*, republican, was born in Johnson in 1830. He is a farmer, receiving his education at the common school and academy. Was a member of the state board of equalization in 1874, and was assistant assessor of internal revenue from 1862 to '67, and deputy collector from 1863 to 1867. Has held the office of justice, lister, selectman, town clerk, and other town offices. Religious preference, Congregationalist.

SYLVESTER N. PALMER, *Morristown*, republican, was born in Elmore, Jan. 6, 1831. He is a farmer, and located in town in 1832. Was educated at the common schools. Has held the office of lister, and has been one of the selectmen since 1875. Religious preference, Congregationalist. P. O. address, Morrisville.

RICHARD R. WAITE, *Stowe*, greenback, was born in Windsor, June 3, 1819. He is a farmer, and located in town in 1842. Was educated at the common schools. Has held the office of constable, selectman, and deputy sheriff. Religious preference, Liberal.

VARNUS P. LOCKE, *Waterville*, republican, was born in Waterville, Jan. 4, 1844. He is a farmer. Was educated at the district schools. Has held the office of superintendent, deputy sheriff, and is constable and collector of taxes, having held the office for seven years. Religious preference, Congregationalist.

ASA M. HARRIMAN, *Wolcott*, republican, was born in Craftsbury, Dec. 19, 1837. He is a farmer, and located in town in 1876. Was educated at the public schools. Religious preference, Methodist. P. O. address, North Wolcott.

ORANGE COUNTY.

JOSEPH W. BLISS, *Bradford*, democrat, was born in Bradford, Jan. 31, 1824. He is a farmer. Is selectman. Was lister several years, and was a member of the general assembly in 1874 and 1876, serving on the general committee.

GEORGE LEVI SPEAR, *Braintree*, democrat, was born in Braintree, April 22, 1842. He is a lumber manufacturer, and represented the town in 1876. Religious preference, Liberal. P. O. address, West Braintree.

BROOKFIELD—not represented.

ALVAH W. WHITNEY, *Chelsea*, republican, was born in Chelsea, Dec. 16, 1832. He is a flour and grain dealer. Was educated at the common schools. Was a selectman in 1867 and '68. Religious preference, Congregationalist.

CALEB C. SARGENT, *Corinth*, republican, was born in Candia, N. H., Dec. 24, 1835. He is a merchant, and located in town in 1860. Was educated at Dartmouth, graduating in the class of 1860. Was a member of the constitutional convention in 1870, and has held the office of town superintendent for ten years; of postmaster since 1867; of justice since 1871, and selectman since 1872. Religious preference, Congregationalist.

WILLIAM H. GILMORE, *Fairlee*, republican, was born in Fairlee, Oct. 17, 1839. He is a farmer. Was educated at the common school and academy. Was quartermaster sergeant of the 8th reg't Vt. Vols., and served as quartermaster of the 7th reg't Vt. Militia. Has been town treasurer, and is now treasurer of the Orange county agricultural association. Religious preference, Episcopalian.

LEVI L. TUCKER, *Newbury*, republican, was born in Newbury in 1815. He is a mason. Has held the office of selectman a number of years, and has been a justice since 1858. Religious preference, Christian. P. O. address, West Newbury.

HOMER DENNISON CAMP, *Orange*, republican, was born in Orange in 1847. He is a farmer. Was educated at Newbury Seminary. Has held the office of selectman since 1876. Religious preference, Universalist.

JOHN BUSWELL, *Randolph*, republican, was born in Randolph, Dec. 29. 1810. He is a farmer. Was educated at the common, and Orange county grammar school. Has held the office of justice of the peace for many years, and has held a number of town offices. Religious preference, Congregationalist. P. O. address, East Randolph.

BENJAMIN F. JEFFERSON, *Strafford*, republican, was born in Parishville, N. Y., Sept. 21, 1845. He is a clergyman, and located in town in 1876. Was educated at Potsdam, N. Y. Religious preference, Freewill Baptist. P. O. address, So. Strafford.

CYREL M. EMERSON, *Thetford*, republican, was born in Thetford, March 21, 1817. He is a farmer, and was educated at the common schools. Has held the office of lister, and is one of the board of selectmen. Religious preference, Congregationalist. P. O. address, East Thetford.

TOPSHAM—not represented.

JAMES L. FARNHAM, *Tunbridge*, republican, was born in Tunbridge in 1836. He is a farmer. Was first lieutenant of Co. D, 12th reg't Vt. Vols. Religious preference, Congregationalist.

GEORGE N. DERBY, *Vershire*, republican, was born in Vershire, Sept. 25, 1841. He is a farmer. Was educated at the common schools and Corinth Academy. Has held the office of selectman, lister, and is justice of the peace. Religious preference, Congregationalist.

WARREN HUNTINGTON, *Washington*, republican, was born in Washington, Sept. 1, 1817. He is a farmer, and was educated at the common schools. Has held the office of justice, selectman, and lister. Religious preference, Universalist.

ELY ELY-GODDARD, *West Fairlee*, independent, was born in the city of New York in 1855. He is not at present engaged in any business. He located in West Fairlee in 1876. Was educated at the institutions of learning in Europe, graduating at Ecole des Sciences Diplomatique, Paris. Religious preference, Roman Catholic. P. O. address, Ely, Vt.

AARON S. MARTIN, *Williamstown*, republican, was born in Williamstown, Nov. 16, 1817. He is a farmer, and was educated at the common schools. He was selectman in 1868, '77 and '78, and justice of the peace in 1874 and '76. Religious preference, Methodist.

ORLEANS COUNTY.

ENOCH C. ROWELL, *Albany*, republican, was born in Plainfield, N. H., October 18, 1835. He is a farmer, and located in town in 1850. Has held a number of military offices in the militia of Vermont. Religious preference, Methodist. P. O. address, East Albany.

IRA D. R. COLLINS, *Barton*, republican, was born in Corinth, Aug. 20, 1831. Previous to 1873, he was a farmer, and had charge of the agricultural department of the Newport Standard, and afterwards of the Monitor. In 1873 he located in Barton, and entered into mercantile pursuits, in which business he is still engaged. He received a liberal academical education. Was a member of the general assembly from the town of Wolcott in 1863 and '64. Has held a number of town offices, both in Wolcott and Craftsbury. Religious preference, Congregationalist. P. O. address, Barton Landing.

GILBERT J. GROSS, *Brownington*, republican, was born in Brownington, Oct. 21, 1844. He is a farmer, and was educated at the district school and academy. Has held the office of lister and first constable, and is selectman.

CHARLES SHERMAN HINMAN, *Charleston*, republican, was born in Derby, Feb. 19, 1846. He is a physician, and located in town in 1871. Is a graduate of the medical department of Dartmouth College, class of 1874. Was a member of the house in 1876, serving on the committee on corporations. Has been superintendent since 1872. Religious preference, Congregationalist. P.O. address, West Charleston.

JOSEPH SOUTHER KIDDER, *Coventry*, republican, was born in Irasburgh, Oct. 20, 1810. He is a farmer, and located in town in 1843. Has held the office of justice, overseer, and lister. Religious preference, Unitarian,

WILLARD W. MILES, *Craftsbury*, republican, was born in Albany, Feb. 6, 1845. He is a lawyer, and located in town in 1873. Was educated in Canada. Was a member of the general assembly from Albany in 1872. Has held the office of superintendent of schools in Albany and in Craftsbury, and was elected town clerk in 1875, which office he now holds. Religious preference, Congregationalist. P. O. address, No. Craftsbury.

BENJAMIN HINMAN, *Derby*, republican, was born in Derby, Aug. 22, 1849. He is a farmer and surveyor. Received an academical education. Has held the office of lister, overseer, and is secretary of the corporation, Derby Academy. He is a grandson of Benjamin Hinman, one of the earliest residents of Derby, and its representative for eight years. P. O. address, Derby Centre.

WILBUR FISK TEMPLETON, *Glover*, republican, was born in Tilton, N. H., Feb. 9, 1836. He is a physician, graduated at the Eclectic Medical College of Pennsylvania in 1857. Served as surgeon on detached service in the civil war. Was a member of the general assembly from Glover in 1876, serving on the committee on public buildings. Religious preference, Rationalist.

WILLIAM W. GOSS, *Greensboro'*, republican, was born in Hardwick, Aug. 4, 1836. He is a mechanic, and located in town in 1859. Has held the office of justice since 1858, and of town clerk since 1870. Religious preference, Congregationalist.

LEMUEL RANKIN TABOR, *Holland*, democrat, was born in Barton, Feb. 6, 1826. He is a farmer, and located in town in 1828. Was educated at the district schools. Has held the office of selectman, and has often officiated in minor town capacities. Religious preference, Methodist.

ZUAR ELDRIDGE JAMESON, *Irasburgh*, republican, was born in Irasburgh, Jan 5, 1835. He is a farmer, occupying the farm on which he was born. Was educated at the common school and academy. Was a member of the Vt. Board of Agriculture from 1870 to 1874 inclusive. Has held the office of justice, and has been superintendent. Religious preference, Methodist.

HARRISON C. SISCO, *Jay*, greenback democrat, was born in Westfield, Aug. 22, 1823. He is a clergyman, and located in town in early life. Was educated at the common schools. Has held a number of town offices. Religious preference, Christian. P. O. address, No. Troy.

DON EUGENE CURTIS, *Lowell*, republican, was born in Lowell, May 3, 1849. He is a merchant, and was a member of the general assembly from Lowell in 1876, serving on the general committee. Religious preference, Congregationalist.

MATTHEW WHITEHILL, *Morgan*, republican, was born in Ryegate in 1837. He is a farmer, and located in town in 1858. Was educated at the common schools. Was a private in Co. E, 15th reg't Vt. Vols, and now holds the offices of selectman, justice of the peace, and grand juror. Religious preference, Congregationalist. P. O. address, Island Pond.

DAVID M. CAMP, *Newport*, republican, was born in Derby, Dec. 11, 1836. He is an editor, and located in town in 1866. Was educated at the academies of Derby and St. Johnsbury. Was assistant clerk of the house in 1868, and held the office of clerk of the house from 1869 to 1876. Was a member of the constitutional convention of 1870. Has held at different times the offices of selectman, constable, superintendent, and for a term of years was a member of the state board of education. Religious preference, Congregationalist.

GEORGE W. WILSON, *Salem*, democrat, was born in Salem, Aug. 25, 1833. He is a farmer, and was educated at the common schools. Has held the office of selectman, lister, and justice of the peace repeatedly. Religious preference, Freewill Baptist. P. O. address, West Charleston.

JOHN W. CURRIER, *Troy*, democrat greenback, was born in Troy, April 5, 1836. He is a lumber manufacturer, and permanently located in town in 1870. Was sergeant of Co. F. 10th reg't. Mass. Vols., transferred to the 1st Eastern Va. brigade, and commissioned first lieutenant and adjutant. Was a member of the house in 1874. P. O. address, North Troy.

JOHN H. BUCK, *Westfield*, republican, was born in Westford, June 22, 1831. He is a merchant, and located in town in 1861. Was educated at the district schools. Has held the office of postmaster, treasurer, and lister. Religious preference, Unitarian.

WENDELL SILSBY, *Westmore*, republican, was born in Lunenburgh, March 28, 1846. He is a farmer and manufacturer of lumber, and located in town in 1854. Was educated at district schools. Was a private in Co. B. 11th reg't Vt. Vols. Has held the office of lister for the last two years. P. O. address, West Burke.

RUTLAND COUNTY.

ROLLIN E. BROWN, *Benson*, republican, was born in Benson, Dec. 27, 1838. He is a farmer. Was educated at the common school and academy. Has held the office of selectman and is justice, lister, town treasurer, and grand juror. Religious preference, Congregationalist.

NATHAN TURNER SPRAGUE, *Brandon*, republican, was born in Mount Holly, June 22, 1828. He is a farmer and banker.

and located in town in 1833. Was educated at the common school and academy. Was a senator from Rutland county in 1872, and represented Brandon in the general assembly of 1876, serving as chairman of the joint committee on the reform school, and was also a member of the committee of ways and means. Religious preference, Baptist.

JOHN HOWE, *Castleton*, republican, was born in Castleton, Oct. 18, 1833. In 1868 he went to Florida, and there resided till 1877, when he resumed his residence in Castleton. He is a lawyer. Was educated at Middlebury, graduating in the class of 1852. Was second lieutenant of Co. B, 2d reg't Vt. Vols. Was a member of the general assembly from Castleton in 1867. Was register of probate, district of Fair Haven, from 1861 to 1864, and was assessor of internal revenue and county supt. of schools during a part of his residence in Florida. Religious preference, Congregationalist.

CHARLES REED HOLDEN, *Chittenden*, republican, was born in Mount Holly, June 3, 1840. He is a manufacturer of and dealer in lumber, and located in town in 1868. Was educated at the district school and Springfield Wesleyan Seminary. P. O. address, Pittsford.

EDWIN CONGDON, *Clarendon*, republican, was born in Clarendon, June 15, 1833. He is a farmer. Was educated at the district school and academy. Was a lister in 1871 and '72, constable from 1859 to 1862, and has held the office of town clerk since 1873. Religious preference, Universalist.

EDWARD J. READ, *Danby*, republican, was born in Danby, Sept. 19, 1835. He was formerly a farmer, but for the past two years has been engaged in the mercantile business. Held the office of selectman in 1871, '72 and '73.

GEORGE M. FULLER, *Fair Haven*, republican, was born in Pittsfield in 1841. He read law, graduated at the Law School of Albany, N. Y., in 1868, and located in town the same year, and is state's attorney of Rutland county. Religious preference, Episcopalian.

ALBERT BRESEE, *Hubbardton*, republican, was born in Hubbardton, April 9, 1822. He is a farmer. Was educated at the district school. Has held the offices of selectman, lister, and justice of the peace.

EBEN B. PERRY, *Ira*, republican, was born in Ira, Aug. 1, 1852. He is a farmer. Was educated at the common and high schools. Has held the office of first constable since 1875. Religious preference, Congregationalist.

HIRAM TEMPLE, *Mendon*, democrat, was born in Mendon in 1834. He is a farmer. Was educated at the common schools. Held the office of selectman in 1877. Religious preference, Universalist.

MILETUS N. PAUL, *Middletown*, republican, was born in Wells, Aug. 14, 1840. He is a farmer, and located in town in

1864. Received a liberal academical education, and has held a number of town offices. Religious preference, Congregationalist.

JUDSON D. S. PACKER, *Mount Holly*, republican, was born in Mount Holly, Sept. 2, 1846. He is a farmer, and was educated at the common schools and academy, and is first constable.

JAMES DOUGAN, *Mount Tabor*, republican, was born in Athol, Warren county, N. Y., in 1850. He is a book-keeper, and located in town in 1875. Was educated at the common schools.

FAYETTE POTTER, *Pawlet*, republican, was born in Pawlet, Sept. 1, 1823. He is a lawyer. Was a graduate of Union College, Schenectady, N. Y., class of 1842.

LOREN B. HOUGHTON, *Pittsfield*, republican, was born in Orange, April 1, 1831. He is a farmer, and located in town in 1864. Was educated at the district school-house. Has held the office of constable and collector for the last seven years. Religious preference, Methodist.

ROLLIN S MEACHAM, *Pittsford*, democrat, was born in Brandon, Sept. 25, 1833. He is a merchant, and located in town in 1866. Was educated at the district school. Was a member of the army, serving in the commissary department. Religious preference, Congregationalist.

NELSON C. HYDE, *Poultney*, republican, was born in Poultney, Jan 13, 1829. He is a farmer. Received a liberal academical education. Held the office of lister in 1865 and for many years since and does now. Mr. Hyde was grand chief patriarch of the order of Odd Fellows in 1875, grand master in 1876, and grand representative in 1877. Religious preference, Congregationalist.

LYMAN WILLIAMS REDINGTON, *Rutland*, democrat, was born in Waddington. St. Lawrence Co., N. Y., March 14, 1849. He is a lawyer, and located in town in 1875. Fitted for college at Williston Seminary, Easthampton, Mass.; entered Yale College, but was compelled by poor health to leave at the expiration of the freshman year. Subsequently graduated in the scientific department of Williston Seminary ; traveled in Europe one year ; attended the law school of Columbia College, concluded his professional studies in the office of the Hon. Matt. H. Carpenter, and was admitted to the practice of his profession in 1871, and to the bar of Rutland county in 1874. Has held the office of town grand juror since 1876. Religious preference, Congregationalist.

RICHARD D. ESTABROOK, *Sherburne*, democrat, was born in Sherburne, Dec. 31, 1828. He is a farmer. Was educated at the common schools. Was a member of the general assembly in 1870. Has held the office of selectman for eight years, and has been overseer. Religious preference, Unitarian. P. O. address, No. Sherburne.

NATHANIEL J. ALDRICH, *Shrewsbury*, republican, was born in Shrewsbury, in 1820. He is a manufacturer of and dealer in lumber. Was educated at the common schools and one term in academy. Has held the office of selectman, and has been a justice of the peace for the last eighteen years. Religious preference, Universalist. P. O. address, No. Shrewsbury.

NATHANIEL A. BUCKLIN, *Sudbury*, independent republican, was born in Sudbury, July 5, 1842. He is a farmer, and was educated at the common schools. Was quartermaster sergeant in the 5th reg't Vt. Vols. Has held the usual town offices. Religious preference, Universalist.

ELIAS E. CLARK, *Tinmouth*, republican, was born in Michigan, in 1840 He is a farmer, and located in town in 1847. Was educated in the common and high schools. Was a member of Co. I. 5th Vt. reg't Vt. Vols., was wounded at Savage Station, taken prisoner and confined on Belle Isle. Has held the office of constable and collector for the last five years. Religious preference, Methodist. P. O. address, Wallingford.

CALVIN M. TOWNSEND, *Wallingford*, republican, was born in Hartford, N. Y., March 17, 1824. He is engaged in mercantile pursuits, and located in town in 1874. Was educated at the common schools. Religious preference, Baptist.

HIRAM W. LEWIS, *Wells*, democrat, was born in Wells, April 1831. He is a hotel keeper. Was educated in the district schools. Was lister in 1866, and has held the office of constable and collector for seventeen years. Religious preference, Liberal.

JACOB WILLIAM JAKWAY, *West Haven*, republican, was born in Greenwich, N. Y., March 29, 1824. He is a farmer, and located in town in 1832. Was educated at the common schools. Has held the office of selectman since 1876. Religious preference, Methodist.

WASHINGTON COUNTY.

J. HENRY JACKSON, *Barre*, democrat, was born in Brome, P. Q., April 19, 1844. He is a physician and surgeon, and located in town in 1870. Was educated at Barre Academy, attended medical lectures at the University of Vermont, and McGill University, Montreal. Religious preference, Congregationalist.

JOHN E. BENJAMIN, *Berlin*, republican, was born in Berlin, July 19, 1833. He is a farmer, and was educated at the common schools, and Barre Academy. Has held the office of justice, lister, and grand juror. Religious preference Calvinist. P. O. address, Montpelier.

TRUE A. TOWN, *Cabot*, national greenback, was born in Woodbury, April 13, 1836. He is a mechanic, and located in town in 1866. Was educated at Newbury Seminary. Religous preference, Methodist. P. O. address, Lower Cabot.

BENJAMIN P. WHITE, *Calais*, democrat, was born in Calais, July 11, 1835. He is a merchant. Was educated at the public schools. Has repeatedly held the office of superintendent, selectman, overseer, lister, and constable, and has held a number of minor town offices. Religious preference, Universalist. P. O. address, East Calais.

LYMAN V. TURNER, *Duxbury*, national greenback, was born in Duxbury, Feb. 1, 1825. He is a farmer, and was educated at the district schools. Has held the office of selectman and town grand juror. Religious preference, Spiritualist. P. O. address, Moretown.

AUSTIN TEMPLETON, *East Montpelier*, republican, was born in East Montpelier, Dec. 20, 1833. He is a farmer, and resides in the house where he was born. Was educated at the district schools, and has held town offices.

SETH BOYCE, *Fayston*, greenback, was born in Fayston, Feb. 11, 1832. He is a farmer. Was educated at the common schools. Has held the offices of selectman and trustee. Religious preference, Methodist. P. O. address, No. Fayston.

DAVID M. PERKINS, Marshfield, republican, was born in Plainfield, June 8, 1833. He is a lumber manufacturer, and located in town in 1861. Has received a common school education. Has held the office of lister for two years in his own town. Religious preference, Methodist. Post Office address, Plainfield.

MYRON W. MILES, *Middlesex*, democrat, was born in Middlesex, April 9, 1834. He is a farmer, and was educated at the common schools. Has held the office of first constable and collector since 1874.

HIRAM A. HUSE, *Montpelier*, republican, was born in Randolph, January 17, 1843. He is a lawyer, and located in town in 1872. Was educated at Dartmouth College, graduating in the class of 1865. Was a resident of Wisconsin from 1845 to 1858. In 1862 he enlisted as a private in Co. F, 12th reg't Vt. Vols. In 1873 he was appointed state librarian, to fill the vacancy occasioned by the death of the Hon. Charles Reed. Religious preference, Episcopalian.

GEORGE HOWES, *Moretown*, democrat, was born in Moretown, July 21, 1835. He is a farmer, and was educated at the common schools. Has held the office of constable and collector for the last two years. Religious preference, Universalist.

NORTHFIELD—not represented.

FRANK A. DWINELL, *Plainfield*, republican, was born in Calais, in 1847. He is a merchant, and located in town in 1873. Was educated at the common schools and Barre Academy, and is town clerk and treasurer. Religious preference, Congregationalist.

WILLIAM B. ORCUTT, *Roxbury*, republican, was born in Roxbury, Jan. 15, 1820. He is a farmer, and dealer in lumber. Was educated at the district school. Was a member of the general assembly from Roxbury in 1859, '60. Was elected assistant judge of the county court in 1874, and has held a number of town offices. Religous preference, Congregationalist.

LUCIUS M. TYLER, *Waitsfield*, republican, was born in Fayston, July 27, 1832. He is a dealer in produce and stock, and located in town in 1864. Is first constable, and was a member of the general assembly from Waitsfield in 1876, serving on the committee on highways, bridges and ferries.

SYLVESTER BANISTER, *Warren*, republican, was born in Bethel, in 1831. He is a miller, and located in town in 1859. Was educated at the district schools. Was a member of Co. A. 6th reg't Vt. Vols., promoted corporal, and made commissary sergeant Oct. 16, 1864. Has been lister, town grand juror, and was elected treasurer in 1873, which position he now occupies. Religious preference, Freewill Baptist.

LEANDER H. HAINES, *Waterbury*, republican, was born in Cabot, Nov. 13, 1833. He is a merchant, and located in town in 1862. Was educated at the district schools and Barre Academy. Has held the offices of justice, overseer, and postmaster. Religious preference, Congregationalist.

MARK P. GOODELL, *Woodbury*, independent, was born in Woodbury, Jan. 29, 1844. He is a farmer. Was educated at the public schools. Was a member of the 15th reg't Vt. Vols. P. O. address, So. Woodbury.

AUGUSTUS A. BLISS, *Worcester*, democrat, was born in Cabot, Sept. 10, 1832. He is a hotel keeper, and located in town in 1870. Was educated at the district schools. Has held the office of first constable and collector of taxes since 1876. Religious preference, Universalist.

WINDHAM COUNTY.

OTHNIEL R. EDWARDS, *Athens*, republican, was born in Shelburne, Mass., June 6, 1828. He is a clergyman, and farmer, and located in town in 1865. Was educated at the common school and Springfield Wesleyan Seminary. Religious preference, Methodist.

WILLIAM H. ROCKWELL, *Brattleboro*, republican, was born in Brattleboro, March 3, 1840. He is a physician. Was educated at the public schools of Brattleboro, and Williston Seminary at East Hampton, Mass.; read medicine with his father, the late William H. Rockwell, M. D.; attended lectures at the medical department of the University of Vermont, and the College of Physicians and Surgeons, New York city. Has been superintendent of the Vt. Asylum for the Insane, and is trustee and treasurer of the Asylum, and director and vice president of the Vermont National Bank of Brattleboro. Religious preference, Episcopalian.

SAMUEL B. HIGGINS, *Brookline*, republican, was born in Newfane in 1835. He is a farmer, and located in town in 1865. Was educated at Brattleboro public schools. Was a member of the 1st Wis. (3 mos.) reg't, and served as musician three years in the 16th reg't of Infantry, regular army. Was selectman in 1868 and '69, and is constable and collector. Religious preference, Free Thinker. P. O. address, Fayetteville.

AUGUSTUS FITCH, Jr., *Dover*, republican, was born in Dover, Feb. 1, 1834. He is a farmer. Was educated at the common schools, and was lister in 1865, '66, and '69. Religious preference, Congregationalist. P. O. address, West Dover.

HORACE R. STODDARD, *Dummerston*, republican, was born in Dummerston, April 3, 1834. He is a farmer. Religious preference, Liberal. P. O. address, West Dummerston.

SAMUEL PHELPS, *Grafton*, republican, was born in Grafton, March 27, 1815. He was educated at the common schools, completing his course at Chester Academy, and Burr & Burton Seminary in Manchester. After the age of seventeen he followed teaching for twenty years. In 1840 he located near Augusta, Ga., where he pursued his vocation, and returning in 1850, re-located in Grafton. During the rebellion he was chairman of the board of selectmen. Has repeatedly held the office of superintendent, treasurer, lister and other town offices. Religious preference Congregationalist.

CHARLES E. ALEXANDER, *Guilford*, republican, was born in Chesterfield, N. H., Jan. 10, 1830. He is a farmer, and located in town in 1865. Was educated at Chesterfield Academy. Is constable and collector, justice, and has held the usual town offices. Was the member from Guilford in 1876, serving on the committee on the grand list. Religious preference, Universalist. P. O. address, Brattleboro.

JOSEPH L. HARRINGTON, *Halifax*, republican, was born in Jamaica, Aug. 5, 1840. He is a physician and surgeon, and located in town in 1866. Is a graduate in medicine of the University of Vermont. Was a member of Co. I, 4th reg't, and was subsequently commissioned assistant surgeon of the 1st Vt. heavy artillery. Was a member of the constitutional convention of 1870, and has held many town offices. He has been justice since 1867, and is town clerk and treasurer. Religious preference, Unitarian.

WILLIAM H. H. HOLTON, *Jamaica*, republican, was born in Jamaica, April 23, 1843. He is a manufacturer. Received a liberal academical education. Was second lieutenant in the 8th reg't Vt. Vols. from its organization till he was discharged for disability arising from wounds received in action. Was appointed second lieutenant in Veteran Reserve Corps, Sept. 17, 1863; promoted to first lieutenant, captain by brevet, and major by brevet, to rank as such from March 13, 1865, for gallant and meritorious services, in which rank he served until Jan. 1, 1868; then as Civilian Agent in the "Bureau of Refugees, Freedmen, and Abandoned Lands," stationed at Orangeburg, S. C. Has held a number of town offices. Religious preference, Baptist.

JAMES LOREN MARTIN, *Londonderry*, republican, was born in Landgrove, Sept. 13, 1846. He is an attorney, and located in town in 1869. He was representative from Londonderry in 1864, and re-elected in 1876, serving that year as chairman of the committee on elections, and as a member of the judiciary committee, and was state's attorney for Windham county the same year. Religious preference, Baptist. P. O. address, South Londonderry.

ZENAS H. WHITNEY, *Marlboro'*, Independent, was born in Marlboro', Jan. 12, 1812. He is a farmer. Was educated at the common schools.

JOHN H. MERRIFIELD, *Newfane*, republican, was born in Newfane, June 12, 1847. He is a farmer. Was educated at the common schools and Springfield Wesleyan Seminary. He held the office of engrossing clerk in 1874 and '76; was superintendent of schools in 1870, '71 and '72, and lister in 1873 '74 and '75. Religious preference, Methodist. P. O. address, Williamsville.

WILLIAM ROBERTSON, *Putney*, republican, was born in Hartford, Conn., April 2, 1828. He is a paper manufacturer, and located in town in 1828. Was educated at the common schools. Has held some town offices.

HENRY C. JOHNSON, *Rockingham*, republican, was born in Newfane, April 1, 1840. He is a merchant, and located in town in 1869. Was educated at the district schools and academies of Newfane, Saxtons River, and West Westminster. Was clerk in the Interior dep't at Washington in 1864, '65, and '66, and was mustered as a private by Gen. Augur when Early menaced the city of Washington in 1864. Religious preference, Baptist. P. O. address, Saxtons River.

SOMERSET—not represented.

ANDREW DEXTER KNIGHT, *Stratton*, republican, was born in Marlboro in 1840. He is a farmer, and located in town in 18_9. Was educated at the public schools. Has held the office of lister. P. O. address, West Wardsboro.

OSCAR R. GARFIELD, *Townshend*, republican, was born in Townshend, Aug. 22, 1824. He is a farmer, and was educated at the common schools, at Chester and Saxton's River Academies. Was a member of the house in 1852, '57 and '58. Has held the usual town offices. P. O. address, West Townshend.

ROSWELL S. WOOD, *Vernon*, republican, was born in Vernon, Nov. 23, 1816. He is a farmer. Was educated at the district schools. Was a member of the constitutional convention of 1870. Has held the office of justice of the peace since 1860. Religious preference, Universalist.

AVERY J. DEXTER, *Wardsboro'*, republican, was born in Wardsboro', April 27, 1818. He is a merchant and farmer. Was a member of the general assembly from Wardsboro' in 1858, '59, and in 1864 and '65. Mr Dexter has been a justice of the peace for the last twenty-six years; selectman and town clerk for the last fourteen years.

DAVID C. GORHAM, *Westminster*, republican, was born in Westminster, March 9, 1818. He is a farmer. Was educated at the common schools. Was a member of the house from Westminster in 1851 and '53. Religious preference, Congregationalist. P. O. address, Westminster West.

WELLS P. JONES, *Whitingham*, republican, was born in Dover in 1845. He is a merchant, and located in town in 1870. Was educated at Powers' Institute, Bernardston, Mass., and at Bryant, Stratton & Co.'s Business College, Providence, R. I. Was representative from Whitingham in 1874. Has been justice of the peace for eight years; was superintendent in 1872 and '73; was chairman of the republican county committee from 1876 to 1878, and is town agent. P. O. address, Jacksonville.

WILMINGTON—not represented.

SAMUEL C. WOODBURN, *Windham*, republican, was born in Windham, Feb. 27, 1819. He is a farmer. Was educated at the common schools. Was a member of the board of selectmen during the war, and at different times holding the same position since. Has held the office of lister, and grand juror repeatedly. Religious preference, Congregationalist.

WINDSOR COUNTY.

FREDERICK A. WAY, *Andover*, republican, was born in Lempster, N. H. in 1820. He is a farmer, and located in town in 1863. Was educated at the district schools. Was a member of the house in 1868 and '69. Has held the office of selectman.

ERVIN C. SHERWIN, *Baltimore*, republican, was born in Baltimore, Dec. 23, 1841. He is a farmer, and was educated at the common schools. Has often held the office of selectman, constable, and other town offices. Religious preference, Baptist. P. O. address, North Springfield.

CHARLES W. BLACK, *Barnard*. democrat, was born in Maine in 1815. He is a blacksmith, and located in town in 1853. Was educated at the district schools. Has held the office of justice of the peace, and is selectman. P. O. address, East Barnard.

MARCUS A. MOODY, *Bethel*, republican, was born in Bethel, Feb. 5, 1840. He is a dealer in groceries and provisions. Was educated at the common schools. Was a member of Co. A, 16th reg't Vt. Vols. Religious preference, Universal't.

George E. Smith, *Bridgewater*, democrat, was born in Bridgewater, Jan. 2, 1842. He is a farmer and teacher. Received his education principally at the common schools. Has held the office of superintendent, except one year, since 1865, and town clerk since 1869. Was lister in 1866, '77 and '78. Religious preference, Universalist.

Henry A. Fletcher, *Cavendish*, republican, was born in Cavendish, Dec. 11, 1839. He is a farmer. Was educated at the common schools and academies. Was first sergeant of Co. C, 16th reg't Vt. Vols., promoted to sergeant major, and to second lieutenant of his company, April 2, 1863. Was a member of the house in 1867 and '68. Has held a few town offices. Religious preference, Baptist. P. O. address, Proctorsville.

Nehemiah Adams Edson, *Chester*, republican, was born in Chester, May 30, 1828. He is a farmer, and was educated at the common schools and Chester Academy. Religious preference, Universalist. P. O. address, North Chester.

Noah B. Hazen, *Hartford*, republican, was born in Hartford, April 2, 1841. He is a farmer, and was educated at Dartmouth College, class of 1863. Has held the office of superintendent of schools for nine consecutive years, and for the last two years has been clerk of the board of examination for common school teachers of Windsor county. Religious preference, Congregationalist.

Charles C. Thornton, *Hartland*, republican, was born in Springfield, Nov. 20, 1826. He is a merchant, and located in town in 1871. Is town treasurer, and was representative in 1872 and '76, serving the latter year on the committee of elections. Religious preference, Universalist. P. O. address, Hartland 4 Corners.

Elwin A. Howe, *Ludlow*, republican, was born in Londonderry, Sept. 18, 1843. He is agent and superintendent of the Ludlow Toy Mfg. Co., and located in town in 1869. Was educated at the common schools and West River Academy. Was a private of Co. G, 11th reg't Vt. Vols., promoted corporal Jan , 1864; was first lieutenant Co. I, 108th U. S. C. I.; aide-de-camp to Gen. James Oakes, and captain Co. K, 108th C. I. Was superintendent of schools in Londonderry. Has been constable and collector in Ludlow. Religious preference, Congregationalist.

William E. Lewis, *Norwich*, republican, was born in Norwich, May 25, 1815. He is a farmer, and an alumnus of Norwich University. Was a member of the house in 1856, '57, '63 and '72. Has held the office of town clerk since 1842, was selectman from 1842 to '55; constable and deputy sheriff from 1839 to '65; assistant assessor internal revenue from 1867 to 1871, and is town treasurer. Religious preference, Episcopalian.

ALONZO F. HUBBARD, *Plymouth*, republican, was born in Plymouth, Nov. 28, 1843. He is a farmer and merchant. Was educated at the common schools and Woodstock Academy. Has held the office of justice of the peace for six years. Religious preference, Spiritualist. P. O. address, Tyson Furnace.

WILLIAM CLEMENT WHIPPLE, *Pomfret*, republican, was born in Pomfret, Jan. 7, 1830. He is a farmer. Was educated at the district schools. Was quartermaster sergeant in the 147th Ill. Vols. Has held the office of superintendent, and is justice of the peace. Religious preference, Universalist. P. O. address, North Pomfret.

READING—not represented.

ROCHESTER—not represented.

MARTIN S. ADAMS, *Royalton*, republican, was born in Royalton, March 2, 1835. He is a merchant. Was educated at Royalton Academy. He has been engaged in the mercantile business since 1848, in the towns of Royalton and Northfield, permanently locating in Royalton in 1860. Has held town offices, and positions of trust in various benevolent associations. Religious preference Congregationalist. P. O. address, South Royalton.

LEVI BARTLETT STEELE, *Sharon*, republican, was born in Buxton, Maine, April 28, 1829. He is a clergyman, and located in town in 1874. Was educated at the common schools of Buxton, and at the New Hampton Institute in Fairfax. Has held the office of superintendent of schools in Johnson, Bolton and Sharon. Religious preference, Baptist.

FREDERICK W. PORTER, *Springfield*, republican, was born in Springfield, Oct. 27, 1823. He is a manufacturer. Was educated at Kimball Union Academy, Meriden, N. H. Has held the office of postmaster. Religious preference, Swedenborgian.

NATHAN DAVIS, *Stockbridge*, republican, was born in Pomfret, May 5, 1818. He is a farmer, and located in town in 1822. Was educated at the district schools. Has frequently held two offices and has been justice of the peace for the last twelve years. Religious preference, Methodist. P. O. address, Gaysville.

JUSTUS DARTT, *Weathersfield*, republican, was born in Weathersfield, Feb. 17, 1836. He was formerly a teacher, but is now a farmer. Was educated at the Springfield Wesleyan, and Newbury Seminaries. Was second lieutenant of Co. D, 9th reg't Vt. Vols. Was a member of the house in 1874. Has been superintendent, lister, auditor, and selectman. Religious preference, Congregationalist. P. O. address, Springfield.

JAMES M. TAYLOR, *Weston*, republican, was born in Weston, July 11, 1818. He is a farmer, Has repeatedly held the offices of lister, selectman and overseer. Religious preference, Universalist.

EUGENE H. SPAULDING, *West Windsor*, republican, was born in Weston, Mass., Oct. 2, 1838. He is a farmer, and located in town in 1842. Was a member of the house in 1868, '69 and '74, and is town clerk and treasurer. Religious preference, Universalist. P. O. address, Brownsville.

JAMES ADDISON POLLARD, *Windsor*, republican, was born in Plymouth, Nov. 19, 1817. He is a merchant, and located in town in 1863. Was representative from Plymouth in 1857-8, was representative from Windsor in 1865-7-8 and '76, serving that year on the committee of ways and means, and was senator from Windsor county in 1862-3. Was superintendent of the state prison from 1863 to 1874. Religious preference, Baptist.

HORACE C. LOCKWOOD, *Woodstock*, republican, was born in Woodstock, Jan. 12, 1830. He is a farmer. Was educated at the common schools. Has been chairman of the board of selectmen since 1871, with the exception of one year. Religious preference, Episcopalian.

OFFICERS OF THE HOUSE.

HENRY NELSON NEWELL, Shelburne, Clerk, republican, was born in Charlotte, June 18, 1843. He is a farmer, and located in town in 1844. Received a liberal academical education. Was assistant clerk of the house in 1868, '69 and '70, and was a member of the general assembly from Shelburne in 1874. Has held the usual town offices. Religious preference, Methodist.

WILLIAM WALLACE STICKNEY, Ludlow, First Assistant Clerk, republican, was born in Plymouth, Vt., March 21, 1853. He is a law student, and located in town in 1877. Was educated at Phillips Exeter Academy, class of 1877. Was second assistant clerk of the House in 1872. Religious preference, Unitarian.

OLIN MERRILL, Enosburgh, Second Assistant Clerk, republican, was born in Plainfield, March 11, 1854. He is a law student, and located in town in 1873. Was educated at the Vermont Methodist Seminary. Religious preference, Methodist. P. O. address, Enosburgh Falls.

HAYNES PORTER CUSHING, Burke, Chaplain, republican, was born in Burke, June 10, 1816. He is a clergyman. Was educated at Lyndon and Newbury Seminaries. Was a member of the General Assembly from Barton in 1864 and '65. Religious preference, Methodist. P. O. address, East Burke.

HIRAM SKEELS, Highgate, Doorkeeper, republican, was born in Highgate, April 21, 1830. He is a farmer. Was educated at the common schools and academy. Was a member of the General Assembly in 1876. Was Inspector of Customs in 1868, '69, '70; Deputy Collector of Customs, from 1870 to '72, and Consular Agent at Stanbridge, P. Q., from 1873 to 1875. Religious preference, Liberal. P. O. address, Highgate Centre.

WILLIAM E. BAILEY, Albany, Assistant Doorkeeper, republican, was born in Craftsbury in 1855. He is a student. P. O. address, East Albany.

GRANT M. SPRAGUE, St. Albans, Page, was born in Weybridge, Vt., December 2, 1763. He is a student, and was Assistant Librarian in St. Albans Free Library in 1875 and '76. Religious preference, Methodist.

ERNEST A. BLODGETT, St. Johnsbury, Page, was born in Randolph, Vt., January 31, 1866; located in St. Johnsbury the same year. He is a student. Religious preference, Congregationalist.

CHARLES W. HOLTON, Jamaica, Page, was born in Jamaica, in 1867. He is a student. Religious preference, Baptist.

JED. P. LADD, JR., Alburgh, Page, was born in Alburgh in 1868. He is a student. Religious preference, Congregationalist. P. O. address, Alburgh Springs.

ANDREW C. BROWN, Montpelier, Reporter, republican, was born in Sutton, July 10, 1828, and located in Montpelier in 1854. Is an insurance agent. Was Lieut.-Col. of the 13th regiment Vermont Volunteers, and Commissioner of the Board of Enrollment from 1863 to 1865. Has been reporter since 1864. Religious preference, Congregationalist.

EDWARD DANA, of Rutland, Reporter, republican, was born in Woodstock, May 6, 1852. He is a law student, and located in town in 1867. Is a graduate of Middlebury College, class of '76. Religious preference, Congregationalist.

RECAPITULATION OF THE HOUSE.

The House of Representatives consists of 232 members, of which 175 are Republicans, 43 are Democrats, 5 are Greenbacks, 5 are Independent, 3 are Democratic Greenbacks, and 1 is National Greenback Labor; nine towns are not represented. Twenty representatives were members of the House in the last General Assembly. Forty-eight have been Representatives before, six have been Senators, one has been a Member of Congress, one has been Clerk, and one Engrossing Clerk. One hundred and twenty represent the towns in which they were born. Benjamin F. Morgan, of Bennington, is the oldest, and Ely Ely-Goddard, of West Fairlee, is the youngest member of the House.

The following tables exhibit the places of birth, the occupations, and the religious preferences of the Representatives:

PLACES OF BIRTH:

Vermont	195	Pennsylvania	1
New Hampshire	11	Michigan	1
New York	9	Province of Quebec	2
Massachusetts	4	Ireland	4
Maine	3	Scotland	1
Connecticut	1		

OCCUPATIONS:

Farmers	141	Produce Dealers	2
Merchants	22	Farmer and Banker	1
Lawyers	12	Farmer and Mechanic	1
Physicians	8	Treasurer	1
Manufacturers	10	Miller	1
Hotel Keepers	5	Iron Founder	1
Clergymen	4	Groceries and Provisions	1
Mechanics	3	R. R. Conductor	1
Farmers and Merchants	3	Blacksmith	1
Farmers and Lumbermen	3	Harness Maker	1
Farmers and Speculators	2	Teacher	1
Accountants	2	Superintendent	1
Editors	2	No business	2

RELIGIOUS PREFERENCES:

Congregationalists	54	Spiritualists	3
Universalists	31	Friends	2
Methodists	31	Christians	2
Baptists	14	Protestant	1
Episcopalians	9	Calvinist	1
Liberals	9	Swedenborgian	1
Freewill Baptists	7	Free Thinker	1
Unitarians	5	Rationalist	1
Roman Catholics	5	No preference	52
Presbyterians	3		

ARRIVAL AND DEPARTURE OF MAILS.

WESTERN closes at 9 A. M., 3.30 and 9 P. M.

NORTHERN closes at 3.30 and 9 P. M.
Arrives at 10 A. M. and 9 P. M.

SOUTHERN AND EASTERN closes at 9 A. M. and 9 P. M.
Arrives at 7 A. M. and 5 P. M.

NEW YORK closes at 9 A. M., 3.30 and 9 P. M.
Arrives at 7 A. M. and 5 P. M.

BARRE MAIL arrives at 8 A. M. and 2 P. M.
Leaves at 9 A. M. and 3.30 P. M.

MONTPELIER & WELLS RIVER MAIL closes at 7 A. M.
Arrives at 6 P. M.

MORRISVILLE STAGE arrives every day (except Sundays) at 4 P. M. Leaves every day (except Sundays) at 9.30 A. M.

CALAIS, arrives and departs three times a week—Tuesdays, Thursdays and Saturdays. Arrives at 12 M., and departs at 4 P. M.

BERLIN, arrives and departs every day, except Sundays. Arrives at 3 P. M., and departs at 4.30 P. M.

☞ All matter for the above mails, by railroad, must be in the office promptly at the hour of closing.

OFFICE HOURS — 7 A. M. to 8 P. M. Sundays—12 M. to 1 P. M.

JOHN W. CLARK, *Postmaster.*

MONTPELIER, October, 1878.

☞ Stamps of 1, 2, 3, 5, 6, 10, 15, and 30 cents, stamped envelopes and stamped paper wrappers, always on hand. Treasury notes, specie and government currency only, received for stamps. Stamps must be put on letters and papers by the forwarder.

RAILROAD TIME TABLE.

CENTRAL VERMONT RAILROAD.

Trains going SOUTH AND EAST leave Montpelier as follows:

Mail Train..9.06 A. M.
Day Express.......................................2.00 P. M.
Mixed Train for Northfield........................9.25 P. M.
Night Express.....................................10.50 P. M.

NORTH AND WEST.

Night Express.....................................3.25 A. M.
Accommodation.....................................6.10 A. M.
Local Passenger...................................11.00 A. M.
Express Mail......................................3.40 P. M.
Accommodation.....................................5.55 P. M.

FOR BARRE.

Leave Montpelier at 6.32 A. M., 12.15 P. M., and 4.25 P. M.

MONTPELIER & WELLS RIVER RAILROAD.

Trains leave Montpelier as follows:

Mail..7.25 A. M.
Express Passenger.................................2.20 P. M.
Mixed...4.35 P. M.

RELIGIOUS SERVICES.

EACH SUNDAY.

At Bethany Church, (Congregationalist,) corner of Main and School Streets, Rev. Mr. Hincks, at 10.30 A. M. and 7 P. M. Lecture and Social Meeting Wednesday evening.

Christ Church, (Episcopal,) State Street, Rev. Dr. Hull, at 10.30 A. M. and 7 P. M.

Trinity M. E. Church, Main Street, Rev. Mr. Parkhurst, at 10.30 A. M. and 7 P. M. Prayer Meeting on Tuesday evening, and Class Meeting on Thursday evening at 7 o'clock.

Church of the Messiah,—(Independent,)—Main Street, Rev. Mr. Wright, at 10.30 A. M. and 7 P. M.

Baptist Church, School Street, Rev. Mr. Rogers, at 10.30 A. M. and 7 P. M. Prayer Meeting on Thursday evening, at 7 o'clock.

St. Augustine, (Roman Catholic,) Court Street, Rev. Father Savoie. High Mass at 10.30 A. M.; Vespers at 3.30 P. M.

ALPHABETICAL INDEX TO HOUSE DIAGRAM.

Member.	*Seat.*
Adams, of Royalton	8
Aldrich, of Shewsbury	212
Alexander, of Guilford	124
Allen, of Westford	4
Atwood, of Salisbury	151
Ball, of Sutton	148
Bannister, of Warren	184
Barber, of Sandgate	85
Barrows, of Dorset	62
Beals, of Bakersfield	169
Beardsley, of Fletcher	9
Beede, of Maidstone	94
Benjamin, of Berlin	66
Benson, of Winhall	88
Bingham, of Essex	147
Black, of Barnard	126
Bliss, of Bradford	202
Bliss, of Worcester	41
Bowman, of Isle La Motte	105
Boyce, of Fayston	61
Bresee, of Hubbardton	228
Briggs, of Searsburgh	142
Brookins, of Shoreham	194
Brown, of Whiting	42
Brown, of Richford	129
Brown, of Benson	235
Buck, of Westfield	181
Bucklin, of Sudbury	12
Bullard, of Swanton	219
Buswell, of Randolph	110
Camp, of Elmore	6
Camp, of Orange	76
Camp, of Newport	210
Chandler, of Leicester	224
Chase, of Concord	188
Cinnamon, of Hyde Park	204
Clark, of Orwell	217
Clark, of Tinmouth	24
Collins, of Monkton	134
Collins, of Burton	229
Congdon, of Clarendon	60
Cook, of Bloomfield	75
Cramton, of Colchester	5
Currier, of Troy	225
Curtis, of Lowell	3
Damon, of Victory	53
Darling, of Hancock	32
Durtt, of Weathersfield	177
Davis, of Walden	116
Davis, of Peru	80
Davis, of Stockbridge	56
Derby, of Vershire	166
Derrick, of Arlington	175
Dexter, of Wardsboro	103
Dodds, of North Hero	174
Dougan, of Mt. Tabor	161
Dwinell, of Plainfield	40
Eaton, of Danville	153
Eddy, of Glastenbury	92
Edson, of Chester	34
Edwards, of Athens	128
Edwards, of Richmond	97
Ely-Goddard, of W. Fairlee	157
Emerson, of Thetford	163
Estabrook, of Sherburne	215
Farnham, of Tunbridge	171
Fitch, of Dover	192
Fletcher, of Cavendish	179

NUMERICAL INDEX TO HOUSE DIAGRAM.

Seat.	Member.	Seat.	Member.
1	Hartshorn, of Guildhall.	38	Miles, of Middlesex.
2	Poland, of St. Johnsbury.	39	White, of Calais.
3	Curtis, of Lowell.	40	Dwinell, of Plainfield.
4	Allen, of Westford.	41	Bliss, of Worcester.
5	Cramton, of Colchester.	42	Brown, of Whiting.
6	Camp, of Elmore.	43	Monahan, of Underhill.
7	Robertson, of Putney.	44	Potter, of Pawlet.
8	Adams, of Royalton.	45	McGowan, of Grand Isle.
9	Beardsley, of Fletcher.	46	Sprague, of Brandon.
10	White, of South Hero.	47	Winthrop, of Belvidere.
11		48	McCole, of Ryegage.
12	Bucklin, of Sudbury.	49	Mills, of Georgia.
13	Templeton, of E Montpelier.	50	Orton, of Fairfax.
14	White, of Bolton.	51	Holt, of Sunderland.
15		52	Swift, of Manchester.
16	Whitehill, of Morgan.	53	Damon, of Victory.
17		54	Smith, of Newark.
18	Thornton, of Hartland.	55	Mott, of Alburgh.
19	Palmer, of Morristown.	56	Davis, of Stockbridge.
20	Tucker, of Newbury.	57	Lewis, of Norwich.
21	Holden, of Chittenden.	58	Hubbard, of Plymouth.
22	Garfield, of Townshend.	59	Townsend, of Wallingford.
23	Wood, of Vernon.	60	Congdon, of Clarendon.
24	Clark, of Tinmouth.	61	Boyce, of Fayston.
25	Hilliard, of Canaan.	62	Burrows, of Dorset.
26	Steele, of South Burlington.	63	Root, of Rupert.
27	Harrington of Halifax.	64	Townshend, of Burke.
28	Morgan, of Bennington.	65	Fuller, of Fairhaven.
29	Hammond, of Middlebury.	66	Benjamin, of Berlin.
30	Spear, of Braintree.	67	Way, of Andover.
31	Wiley, of Landgrove.	68	Taylor, of Weston.
32	Darling, of Hancock.	69	Steele, of Sharon.
33	Shores, of Granby.	70	Jefferson, of Strafford.
34	Edson, of Chester.	71	Jameson, of Irasburgh.
35	Meacham, of Pittsford.	72	Meader, of Bristol.
36	Hayward, of Addison.	73	Sturtevant, of Weybridge.
37	Howes, of Moretown.	74	Perkins, of Marshfield.

Seat.	*Member.*
75	Cook, of Bloomfield.
76	Camp, of Orange.
77	Paddock, of Pownal.
78	Washburn, of Goshen.
79	Morrissey, of Stamford.
80	Davis, of Peru.
81	Lewis, of Wells.
82	Holton, of Jamaica.
83	Judevine, of Hardwick.
84	Harriman, of Wolcott.
85	Barber, of Sandgate.
86	Moren, of Berkshire.
87	Potter, of Sheldon.
88	Benson, of Winhall.
89	Paul of Middletown.
90	Hyde, of Poultney.
91	Jakway, of West Haven.
92	Eddy, of Glastenbury.
93	Gilkey of Brunswick.
94	Beede, of Maidstone.
95	Thorp, of Charlotte.
96	Nash, of Shelburne.
97	Edwards, of Richmond.
98	Temple, of Mendon.
99	Turner, of Duxbury.
100	Ross, of Waterford.
101	Knight, of Stratton.
102	Ingalls, of Sheffield.
103	Dexter, of Wardsboro.
104	Fuller, of Eden.
105	Bowman, of Isle la Motte.
106	Sheridan, of Highgate.
107	Hinsdill, of St. George.
108	Rowell, of Albany.
109	Town, of Cabot.
110	Buswell, of Randolph.
111	Sisco, of Jay.
112	Martin, of Williamstown.
113	Watts, of Peacham.
114	Goodell, of Woodbury.
115	Perry, of Ira.
116	Davis, of Walden.
117	Weed, of Stannard.
118	
119	
120	Houghton, of Readsboro.

Seat.	*Member.*
121	Higgins, of Brookline.
122	Stoddard, of Dummerston.
123	Garland, of Brighton.
124	Alexander, of Guilford.
125	Whipple, of Pomfret.
126	Black, of Barnard.
127	Stearns, of Lincoln.
128	Edwards, of Athens.
129	Brown, of Richford.
130	
131	Howe, of Castleton.
132	Collins, of Monkton.
133	Woodburn, of Windham.
134	Phelps, of Grafton.
135	Jenne, of Enosburgh.
136	Marsh, of Franklin.
137	Sims, of Lemington.
138	Chase, of Concord.
139	Gloyd, of Jericho.
140	Mueck, of Hinesburgh.
141	Gleason, of Woodford.
142	Briggs, of Searsburgh.
143	Spaulding, of W. Windsor.
144	Sherwin, of Baltimore.
145	Locke, of Waterville.
146	Powers, of Ripton.
147	Bingham, of Essex.
148	Ball, of Sutton.
149	Sargent, of Corinth.
150	Redington, of Rutland.
151	Atwood, of Salisbury.
152	Nash, of New Haven.
153	Eaton, of Danville.
154	Melendy, of Cambridge.
155	Peck, of Barnet.
156	Whitney, of Chelsea.
157	Ely-Goddard, of W. Fairlee.
158	Tabor, of Holland.
159	Houghton, of Pittsfield.
160	Huntington, of Washington.
161	Dougan, of Mount Tabor.
162	Wilson, of Salem.
163	Emerson, of Thetford.
164	Read, of Danby.
165	
166	Derby, of Vershire.

Seat.	Member.	Seat.	Member.
167		205	Martin, of Ferrisburgh.
168		206	Goss, of Greensboro.
169	Beals, of Bakersfield.	207	Holbrook, of Milton.
170	Kennedy, of Fairfield.	208	Talcott, of Williston.
171	Farnham, of Tunbridge.	209	Gross, of Brownington.
172	Rockwell, of Brattleboro.	210	Camp, of Newport.
173	Lockwood, of Woodstock.	211	Kidder, of Coventry.
174	Dodds, of North Hero.	212	Aldrich, of Shrewsbury.
175	Derrick, of Arlington.	213	Hazen, of Hartford.
176	Harrington of Shaftsbury.	214	Thomas, of Lunenburgh.
177	Dartt, of Weathersfield.	215	Estabrook, of Sherburne.
178	Porter, of Springfield.	216	Johnson, of Rockingham.
179	Fletcher, of Cavendish.	217	Clark, of Orwell.
180	Miles, of Craftsbury.	218	Hinman, of Derby.
181	Buck, of Westfield.	219	Bullard, of Swanton.
182	Powers, of East Haven.	220	Greene, of St. Albans.
183	Tyler, of Waitsfield.	221	Kingsley, of Montgomery.
184	Bannister, of Warren.	222	Haines, of Waterbury.
185	Waterman, of Johnson.	223	Williams, of Waltham.
186	Huse, of Montpelier.	224	Chandler, of Leicester.
187	Packer, of Mount Holly.	225	Currier, of Troy.
188	Rogers, of Wheelock.	226	Smalley, of Burlington.
189	Howe, of Ludlow.	227	Silsby, of Westmore.
190	Hinman, of Charleston.	228	Bresee, of Hubbardton.
191	Jones, of Whitingham.	229	Collins, of Barton.
192	Fitch, of Dover.	230	Orcutt, of Roxbury.
193	Williams, of Bridport.	231	Waite, of Stowe.
194	Brookins, of Shoreham.	232	Smith, of Bridgewater.
195	Parker, of Kirby.	233	Moody, of Bethel.
196	Lincoln, of Lyndon.	234	Pollard, of Windsor.
197	Jackson, of Barre.	235	Brown, of Benson.
198	Sherman, of Panton.	236	Scranton, of Vergennes.
199	Fuller, of Starksboro.	237	Gorham, of Westminster.
200	Norton, of Huntington.	238	Templeton, of Glover.
201	Frost, of Cornwall.	239	Whitney, of Marlboro.
202	Bliss, of Bradford.	240	Merrifield, of Newfane.
203	Gilmore, of Fairlee.		
204	Cinnamon, of Hydepark.		

State of Vermont.

JOINT RULES, RULES AND ORDERS

OF THE

Senate and House of Representatives

AND OF THE STATE LIBRARY,

AND

LEGISLATIVE DIRECTORY

BIENNIAL SESSION,

1880.

Prepared pursuant to an Act by the General Assembly,

BY

GEORGE NICHOLS, SECRETARY OF STATE.

TUTTLE & CO.,
OFFICIAL STATE PRINTERS.
1880.

JOINT RULES

OF THE

SENATE AND HOUSE OF REPRESENTATIVES.

1.

A Joint Assembly shall be formed by an union of the Senate and House of Representatives in the Hall of the latter, at such time and for such specific purpose only as may be expressed in a concurrent resolution of both Houses; and may adjourn from time to time during the session of the General Assembly. The President of the Senate shall in all cases preside over, and the Secretary of State, or in his absence, the Secretary of the Senate, shall officiate as Clerk; and the rules of the Senate as far as applicable shall be observed in regulating the proceedings of every Joint Assembly.

2.

The proceedings of every Joint Assembly including the resolution ordering the same, shall be recorded by the Clerk in a book kept for that purpose, which shall be preserved in the office of the Secretary of State, a copy of which shall be furnished to the Governor by the Secretary of State, and shall also be published with the Journal of the proceedings of the House of Representatives.

3.

At the commencement of each session the following Joint Standing Committees, consisting of two Senators and three Representatives, shall be appointed by the presiding officers of the two Houses respectively, to wit:

A Committee on Joint Rules.

A Committee on the Library.

Also the following Joint Standing Committees, to consist of three Senators and five Representatives, to wit:

A Committee on the House of Correction.

A Committee on the Reform School.

A Committee on Game and Fisheries.

4.

A Joint committee of three Senators and three Representatives shall be appointed by the presiding officers of the two Houses respectively, to whom may be referred all documents transmitted by the Governor for the use of the General Assembly, who shall report thereon to that House from which they were received.

5.

The committee of the Senate and House of Representatives, to whom the same subject matter shall have been referred, may, for the purpose of facilitating business, meet together as a joint committee, and make a joint or separate report to either or both Houses, as they may think expedient.

6.

In every case of disagreement between the Senate and House of Representatives, if either shall request a conference and appoint a committee for that purpose, and the other House shall also appoint a committee on its part, such committee shall meet at a convenient hour, to be agreed upon by their chairman, in the conference room, and state to each other, verbally or in writing, the reasons of each House for its vote on the subject matter of disagreement, confer freely thereon, and make a report of their doings to their respective Houses as soon as may be.

7.

Committees of Conference shall consist of an equal number from each House, and shall return the papers referred to them to that House which last voted upon the subject matter of disagreement. The report of the Committee of Conference cannot be amended or altered, as that of other committees may be. In all cases of conference asked after a vote of disagreement, the conferees of the House asking it, are to leave the papers with the conferees of the other.

8.

After each House shall have adhered to the vote of disagreement, a bill or resolution shall be lost.

9.

When bills and resolutions are on their passage between the two Houses, they shall be verified by the attestation of the Secretary or Clerk of each House respectively, and all bills, after their third reading has been ordered, and before being read the third time, shall be duly engrossed, if the House in which they originated, so order; and all joint resolutions shall be fairly engrossed, after their passage, in the House in which they originate, and shall, when finally passed, be signed by the presiding officer of both Houses, in the same manner as bills.

10.

When a bill or resolution, which shall have passed one House, is rejected in the other, notice thereof shall be given to the House in which the same shall have passed; and all such rejected bills or resolutions, with the accompanying papers, shall be returned to and left in the custody of the House which first acted on them.

11.

Each House shall transmit to the other, all papers on which any bill or resolution shall be founded; and should any bill or resolution pass both Houses, the same papers shall be delivered to the Governor.

12.

No bill, which shall have passed one House, shall be sent for concurrence to the other on the last day of the session.

13.

A two thirds vote of all present, shall be required for the suspension of any joint rule.

14.

After bills have passed both Houses, and a certificate showing the one in which they respectively originated has been endorsed thereon, they shall be delivered to a joint standing committee of two Senators and two members of the House of Represen-

AMENDED RULE.

14.

After bills have passed both Houses, and a certificate showing the one in which they respectively originated has been endorsed thereon, they shall be delivered to a joint standing committee of two Senators and two members of the House of Representatives, to be appointed by the presiding officers of the two Houses respectively, to be designated the *Committee on Bills*, who shall make careful examination of all bills, both as regards the original bill and all amendments thereto, and shall see that all bills so ordered, are correctly engrossed; and when satisfied of their accuracy, some member of the committee shall so certify thereon, and shall then present them to the Speaker of the House of Representatives, and then to the President of the Senate, for their official signatures ; and having obtained them, they shall forthwith deliver them to the Governor for his approval, and shall make a true report to both Houses of the day on which each bill was delivered to the Governor, which shall be duly entered upon the journal of each House.

JOINT COMMITTEE ON BILLS.

Of the Senate—Mr. Weed, of Chittenden,
Fuller, of Windham.

Of the House—Mr. Tiffany, of Pittsford,
Allen, of Fair Haven.

tatives, to be appointed by the presiding officers of the two Houses respectively, to be designated the *Committee on Bills*, who shall make careful examination, and see that they are correctly engrossed, both as regard to the original bill, and all amendments thereto; and, when satisfied of their accuracy, shall present them to the Speaker of the House of Representatives, and then to the President of the Senate, for their official signatures; and having obtained them, they shall forthwith deliver them to the Governor for his approval, and shall make a true report to both Houses of the day on which each bill was delivered to the Governor, which shall be duly entered upon the journal of each House.

JOINT RESOLUTION RELATING TO THE REVISED LAWS.

Resolved by the Senate and House of Representatives:

That all bills of a public nature, after being reported by committee and ordered to be read the third time, shall be put into the hands of the joint committee on the revision of the laws, to be formed in accordance with the style adopted in the Revised Laws, without change of substance, and so far as practicable to be put in proper form for their insertion in the Revised Laws, when finally printed; and that, if amendments are made after a bill is read the third time, the secretary of the Senate or clerk of the House, as the case may be, shall return such bills to the committee on the revision for any further changes of the same character that may be necessary, before the bill is put upon its final passage.

JNO. L. BARSTOW,
President of the Senate.

JAMES L. MARTIN,
Speaker of the House of Representatives.

RULES AND ORDERS

OF THE

SENATE.

RULES AND ORDERS OF THE SENATE.

1.

The credentials of Senators shall be presented to the Secretary or Assistant Secretary previous to ten o'clock on the morning of the first Wednesday of October, at which time the Senate shall be called to order. The names of the Senators shall be called over, and when a quorum shall have taken their seats, they shall take the following oath, viz.: "I, ——, Senator of the County of ——, in the State of Vermont, October Session, 18——, do solemnly swear that I will be faithful and true to the State of Vermont, and that I will not, directly or indirectly, do any act or thing injurious to the constitution or government thereof as established by convention. So help me God. And I also solemnly swear that, as a member of this Senate, I will not propose or assent to any bill, vote, or resolution, which shall appear to me injurious to the people, nor do or consent to any act or thing whatever, that shall have a tendency to lessen or abridge their rights and privileges, as declared by the Constitution of this State; but will in all things conduct myself as a faithful, honest representative and guardian of the people, according to the best of my judgment and abilities. So help me God." Whereupon, they shall, on nomination of the President appoint a *Canvassing Committee*, consisting of one Senator from each county, to join such committee as the House of Representatives may appoint, whose duty shall be to receive, sort, and count the votes for Governor, Lieutenant Governor, and Treasurer; and shall, in like manner, appoint a committee of one Senator from each county to join such committee as the House of Representatives may appoint, whose duty shall be to canvass the votes for County and Probate officers, and make report thereof to the Joint Assembly of both Houses.

2.

The Senate shall meet every day (Sundays excepted) at ten o'clock in the morning, and two o'clock in the afternoon, unless otherwise specially ordered.

3.

The President having taken the chair, and a quorum being present, the journal of the preceding day shall be read, and all errors therein corrected.

4.

In case no quorum shall assemble within fifteen minutes after the time to which the Senate was adjourned, those present shall have the power to send the Sergeant-at-Arms, or other officer, after the absentees, and compel their attendance.

5.

Whenever the Senate shall assemble, according to adjournment, or at the commencement of a session, and the President shall be absent, it shall be the duty of the Secretary, if present, if not, of a Senator, to call to order; and the Senators present, if a quorum, shall by ballot elect a President *pro tempore*.

6.

No Senator shall be absent without leave, unless he is sick, or otherwise necessarily detained.

7.

No Senator shall audibly speak to another, or otherwise interrupt the business of the Senate, while the journal or other public papers are being read, or while a Senator is orderly speaking in debate.

8.

Every Senator, when he speaks, shall, standing in his place, address the President, and when he has finished shall sit down.

9.

No member shall speak more than twice on the same question, without leave of the Senate; and Senators who have once spoken, shall not again be entitled to the floor (except for the purpose of explanation,) to the exclusion of another who has not spoken.

10.

In all cases, the Senator first arising and addressing the President (subject to the restriction of rule 9,) shall be entitled to the floor, and when two or more arise at the same time, the President shall name the one who is to speak.

11.

When a Senator shall be called to order he shall sit down; and every question of order shall be decided by the President without debate, subject to an appeal to the Senate.

12.

If a Senator be called to order for words spoken, the exceptional words shall be immediately taken down in writing by the Senator calling to order, that the President may be better enabled to judge of the matter.

13.

The first hour of each morning's sitting may be devoted to the reception and disposal of petitions, memorials and remonstrances, motions, resolutions, and the introduction of bills ; after which the orders of the day, or other proper business, shall be announced, always commenciug with the unfinished business of the last sitting. The first hour of the afternoon's sitting may be occupied in receiving and disposing of reports of committees, and in completing the business of the morning hour ; at the expiration of which, the Senate will again take up the orders of the day.

14.

Reports of committees may be signed by any member in behalf of the committee, and shall be by him presented to the Senate, when the call for reports is made. The signer of each report shall be held responsible for the accuracy of its statements, and the propriety of its language, and when the same shall be under consideration, he shall be further liable to give additional statements of facts or other explanations, in answer to the call of any Senator.

15.

The proceedings of the Senate, except when acting as in Committee of the Whole, embracing the titles of bills and such parts thereof as may be affected by the proposed amendments, and also the names of the Senators, and the votes which they give on every question decided by yeas and nays, shall be, by the Secretary, accurately and concisely inserted in the journal.

16.

The Senate shall biennially, within the first four days of actual sitting, elect, by ballot, a Secretary, and an Assistant Secretary, who shall be severally sworn to the faithful dischage of their duties, and shall hold their offices until superseded by a new election. The Assistant Secretary shall be *ex-officio*, engrossing clerk.

17.

The Senate shall at each biennial session appoint the following committees, to consist of three members each, except that the committees on the Judiciary and on Railroads shall consist of seven members each, and the committees on Claims, and on Education shall consist of five members each :

A Committee on Rules.
A Committee on Finance.
A Committee on Judiciary.
A Committee on Claims.
A Committee on Education.
A Committee on Agriculture.
A Committee on Manufactures.
A Committee on Elections.
A Committee on Military Affairs.

A Committee on Railroads.
A Committee on Highways and Bridges.
A Committee on Banks.
A Committee on Land Taxes.
A Committee on Printing.
A General Committee.
A Committee on Federal Relations.
A Committee on the State Prison.
A Committee on the Insane Asylum.
A Committee on Grand List.

18.

All bills after the second reading, and all petitions, memorials, remonstrances, resolutions and other papers, calling for legislative action (except such as have been reported by a committee), no objection being made, shall be referred by the President to appropriate committees.

19.

Before any resolution, any petition, or other paper addressed to the Senate, shall be received and read, whether the same shall be introduced by the President or a Senator, the title shall be fairly endorsed thereon, and a brief statement of its objects or contents shall be made by the introducer.

20.

Every motion shall be reduced to writing by the mover, if required thereto by the President or a Senator, and a motion to lay another motion, the latter not being in writing, on the table, or otherwise to dispose of it, shall not be in order.

21.

Every bill shall receive three readings before it is passed; the President shall give notice at each reading whether it be the first, second, or third; the last of which reading of public bills shall be at least twenty-four hours after the first reading, unless the Senate unanimously direct otherwise; provided, that the bills may be read the second time by their title. Resolutions requiring the approbation and signature of the Governor shall be treated in all respects as bills; and the third reading of all bills of a public nature shall be ordered for some particular day. Each and every nomination made by the Governor, to be confirmed by the Senate, shall lie over at least twenty-four hours between such nomination and the confirmation thereof.

22.

On motion of a Senator, public bills, after the second reading, may be referred to a committee of the whole.

23.

No amendment to a bill originating in the Senate shall be received at the third reading, but the bill may be committed to a Senator for amendment at any time before its passage.

24.

Motions on bills and resolutions shall be sustained in the following order: 1. To postpone indefinitely. 2. To lay on the table. 3. To commit. 4. To amend.

25.

A call for the previous question shall not at any time be in order. A motion to adjourn shall always be in order.

26.

If the question in debate contains several points, the same may be divided on the demand of a Senator. A motion to strike out and insert shall not be divided, but the rejection of a motion to strike out and insert one proposition shall not preclude a motion to strike out and insert a different one, or a motion to simply strike out; nor shall the rejection of a motion simply to strike out, prevent a subsequent one to strike out and insert.

27.

In filling blanks, the largest sum and the longest time shall be first in order.

28.

When the reading of a paper is called for, and the same is objected to by a Senator, the question shall be determined by a vote of the Senate.

29.

The yeas and nays shall be taken on the call of a Senator, and every Senator present shall vote unless excused by the Senate; but no Senator shall be compelled to vote who was absent when the question was stated by the President.

30.

No Senator in the minority, nor one who did not vote on the decision of the question, shall have a right to move a reconsideration thereof; nor shall any motion for reconsideration be in order unless made before the close of the next day of actual sitting of the Senate, after that in which the vote was taken, and before the bill, resolution, report, amendment, address, or motion upon which the vote was taken, shall, in the regular progress of business, have gone out of the possession of the Senate.

31.

On all questions, in the decision of which a simple majority is required, when the Senate is equally divided, the Secretary shall take the casting vote of the President. In all such cases a motion for reconsideration, if made in time, shall be in order from any Senator who voted on the question.

32.

The President shall have the right to call upon any Senator to discharge the duties of the Chair, whenever he shall find it necessary temporarily to retire ; but such substitution shall not extend beyond more than one adjournment.

33.

The Senate having taken the final vote on any question the same shall not again be in order during the same session, in any form whatever, except by way of reconsideration ; and when a motion for reconsideration has been decided, that decision shall not be reconsidered.

34.

No proposition to amend the rules of the Senate, or the joint rules of both Houses, shall be acted on until the same shall have been before the Senate at least twenty-four hours ; and no rule of the Senate shall be suspended except by the vote of three fourths of the members present.

35.

Messages shall be sent to the House of Representatives by the Secretary or Assistant Secretary.

36.

Reporters may be placed on the floor of the Senate, under the direction of the Secretary, with the approbation of the President.

37.

No person shall be admitted within the lobby of the Senate Chamber except the Governor, Treasurer of the State, Secretary of State, Auditor of Accounts, members of the other House, Judges of the Supreme Court, Circuit Judges, Senators and Representatives in Congress, Ex-Governors and Lieutenant Governors, Ex-Judges of the Supreme Court, Ex-Senators of the State Senate, District Judge and Attorney of the United States, members of other State Legislatures, Clerk and Assistant Clerk of the House of Representatives, and the Secretary of Civil and Military Affairs, and such ladies and gentlemen as the President or a Senator may introduce.

38.

When in session the Senators shall sit with their heads uncovered.

39.

Upon any disorderly conduct in the gallery, the President may order the same to be cleared.

40.

Whenever a bill or resolution is laid on the table, by order of the Senate, and shall have remained on the table twenty-four hours, it shall be subject to be taken up by the Chair, and presented for the consideration of the Senate, without a call or order on the subject.

41.

There shall be one Door-Keeper, one Assistant Door-Keeper, and two Messengers of the Senate.

42.

CHOICE OF SEATS.

At nine o'clock on the morning of the first day of the Senate, and before the session shall be called to order, the Secretary shall place in a box prepared for the purpose, fourteen ballots, designating by name the several counties in the State, and shall proceed to draw therefrom, impartially, one ballot at a time until all are drawn. And as each ballot is drawn, the Senator or Senators from the county designated by such ballot, shall, personally, if present, or may by proxy, if absent, select his or their seat or seats. If any Senator or Senators, from any county so drawn, should not be present, either personally or by proxy, at the time of such drawing, the county next drawn shall have preference.

43.

The subject matter of each and every bill and resolution shall be briefly indicated in its title by the mover ; and every bill and resolution shall be properly folded, and the name of the mover legibly written at the bottom of the same, before its introduction.

44.

After the second reading of any Senate bill of public character, the Secretary shall cause not less than three hundred copies of the same to be forthwith printed for the use of the General Assembly, unless already printed, and he shall furnish five copies thereof to the Librarian.

45.

The President of the Senate shall appoint a special committee of seven members, to whom shall be referred all proposals of amendment to the Constitution of the State.

RULES AND ORDERS

OF THE

HOUSE.

RULES AND ORDERS

OF THE

HOUSE OF REPRESENTATIVES.

RULE 1.

At half-past eight o'clock on the morning of the second day of the session, and before the House shall be called to order, the Speaker shall direct the Sergeant-at-Arms to cause the seats to be vacated, and the Clerk shall place in a box prepared for the purpose, ballots designating by name the several towns in the State, and shall proceed to draw therefrom, impartially, one ballot at a time, until all are drawn; and as each ballot is drawn, the member from the town designated by such ballot shall personally, if present, or may by proxy, if absent, select his seat, and shall occupy the same during the drawing, either by himself or his proxy. If any member from any town so drawn shall not be present, either himself or by his proxy, at the time of such drawing, the town next drawn shall have preference.

RULE 2.

The House shall meet every day (Sundays excepted), at ten o'clock in the morning, and at two o'clock in the afternoon, unless otherwise ordered.

Rule 3.

OF COMMITTEES.

At the commencement of each session the following Standing Committees shall be appointed, viz: A committee of three members, to report rules of the House.

A committee of seven members, to whom shall be referred all matters relating to the election of members; to be denominated the Committee on *Elections.*

A committee of seven members, to whom shall be referred all matters relating to the Government of the United States, and the relations of this State to it; to be denominated the Committee on *Federal Relations.*

A committee consisting of nine members, to whom shall be referred all matters affecting the revenue of the State, and who shall inquire into the state of the Treasury; ascertain the amount of debts due the State, and the claims against it; report the amount of taxes necessary to be raised for the support of Government, and inquire what measure, if any, ought to be adopted, the better to equalize the public burdens, secure the accountability of public agents, and otherwise improve the financial concerns of the State; to be denominated the Committee of *Ways and Means.*

A committee consisting of seven members, to whom shall be referred all matters relating to the militia; to be denominated the Committee on *Military Affairs.*

A committee consisting of nine members, to whom shall be referred all matters relating to the Judiciary; to be denominated the *Judiciary Committee.*

A committee consisting of seven members, to whom shall be referred all matters relating to literary and scientific subjects; to be denominated the Committee on *Education.*

A committee consisting of nine members, to whom shall be referred all claims against the State; to be denominated the Committee of *Claims.*

A committee consisting of nine members, to whom shall be referred all matters relating to Railroads; to be denominated the Committee on *Railroads.*

A committee consisting of seven members, to whom shall be referred all matters relating to Highways, Bridges and Ferries; to be denominated the Committee on *Highways, Bridges and Ferries.*

A committee consisting of seven members, to whom shall be referred all matters relating to Banks; to be denominated the Committee on *Banks.*

A committee consisting of seven members, to whom shall be referred all matters relating to Domestic Manufactures; to be denominated the Committee on *Manufactures.*

A committee consisting of one member from each county, to whom shall be referred all matters relating to Agriculture; to be denominated the Committee on *Agriculture.*

A committee consisting of one member from each county, to whom shall be referred all matters relating to Land Taxes; to be denominated the *Land Tax Committee.*

A committee of one member from each county, to whom shall be referred all matters relating to the Grand List; to be denominated the committee on *Grand List.*

A committee of one member from each county, to whom shall be referred all subjects for which there shall be no other appropriate committee; to be denominated the *General Committee.*

A committee of one member from each county, whose duty it shall be to receive and distribute all public documents and papers, printed for the use of the members; to be denominated the *Distributing Committee.*

A committee consisting of seven members, to whom shall be referred all matters relating to the State Prison; to be denominated the Committee on the *State Prison.*

A committee of seven members, to whom shall be referred all bills and other matters relative to private corporations; to be denominated the Committee on *Corporations.*

A committee of seven members, to whom shall be referred all bills and other matters relative to town lines; to be denominated the Committee on *Town Lines.*

A committee consisting of one member from each county, who shall consider all matters relating to the mileage and debentures of the members of the House; to be denominated the Committee on *Mileage and Debentures.*

A committee consisting of seven members, to whom shall be referred all matters relating to the

Public Buildings ; to be denominated the Committee on *Public Buildings.*

A committee consisting of seven members, to whom shall be referred all matters relating to the Insane Asylum, to be denominated the Committee on *the Insane.*

RULE 4.

No committee shall sit during the session of the House, without leave from the House.

RULE 5.

Committees shall consider and report to the House upon all matters referred to them, and they may report by bill or otherwise.

RULE 6.

Committees shall be made by the Speaker, but any appointment so made, may, on motion of a member, be overruled by the House ; in which case the House shall, on nomination of a member, immediately fill the vacancy.

RULE 7.

A member shall be excused from service on any committee upon his request, if, at the time of his appointment, he is a member of two other committees.

RULE 8.

Whenever the House orders the appointment of a committee, the Speaker shall be entitled to one recess of the House in which to make the appointment.

RULE 9.

OF THE RIGHTS AND DUTIES OF THE SPEAKER AND OTHER MEMBERS.

The Speaker shall take the chair at the hour to which the House adjourned, call it to order and proceed to business; causing the journals of the previous day to be read at the opening of the House on each day, unless otherwise ordered by the House. He shall preserve order, and may speak on questions of order in preference to any other member, rising from his seat for that purpose; and shall decide on all questions of order, subject to an appeal to the House.

RULE 10.

In case of any disturbance or disorderly conduct in the gallery or lobby, the Speaker may cause the same to be cleared.

RULE 11.

If any member, in speaking, or otherwise, transgress the rules of the House, the Speaker shall, or any other member may, call to order, in which case, the member so called to order shall immediately sit down, unless permitted to explain; and the House shall, if appealed to, decide the same without debate. If the decision be in favor of the member called to order, he shall be at liberty to proceed; if otherwise, and the case require, he shall be liable to the censure of the House.

RULE 12.

No member shall speak more than twice to the same question without permission from the House; nor shall he speak the second time while the floor is claimed by a member who has not spoken to the question under consideration.

RULE 13.

No member shall absent himself from the service of the House unless he have leave of absence, is sick, or unable to attend.

RULE 14.

The yeas and nays shall be ordered on any question, on demand of a member, and when taken, and also on a division of the House, every member present, except the Speaker, shall vote, unless excused by the House ; but no member shall be compelled to vote who was not present when the question was stated from the Chair ; nor shall any one, in taking the yeas and nays, be permitted to vote, except by unanimous consent, who was not within the bar of the House when his name was called ; and when any member asks leave to vote, the Speaker shall propound to him the question: "Were you within the bar of the House when your name was called?" Nor shall any member be permitted to vote on any question in which he is immediately or directly interested. No member or other person, shall visit or remain by the Clerk's table while the yeas and nays are being called, or the ballots are being counted.

RULE 15.

In all cases of ballot, the Speaker shall vote ; in other cases he shall not be required to vote, unless the House be equally divided, or unless his vote, if given to the minority, will make the division equal ; and in case of such equal division, the question shall be lost.

RULE 16.

A member in the minority or one who did not vote on any question, shall not have a right to move a reconsideration thereof, nor shall a motion for reconsideration be in order, unless made before the close of the next day of actual session after that on which the vote was taken.

RULE 17.

A member, on presenting a resolution, shall state, shortly, the object of it, and be held responsible for the propriety of expression therein used.

RULE 18.

Every motion shall be reduced to writing by the mover, if required by the Speaker, or any other member.

RULE 19.

The Speaker may call upon any member to discharge the duties of the chair whenever he shall find it necessary to retire from it ; and such member shall discharge all the duties devolving upon the Speaker, for a time not exceeding four regular sessions, and, if at the expiration of said time the Speaker shall be unable to occupy the chair, the House shall elect from its members a Speaker pro tem, who shall serve until the Speaker shall be able to resume the duties of his office ; and when the House shall go into Committee of the Whole, the chairman shall be named by the Speaker.

RULE 20.

All petitions shall be referred to a Committee without reading, unless the reading be demanded by a member.

RULE 21.

The House having once decided on any question, it shall not again be brought before the House by any member thereof, in any form whatever, during the same session.

RULE 22.

When a motion shall be made for a call of the House, the call shall be ordered, if said motion is sustained by a majority of the members present.

RULE 23.

No motion to amend the rules of the House shall be acted upon until it shall have been before the House at least twenty-four hours.

RULE 24.

The Governor, Lieutenant Governor, the Treasurer, and Secretary of State, Auditor of Accounts, Secretary of Civil and Military Affairs, and members of the State Senate, Senators and Members of Congress, the Judges of the Supreme and Circuit Courts, the District Judge, Collector, Attorney, and Marshal of the United States, and such as have previously held those offices ; the clergy, and such as may be introduced by a member, shall be admitted to seats on the floor of the House.

Rule 25.

Counsel may be admitted to advocate any cause if permitted by three-fourths of the members present.

Rule 26.

No bill shall pass the House until it shall have been read three several times, the last of which shall be at least twenty-four hours after the first reading, and the third reading of all bills of a public nature shall be ordered for some particular day.

Rule 27.

All bills shall be read a second time by their titles only, unless the reading shall be demanded by a member ; and all bills after the second reading, and all petitions, memorials, remonstrances, resolutions and other papers, calling for legislative action (except such as have been reported by a committee), no objection being made, shall be referred by the Speaker to appropriate committees.

Rule 28.

No bill for the charter, re-charter, or increase of capital of any bank, or for the alteration of county or town lines, or the removal or alteration of shires, shall be entertained by the House, unless it is made to appear to the committee to which it may have been referred that the required notice has been given.

Rule 29.

The subject matter of a bill shall be briefly indicated in the title by the mover, at the time of its introduction ; and every bill and resolution shall be properly folded, and the name of the mover, and the town he represents, shall be legibly written on the bottom of the same before it shall be offered.

RULE 30.

A two thirds vote of all present shall be required for the suspension of any rule of the House.

RULE 31.

MOTIONS.

A motion to adjourn shall always be in order, and shall be determined without debate.

RULE 32.

Motions on bills and resolutions shall be sustained in the following order:

1. To dismiss.
2. To postpone to a day certain.
3. To lay on the table.
4. To commit.
5. To amend.

RULE 33.

If the question in debate contains several points, the same shall be divided on the demand of a member. A motion to strike out or insert shall not be divided, but the rejection of a motion to strike out and insert one proposition shall not preclude a motion to strike out and insert a different one, or a motion simply to strike out prevent a subsequent one to strike out and insert.

RULE 34.

In filling blanks, the largest sum and the longest time shall be the first in order.

RULE 35.

ORDER OF BUSINESS.

The first hour of each morning's sitting may be devoted to the reception and disposal of petitions, memorials, remonstrances, motions, resolutions and the introduction of bills; after which the orders of the day, or other proper business, shall be announced, always commencing with the unfinished business of the last sitting. The first hour of the afternoon's sitting may be occupied in the receiving and disposing of reports of committees, and in completing the business of the morning hour; at the expiration of which, the House will again take up the orders of the day.

RULE 36.

REPORTS.

Reports of committees may be signed by any member in behalf of the committee, and made to the House, by laying the same on the Speaker's table during a session. The signer of such report shall be held responsible for the accuracy of its statements, and the propriety of its language, and when the same shall be under consideration, he shall be further liable to answer all proper calls of any member of the House, for additional statements of facts.

RULE 37.

All bills and other matters reported to the House by committee requiring the action of the House, shall be taken up and considered in the same order in which they are reported, unless the House should otherwise direct.

Rule 38.

All incidental questions of order, arising after a motion is made for the previous question, and pending such motion, shall be decided, whether on appeal or otherwise, without debate.

Rule 39.

After the second reading of all bills of a public character, the Clerk shall cause not less than three hundred copies of the same to be forthwith printed for the use of the members of the General Assembly.

Rule 40.

All messages from the House of Representatives to the Senate, shall be transmitted by its Clerk, or one of his assistants.

RULES AND BY-LAWS

OF THE

STATE LIBRARY.

RULES AND BY-LAWS OF THE STATE LIBRARY.

1.

The Library shall be kept open each day, at suitable hours, of every session of the Legislature and Constitutional Convention, when the Librarian or his Assistants shall be present. And no person shall be allowed access to the Library at any time except in the presence of the Librarian or his Assistants.

2.

Books may be taken from the Library by the Governor and Lieutenant Governor ; the Secretary of Civil and Military Affairs ; members of the Senate and House and their Clerks ; members of the Constitutional Convention and its Clerks ; Heads of Departments ; Judges of the Supreme Court ; Trustees of the Library ; Secretary and members of the Board of Education.

3.

The right to take and keep books by the members and Clerks of a Legislature, or Constitutional Convention, is limited to the time said Legislature or Convention may be in session, and no other person shall keep a book from the Library more than twenty days.

4.

The Librarian shall keep records in which he shall enter all books taken from the Library; and every person taking a book shall be responsible for its return agreeably to the rules of the Library until the Librarian shall cancel the charge. And no book shall be taken from the Library until the same has been so charged.

5.

Every book placed on the shelves of the Library shall be stamped on the outside and inside, when practicable, with the words, "Vermont State Library," in such a manner as to be indelibly inscribed.

6.

The Librarian in suitable books shall keep a record of all the transactions of the Library in the purchase and exchange of books, and also of all the expenses of the Library, for the examination of the Trustees and the Committee on the Library.

7.

The Librarian, in the discharge of his duties, shall in all matters be subject to the control of the Trustees of the Library, and shall keep a full record of all their proceedings.

8.

The Library and Library Rooms shall be under the control and charge of the Librarian, and he shall carefully preserve the books and all other property belonging to the Library; and if any loss or damage to the same shall happen from his want of care, or any violation of the rules of the Library, by him permitted, he shall be personally responsible for the same.

9.

If on notice to any person that the time for which any book or books have been drawn from the Library by such person, has expired, such person shall neglect to return such book or books to the Library for more than three days after such notice, such person shall be liable to pay the State double the value of such book or books, which value shall be estimated at the cost of replacing the same.

10.

If any person shall take from the Library any book or other article belonging to the same, without being properly authorized so to do, such person shall be liable to pay to the State double the value of such book or other article, and shall also pay a penalty of ten dollars.

11.

If any person shall have in his possession any book or other article belonging to the Library, and shall neglect to return the same to the Library on demand, such person shall be liable to pay to the State double the value of such book or other article, and also a penalty of ten dollars.

12.

If any book shall be damaged while the same shall be drawn from the Library by any person, such person shall be liable to pay to the State the amount of such damage.

OATHS.

THE following oaths are required to be administered by the Constitution of the State of Vermont, and by statutory provision, to officers under the civil government thereof, to wit:

The Representatives, having met and chosen their Speaker and Clerk, shall, each of them, take and subscribe the following oaths, or affirmations, (except when they shall produce certificates of their having heretofore taken and subscribed the same,) to wit:

You do solemnly swear (or affirm) that, as a member of this assembty, you will not propose or assent to any bill, vote, or resolution, which shall appear to you injurious to the people, nor do or consent to any act or thing whatever, that shall have a tendency to lessen or abridge their rights and privileges, as declared by the Constitution of this State; but will in all things conduct yourself as a faithful, honest representative and guardian of the people, according to the best of your judgment and abilities. So help you God (in case of an oath); under the pains and penalties of perjury (in case of an affirmation).

Rule 1 of the Senate requires the following oath to be taken by the members of that body, to wit:

I, ———, a Senator from the County of———, in the State of Vermont, October session, 18——, do solemnly swear that I will be true and faithful to the State of Vermont, and that I will not directly or indirectly, do any act or thing injurious to the Constitution or Government thereof, as established by convention. So help me God. And I also solemnly swear that, as a member of this Senate, I will not propose or assent to any bill, vote or resolution, which shall appear to me injurious to the people, nor do or consent to any act or thing whatever, that shall have a tendency to lessen or abridge their rights and privileges, as declared by the Constitution of this State ; but will in all things conduct myself as a faithful, honest representative and guardian of the people, according to the best of my judgment and abilities. So help me God.

Every officer, whether judicial, executive, or military, in authority under this State, shall take and subscribe the following oaths or affirmations of allegiance to this State, and of office, (unless he shall produce evidence that he has before taken the same, except military officers, who are to take only the oath of allegiance, and such as shall be exempted by the Legislature.)

OATH OR AFFIRMATION OF ALLEGIANCE.

You do solemnly swear (or affirm) that you will be true and faithful to the State of Vermont, and that you will not, directly or indirectly, do any act or thing injurious to the Constitution or Government thereof, as established by Convention. So help you God (if an oath), under the pains and penalties of perjury (if an affirmation).

OATH OR AFFIRMATION OF OFFICE.

You ———, do solemnly swear (or affirm) that you will faithfully execute the office of ———for the ———of ———, and will therein do equal right and justice to all men, to the best of your judgment and abilities, according to law. So help you God (if an oath), under the pains and penalties of perjury (if an affirmation).

The form of oath to be administered to persons appointed in pursuance of the provision of law, to perform any duty or execute any office, commission, or trust whatsoever, where an oath is required, and no specific form is provided, is as follows :

OATH TO BE ADMINISTERED TO COMMITTEES, ETC.

You solemnly swear that you will faithfully execute the office (duty or trust) of ——— to the best of your judgment and abilities, according to law. So help you God.

REGULATIONS

IN THE

DEPARTMENT OF THE CLERK.

HENRY N. NEWELL, *Clerk.*
WILLIAM W. STICKNEY, *First Assistant Clerk.*
OLIN MERRILL, *Second Assistant Clerk.*

To insure a systematic and correct performance of the duties in this Department, the Clerk of the House of Representatives establishes the following Regulations:

DUTIES OF ASSISTANTS.

First Assistant Clerk.—It shall be his special duty:

I.

To officiate at the Reading Desk when required by the Clerk, and in case of his absence to perform his duty generally.

II.

To file all bills, resolutions, etc., disposed of by the Speaker.

III.

To distribute to the proper committee or officer, all bills, petitions and other papers referred.

Second Assistant Clerk.—It shall be his special duty:

I.

To make copies of all resolutions instructing committees.

II.

To make all proper entries in the Senate and House bill-books, and send to the printer all bills to be printed.

HENRY N. NEWELL, *Clerk.*

HOUSE OF REPRESENTATIVES,
Montpelier, Oct. 6, 1880.

SENATORS IN CONGRESS.

AN ACT TO REGULATE THE TIME AND MANNER OF HOLDING ELECTIONS FOR SENATORS IN CONGRESS.

Be it enacted by the Senate and House of Representatives of the United States of America in Congress assembled:

That the Legislature of each State which shall be chosen next preceding the expiration of the time for which any Senator was elected to represent said State in Congress, shall, on the second Tuesday after the meeting and organization thereof, proceed to elect a Senator in Congress, in place of such Senator so going out of office, in the following manner: Each house shall openly, by a *viva voce* [vote] of each member present, name one person for Senator in Congress from said State, and the name of the person so voted for, who shall have a majority of the whole number of votes cast in each house, shall be entered on the journal of each house by the clerk or secretary thereof; but if either house shall fail to give such majority to any person on said day, that fact shall be entered on the journal. At twelve o'clock, meridian, of the day following that on which proceedings are required to take place, aforesaid, the members of the two houses shall convene in joint assembly and the journal of each house shall then be read, and if the same person shall have received a majority of all the votes in each house, such person shall be declared duly elected Senator to represent said State in the Congress of the United States; but if the same person shall not have received a majority of the votes in each house, or if either house shall have failed to take proceedings as required by this act, the joint assembly shall then proceed to choose, by a *viva voce* vote of each member present, a person for the purpose aforesaid, and the person having a majority of all the votes of the said joint assembly, a majority of all the members elected to both houses being present and voting, shall be declared duly elected; and in case no person shall receive such majority on the first day, the joint assembly shall meet at twelve o'clock, meridian, of each succeeding day during the session of the legislature, and take at least one vote until a Senator shall be elected.

SEC. 2. *And be it further enacted*, That whenever, on the meeting of the Legislature of any State, a vacancy shall exist in the representation of such State in the Senate of the United States, said Legislature shall proceed, on the second Tuesday after the commencement and organization of its session, to elect a person to fill such vacancy, in the manner hereinbefore provided for the election of a Senator for a full term; and if a vacancy shall happen during the session of the Legislature, then on the second Tuesday after the Legislature shall have been organized and shall have notice of such vacancy.

SEC. 3. *And be it further enacted*, That it shall be the duty of the Governor of the State from which any senator shall have been chosen as aforesaid to certify his election, under the seal of the State, to the President of the Senate of the United States, which certificate shall be countersigned by the Secretary of State of the State.

Approved July 25, 1866.

LIST OF THE

EXECUTIVE AND LEGISLATIVE DEPARTMENTS

OF THE GOVERNMENT

OF THE

STATE OF VERMONT,

AND OFFICERS CONNECTED THEREWITH, WITH PLACES OF RESIDENCE,

1880.

Executive Department.

His Excellency, ROSWELL FARNHAM,
of Bradford,
GOVERNOR.
Pavilion, 27 and 28.

Charles C. Farnham, Bradford, *Messenger.*
Pavilion, 28.

Secretary of Civil and Military Affairs,
LESTER F. THURBER, Bradford.
American, 52.

Frank H. Brown, Rockingham, *Clerk.*
American, 42.

His Honor, JOHN L. BARSTOW, Shelburne,
LIEUT. GOVERNOR.
Riverside, 2.

JOHN A. PAGE, Montpelier,
TREASURER.
at Home.

HORACE W. KEMPTON, Montpelier........*Clerk.*
at Home.

Inspector of Finance,

WILLIAM H. DUBOIS, Randolph.

Secretary of State,

GEORGE NICHOLS, Northfield.
Fred E. Smith's.

CHARLES W. PORTER, Montpelier, *Deputy.*
Pavilion, 91.

EUGENE W. J. HAWKINS, Starksboro, *Eng. Clerk.*
O. D. Scribner's.

Everett C. Benton, Guildhall.......... *Messenger.*
Riverside, 20.

Auditor of Accounts,

E. HENRY POWELL, Richford,
Pavilion. 68.

ALBERT W. FERRIN, Montpelier,.......... *Clerk.*
At Home.

Sergeant-at-Arms,

TRUMAN C. PHINNEY, Montpelier.
At Home.

ARTHUR L. JAMESON, Irasburgh,.......... *Clerk.*
D. S. Wheatley's.

Herman D. Hopkins, Jr., Montpelier,... *Messenger.*
At Home.

Harry C. Briggs, Brandon,............. *Messenger.*
Edward Demeritt's.

Railroad Commissioner,

DAN P. WEBSTER, Putney.

Elective Trustees of the University of Vermont and State Agricultural College,

JUSTIN S. MORRILL, Strafford, WALDO P. BRIGHAM, Hyde Park, ELIAKIM P. WALTON, Montpelier.	Term expires 1881.
*ASAHEL PECK, Jericho, PAUL DILLINGHAM, Waterbury, CROSBY MILLER, Pomfret.	Term expires 1883.
LUKE P. POLAND, St. Johnsbury, ROSWELL FARNHAM, Bradford, JUSTUS DARTT, Weathersfield.	Term expires 1885.

Supervisors of the Insane,

JOSEPH L. HARRINGTON, Halifax;
WILLIAM H. WALKER, Ludlow;
JOSIAH O. CRAMTON, Colchester.

Directors of State Prison and House of Correction.

WILLIAM H. H. BINGHAM, Stowe;
NER P. SIMONS, Rutland;
JOSEPH C. PARKER, Hartford.

Superintendent of the State Prison,

WENDELL P. RICE, Windsor.

Superintendent of the House of Correction,

GEORGE N. EAYRES, Rutland.

Trustees of the Vermont Reform School,

WILLIAM P. DILLINGHAM, Waterbury;
CYRUS M. SPAULDING, Burlington;
DAVID M. CAMP, Newport.

Superintendent of the Vermont Reform School,

WILLIAM G. FAIRBANK, Vergennes.

*Deceased.

State Superintendent of Education,
EDWARD CONANT, Randolph.

State Superintendent of Agricultural Affairs,
JOHN B. MEAD, Randolph.

State Library.

HIRAM A. HUSE, Montpelier, *Librarian.*
At Home.

THOMAS L. WOOD, Montpelier,.........*Assistant.*
O. D. Scribner's.

Edward L. Smith, Montpelier..........*Messenger.*
At Home.

State Cabinet.

HIRAM A. CUTTING, Lunenburgh, *Curator of Cabinet.*
Mrs. Chas. Reed's.

STATE HOUSE EMPLOYES.

George Richardson, Montpelier...........*Janitor.*
At Home.

Zed S. Stanton, Roxbury..............*Watchman.*
E. Wright's.

John W. Peck, Montpelier ....*Engineer.*
At Home.

Edward P. Richardson, Montpelier..*Ass't Engineer.*
At Home.

William H. Kelton, Calais...............*Sweeper.*
Mrs. True's.

James Evans, Northfield...................*Sweeper.*
Geo. Richardson's.

Joseph Yatta, Montpelier.................*Sweeper.*
At Home.

Oscar F. George, Calais ....*Sweeper.*
Seminary Building.

MILITARY DEPARTMENT.

Governor and Commander in Chief,
ROSWELL FARNHAM, Bradford.
Pavilion, 27 and 28.

Adjutant & Inspector General,
JAMES S. PECK, Montpelier.
At Home.

Quarter Master General,
LEVI G. KINGSLEY, Rutland.

Judge Advocate General,
FRANK G. BUTTERFIELD, Rockingham.

GOVERNOR'S STAFF.

Surgeon General,
LEROY M. BINGHAM, Burlington.

Aides-de-Camp,

Colonel George T. Childs, St. Albans.
" William R. Rowell, Troy.
" Ely Ely-Goddard, Ely.
" Horace J. Brooks, Burlington.
" Milton K. Paine, Windsor.
" Olin Scott, Bennington.

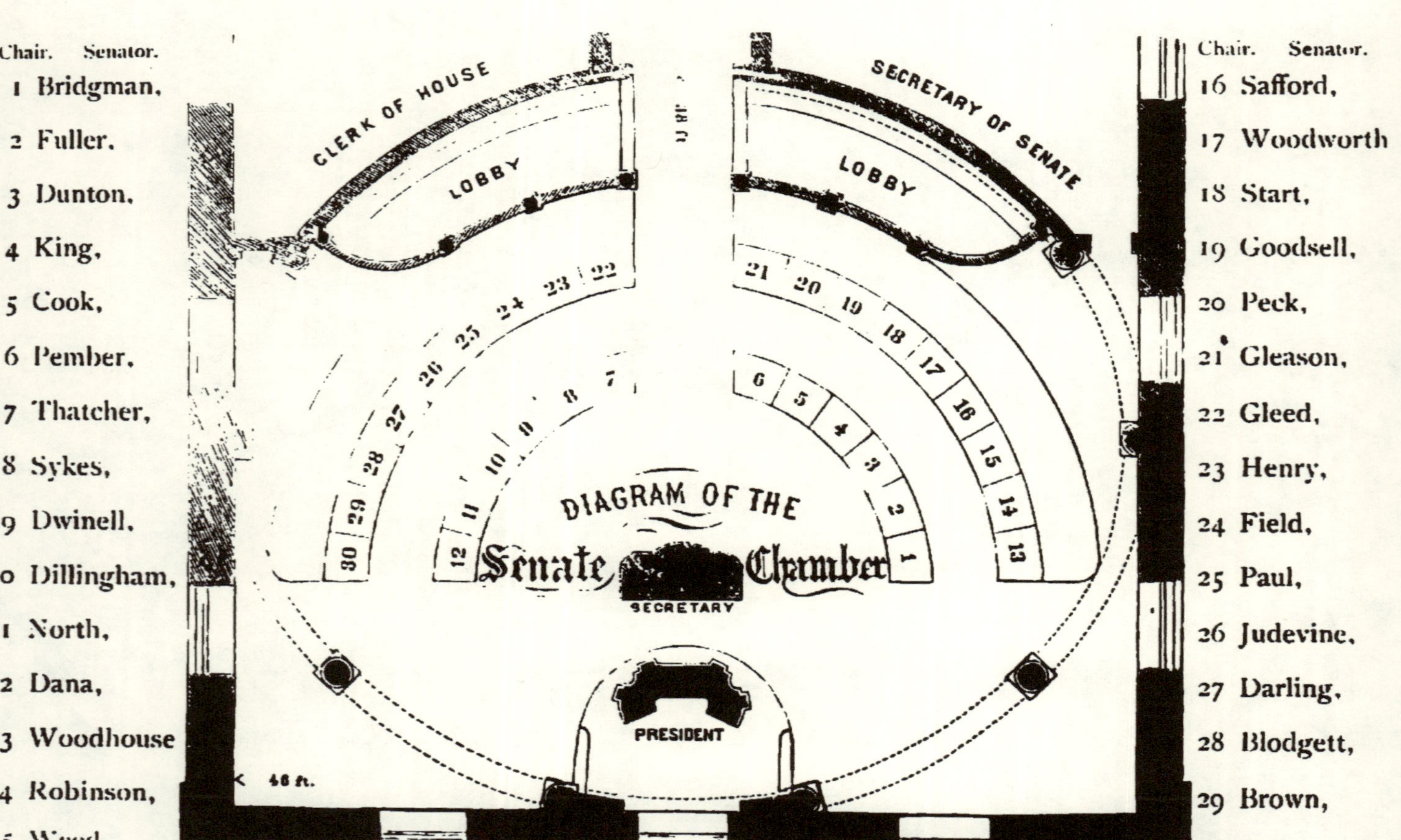

Chair.	Senator.
1	Bridgman,
2	Fuller,
3	Dunton,
4	King,
5	Cook,
6	Pember,
7	Thatcher,
8	Sykes,
9	Dwinell,
10	Dillingham,
11	North,
12	Dana,
13	Woodhouse
14	Robinson,
15	Weed.

Chair.	Senator.
16	Safford,
17	Woodworth
18	Start,
19	Goodsell,
20	Peck,
21	Gleason,
22	Gleed,
23	Henry,
24	Field,
25	Paul,
26	Judevine,
27	Darling,
28	Blodgett,
29	Brown,
30	Lane.

Legislative Department.

SENATE,

Arranged Alphabetically by Counties; with Senators' Names, Residences, Rooms, the Number of their Chairs, respectively; and the Officers of the Senate.

HIS HONOR, JOHN L. BARSTOW, LIEUT. GOVERNOR, *President.*

Counties.	Senators.	Residences.	Rooms.	No. of Chair
Addison	Edward S. Dana........	New Haven......	Pavilion, 13.........	12
"	Julius N. North........	Shoreham........	Pavilion, 44.........	11
Bennington	Gilbert M. Sykes	Dorset...	H. D. Hopkius'......	8
"	Charles Thatcher.......	Bennington......	Pavilion, 29.........	7
Caledonia	Jonathan R. Darling ...	Groton	Mrs. Newcomb's....	27
"	Elijah D. Blodgett......	St. Johnsbury ...	Pavilion, 23.........	28
Chittenden	Asher C. Robinson.....	Westford	Mrs. True's, 29	14
"	Charles W. Woodhouse,.	Burlington.......	Pavilion, 40.........	13
"	Walter A. Weed.......	Shelburne	Pavilion, 75.........	15

Essex	Harvey Judevine	Concord	Riverside, 13	26
Franklin	Henry R. Start	Bakersfield	Pavilion, 68	18
"	Arthur W. Woodworth	Enosburgh	Pavilion, 67	17
"	Alfred G. Safford	St. Albans	Pavilion, 21	16
Grand Isle	Elisha R. Goodsell	Isle La Mott	Bishop's, 30	19
Lamoille	Philip K. Gleed	Morristown	O. Fifield's	22
Orange	Marcus Peck	Brookfield	American, 80	20
"	Samuel M. Gleason	Thetford	Pavilion, 89	21
Orleans	Elisha Lane	Derby	Pavilion, 53	30
"	James Brown	Lowell	Huntington's	29
Rutland	Walter C. Dunton	Rutland	Riverside, 10	3
"	Royal D. King	Benson	D. S. Wheatley's	4
"	Orel Cook	Mendon	Bishop's	5
"	Emmett R. Pember	Wells	Mrs. True's, 20	6
Washington	William P. Dillingham	Waterbury	Pavilion, 55	10
"	Albert Dwinell	Calais	Pavilion, 87	9

Counties.	Senators.	Residences.	Rooms.	No. of Chair
Windham	Levi K. Fuller	Brattleboro	Pavilion, 60	2
"	Jabez D. Bridgman	Rockingham	Pavilion, 51	1
Windsor	Ora Paul	Pomfret	Mrs. True's, 24	25
"	Frederic G. Field	Springfield	Pavilion, 115	24
"	Hugh Henry	Chester	Pavilion, 54	23

OFFICERS OF THE SENATE.

Names.	Residences.	Offices.	Rooms.
CHAUNCEY W. BROWNELL, Jr.,	Burlington,	*Secretary,*	Riverside, 21.
FRANK A. DWINELL,	Plainfield,	*Ass't Secretary,*	Pavilion, 87.
EDWIN WHEELOCK,	Cambridge,	*Chaplain,*	C. C. Eaton's.
ALVIN D. WHITE,	Huntington,	*Doorkeeper,*	Mrs. True's, 17.
CHARLES S. DANA,	New Haven,	*Ass't Doorkeeper,*	Bishop's, 42.

William G. Stearns, . . . Bethel, . . . *Page*, ... O. D. Scribnėr's.
Julius B. North, ... Shoreham, . . *Page*, ... Pavilion, 44.

REPORTER.

Robert Roberts, ... Burlington, ... Riverside, 21.

HOUSE OF REPRESENTATIVES,

Arranged with reference to towns; Names of Members, their Rooms, the Number of their Seats, respectively; and the Officers of the House.

Hon. JAMES L. MARTIN, Londonderry, *Speaker*.

Towns.	Counties.	Representatives.	Rooms.	No. of Seat.
Addison........	Addison	Gideon W. Whitford....	Mrs. True's, 43......	204
Albany.........	Orleans	Hiram W. Chafey......	Mrs. Camp's.........	141
Alburgh.........	Grand Isle.......	Henry Mott	Morse's.............	120
Andover........	Windsor	Isaiah Lovejoy.........	C. C. Eaton's........	83
Arlington.......	Bennington......	Martin H. Deming.....	Pavillion, 50.........	236
Athens....... ..	Windham........	George N. Ober........	Orrin Daley's, 4.....	56
Bakersfield......	Franklin.........	William H. Giddings...	Pavilion, 81.........	47
Baltimore.......	Windsor.........	Thomas Preston........	Bennett's, 21........	42
Barnard.........	"	Isaac D. Davis.	American, 62........	106
Barnet	Caledonia........	George P. Blair........	Mrs. Newcomb's....	222

Barre	Washington	Henry Priest	At home	21
Barton	Orleans	Richard B. Skinner	Huntington's	98
Belvidere	Lamoille	Thomas M. Potter	Bennett's, 1	66
Bennington	Bennington	Lyman F. Abbott	Pavilion, 65	235
Benson	Rutland	Willard E. Strong	D. S. Wheatley's	32
Berkshire	Franklin	Leander C. Leavens	Pavilion	58
Berlin	Washington	Martin W. Wheelock	At home	77
Bethel	Windsor	Joseph G. Sargent	American, 28	226
Bloomfield	Essex	Fred A. Roby	Mrs. True's, 27	174
Bolton	Chittenden	Thomas B. Whalen	C. F. Ahn's	61
Bradford	Orange	Moses R. Chamberlain	Bishop's, 28	178
Braintree	"	Victor I. Spear	American, 80	6
Brandon	Rutland	George Briggs	Pavilion, 14	237
Brattleboro	Windham	George W. Hooker	Pavilion, 61, 62	187
Bridgewater	Windsor	Charles Babcock	Bishop's, 36	227
Bridport	Addison	John H. Witherell	Bishop's, 17	198

Towns.	Counties.	Representatives.	Rooms.	No. of Seat.
Brighton	Essex	Cephas G. Adams	Mrs. Camp's	60
Bristol	Addison	Erasmus M. Kent	Mrs. Trne's, 18	63
Brookfield	Orange	Almon Shepherd	Mrs. Hibbard's	27
Brookline	Windham	Erastus Whitney	Orrin Daley's	171
Brownington	Orleans	Ahira O. Joslyn	Mrs. Camp's	218
Brunswick	Essex	William W. Fitch	Riverside, 20	211
Burke	Caledonia	John S. J. Bemis	Hathaway's	8
Burlington	Chittenden	Russell S. Taft	Riverside, 8.	1
Cabot	Washington	George Gould	Pavilion, 94	39
Calais	"	Joseph W. Leonard	C. C. Eaton's	116
Cambridge	Lamoille	Lowell A. Blaisdell	Bennett's, 16	200
Canaan	Essex	William Morrill	Mrs. Newcomb's	100
Castleton	Rutland	Samuel-L. Hazard	Pavilion, 111	14
Cavendish	Windsor	Henry A. Fletcher	American, 63	231

Charleston	Orleans	Thomas L. Dolloff	Hathaway's	69
Charlotte	Chittenden	Charles D. Prindle	American, 61	101
Chelsea	Orange	Lyman G. Hinckley	Pavilion, 25	150
Chester	Windsor	Daniel W. Davis	Mrs. Walling's	232
Chittenden	Rutland	Edwin Horton	Hathaway's	29
Clarendon	"	Noel Potter	Bennett's	162
Colchester	Chittenden	Francis Le Clair	Bishop's	52
Concord	Essex	Selim E. Grout	Mrs. Newcomb's	36
Corinth	Orange	Not represented.		
Cornwall	Addison	William H. Bingham	Bishop's, 3	199
Coventry	Orleans	Henry F. Black	Mrs. Camp's	140
Craftsbury	"	James W. Simpson	Mrs. Camp's	95
Danby	Rutland	Erastus Kelly	Bennett's, 20	159
Danville	Caledonia	Silas H. Stone	Bishop's, 32	12
Derby	Orleans	Warren Goodwin	Mrs. Newcomb's	17
Dorset	Bennington	Orrin E. Whitney	Mrs. Walling's, 3	115

Towns.	Counties.	Representatives.	Rooms.	No. of Seat.
Dover	Windham	Henry I. Turner	Mrs. Hibbard's, 2	31
Dummerston	"	Stephen L. Dutton	Mrs. True's, 19	215
Duxbury	Washington	Not represented.		
East Haven	Essex	Solomon S. Hudson	D. S. Wheatley's	62
East Montpelier.	Washington	Andrew A. Tracy	At home	16
Eden	Lamoille	Martin Shattuck	Bennett's	104
Elmore	"	Judson T. Parker	S. Kimball's	54
Ely	Orange	Ely Ely-Goddard	Pavilion, 34 & 35	19
Enosburgh	Franklin	Charles Allen	H. D. Hopkins's	38
Essex	Chittenden	Charles H. Nichols	Bennett's, 23	45
Fairfax	Franklin	David A. Shepardson	Orrin Daley's	86
Fairfield	"	Samuel H. Soule	Bishop's, 62	87
Fair Haven	Rutland	Edward L. Allen	L. G. Camp's	13
Fairlee	Orange	Myron W. Smith	Mrs. Newcomb's	48

Fayston	Washington	Nathan Boyce	American, 82	134
Ferrisburgh	Addison	Jared Booth	Mrs. True's, 43	203
Fletcher	Franklin	Peter McGettrick	Bennett's, 17	121
Franklin	"	Bart Whitney	H. D. Hopkins's	57
Georgia	"	James K. Curtis	Orrin Daley's	85
Glastenbury	Bennington	Trenor P. Harbour	Bishop's, 13	122
Glover	Orleans	Wilbur F. Templeton	P. P. Pitkin's	238
Goshen	Addison	George E. Dutton	C. F. Ahn's	103
Grafton	Windham	Charles W. Haskell	D. S. Wheatley's	182
Granby	Essex	Charles W. Matthews	M. Russell's	137
Grand Isle	Grand Isle	James A. Brown	Bishop's 24	128
Granville	Addison	Alvin Ford	C. C. Eaton's	78
Greensboro	Orleans	John Simpson	D. W. Dudley's	221
Groton	Caledonia	Samuel P. Welch	Mrs. Hibbard's	72
Guildhall	Essex	Eldad A. Rhodes	Mrs. Newcomb's	196
Guilford	Windham	William W. Barney	Mrs. True's	190

Towns.	Counties.	Representatives.	Rooms.	No. of Seat.
Halifax	Windham	Lewis W. Sumner	Mrs. True's, 23	26
Hancock	Addison	Hiram R. Perry	C. C. Eaton's	88
Hardwick	Caledonia	Alden E. Judevine	Riverside, 11	225
Hartford	Windsor	Samuel J. Allen	Riverside, 17	149
Hartland	"	Elam M. Goodwin	Mrs. True's, 21	124
Highgate	Franklin	Oscar S. Searle	Morse's	35
Hinesburgh	Chittenden	John H. Allen	Mrs. True's, 22	148
Holland	Orleans	George R. Caswell	L. G. Camp's	129
Hubbardton	Rutland	Allen St. John	Bishop's, 34	161
Huntington	Chittenden	Orvis H. Ellis	American, 61	10
Hyde Park	Lamoille	Harrison W. Hendrick	M. Russell's	43
Ira	Rutland	Eben B. Perry	Bennett's, 8	76
Irasburgh	Orleans	Laforrest H. Thompson	Pavilion, 57	142
Isle La Motte	Grand Isle	James Hurst	Bishop's, 30	119

Jamaica	Windham	Warren C. Cushing	Mrs. True's, 31	153
Jay	Orleans	Jonathan E. Chase	M. Pearson's	125
Jericho	Chittenden	Cornelius S. Palmer	Mrs. True's, 30	147
Johnson	Lamoille	Isaac A. Manning	H. M. Pierce's	68
Kirby	Caledonia	Henry Ranney	Mrs. Newcomb's	233
Landgrove	Bennington	James H. Abbott	Bennett's, 19	97
Leicester	Addison	Walter J. Thomas	D. W. Dudley's	136
Lemington	Essex	Barnard O. Neil	Mrs. True's, 27	229
Lincoln	Addison	Samuel D. OBrian	American, 55	70
Londonderry	Windham	James L. Martin	Smilie's—Front room—first floor.	Chair
Lowell	Orleans	Carlos Farman	D. S. Wheatley's	84
Ludlow	Windsor	Elwin A. Howe	L. G. Camp's	189
Lunenburgh	Essex	Martin J. Pond	Russell's	81
Lyndon	Caledonia	Welcome A. Bemis	Bennett's, 24	144
Maidstone	Essex	Ira C. Cameron	L. B. Poor's	79
Manchester	Bennington	David S. Wilson	Bishop's, 4	194

Towns.	Counties.	Representatives.	Rooms.	No. of Seat.
Marlboro	Windham	Albert M. Prouty	Mrs. True's, 23	25
Marshfield	Washington	Mark Mears	C. C. Eaton's	96
Mendon	Rutland	Henry H. Shedd	Bennett's, 11	89
Middlebury	Addison	Joseph Battell	Pavilion	206
Middletown	Rutland	Leonidas Gray	Pavilion, 37	201
Middlesex	Washington	William Chapin	American, 82	216
Milton	Chittenden	Henry H. Rankin	Bishop's, 5	160
Monkton	Addison	Lucius E. Smith	Pavilion, 58	3
Montgomery	Franklin	Samuel N. Dix	M. Russell's	37
Montpelier	Washington	Benjamin F. Fifield	At home	34
Moretown	"	Russell Sawyer	American, 82	133
Morgan	Orleans	Jeremiah S. Wilcox	Mrs. Camp's	131
Morristown	Lamoille	Isaac P. Booth	Huntington's	92
Mount Holly	Rutland	Charles W. Priest	Hathaway's, 3	30

Mount Tabor	Rutland	Daniel H. Lane	Walling's, 5	114
Newark	Caledonia	Jabez Smith	Hathaway's	9
Newbury	Orange	Daniel P. Kimball	Bishop's, 28	177
Newfane	Windham	John H. Merrifield	Mrs. True's, 28	240
New Haven	Addison	Edson A. Doud	Pavilion, 13	152
Newport	Orleans	Theophilus Grout	Pavilion, 53	210
Northfield	Washington	Andrew E. Denny	American	219
North Hero	Grand Isle	Holland J. Fefee	John Witt's, 1	118
Norwich	Windsor	Samuel H. Currier	Mrs. Newcomb's	105
Orange	Orange	Lewis Hutchinson	Mrs. Hibbard's	41
Orwell	Addison	William B. Wright	Pavilion, 14	234
Panton	"	Norman J. Towsley	Riverside, 18	64
Pawlet	Rutland	Amos W. Wilcox	Bishop's, 63	220
Peacham	Caledonia	Plynn Bolton	Mrs. Newcomb's	33
Peru	Bennington	Marshall J. Hapgood	D. W. Dudley's	195
Pittsfield	Rutland	Edward Atwood	Bishop's, 15	164

Towns.	Counties.	Representatives.	Rooms.	No. of Seat.
Pittsford	Rutland	Amos D. Tiffany	S. Dewey's	7
Plainfield	Washington	Dudley B. Smith	At home	59
Plymouth	Windsor	Alonzo F. Hubbard	Bennett's, 7	214
Pomfret	"	William H. Adams	Mrs. True's, 24	123
Poultney	Rutland	Charles Ripley	Mrs. True's, 20	113
Pownal	Bennington	Abraham G. Parker	Pavilion, 20	20
Putney	Windham	Denison Davis	Bishop's, 14	212
Randolph	Orange	James G. Fowler	Mrs. Hibbard's	5
Reading	Windsor	Eleazer Dexter	D. W. Dudley's	23
Readsboro	Bennington	Tyler D. Goodell	Mrs. Hibbard's	192
Richford	Franklin	Alonzo Button	Pearson's, 1	126
Richmond	Chittenden	Henry A. Hodges	Pavilion	202
Ripton	Addison	William N. Cobb	Bennett's, 10	109
Rochester	Windsor	Albert Richmond	Huntington's	99

Rockingham	Windham	Charles Smith	Pavilion, 112	179
Roxbury	Washington	William B. Orcutt	American, 46	15
Royalton	Windsor	Charles West	Mrs. Walling's	156
Rutland	Rutland	John B. Page	Pavilion, 22	185
Rupert	Bennington	Edgar H. Beebe	Bishop's, 18	208
Ryegate	Caledonia	Jefferson Renfrew	Mrs. Hibbard's	73
Salem	Orleans	David Hopkinson	Mrs. Newcomb's	139
Salisbury	Addison	Loyal N. Waterhouse	D. W. Dudley's, 5	91
Sandgate	Bennington	Crawford R. Woodard	Bishop's, 18	205
Searsburgh	"	Rosel H. Stanley	Bennett's, 22	117
Shaftsbury	"	Milo Pierce	Bishop's, 4	193
Sharon	Windsor	Ammi Follett	Bishop's, 33	155
Sheffield	Caledonia	Charles Ingalls	Riverside, 19	102
Shelburne	Chittenden	David C. Smith	Orrin Daley's, 1	50
Sheldon	Franklin	Albert T. Leach	American, 29	11
Sherburne	Rutland	Edwin S. Colton	Bennett's, 11	90

Towns.	Counties.	Representatives.	Rooms.	No. of Seat.
Shoreham	Addison	Franklin Moore	Bishop's, 3	197
Shrewsbury	Rutland	George W. Foster	Mrs. True's, 25	18
Somerset	Windham	Franklin D. Chase	D. S. Wheatley's	107
So. Burlington	Chittenden	Seymour E. Thayer	Bishop's, 38	51
South Hero	Grand Isle	David S. Dillon	Bishop's, 23	172
Springfield	Windsor	Robert M. Colburn	Pavilion, 114	132
Stamford	Bennington	Wheeler C. Bratton	Bennett's, 22	173
Stannard	Caledonia	Alvah S. Ayer	Morse's	74
Starksboro	Addison	J. Sylvester Hill	American, 55	108
St. Albans	Franklin	Herbert Brainerd	Pavilion, 64	135
St. George	Chittenden	Mitchell W. Hinsdill	Mrs. True's, 22	228
St. Johnsbury	Caledonia	Walter P. Smith	Pavilion, 26	223
Stockbridge	Windsor	Orlando J. Richardson	Orrin Daley's	82
Stowe	Lamoille	Paphro D. Pike	Bishop's, 62	67

Strafford	Orange	Nathan B. Cobb	H. D. Hopkins's	24
Stratton	Windham	Andrew D. Knight	D. S. Wheatley's	112
Sudbury	Rutland	Benoni Griffin	M. Russell's	186
Sunderland	Bennington	Arnold R. Webb	Bishop's, 18	175
Sutton	Caledonia	Charles W. Willey	Riverside, 22	146
Swanton	Franklin	Hiram Platt	American, 86	166
Thetford	Orange	Jeduthan Taylor	Orrin Daley's	75
Tinmouth	Rutland	Isaac D. Tubbs	Bishop's, 8	158
Topsham	Orange	Roney M. Harvey	Mrs. Hibbard's	40
Townshend	Windham	Joseph B. Ware	Mrs. Walling's	55
Troy	Orleans	Daniel H. Buck	Bishop's, 31	213
Tunbridge	Orange	Orvis P. Cilley	American, 65	154
Underhill	Chittenden	Geo. W. Woodworth, Jr.	Mrs. True's, 14	145
Vergennes	Addison	Walter Scranton	Pavilion, 56	4
Vernon	Windham	Josiah M. Morrill	Mrs. Walling's	170
Victory	Essex	Charles Damon	Riverside, 25	53

Towns.	Counties.	Representatives.	Rooms.	No. of Seat.
Waitsfield	Washington	Walter A. Jones	Riverside, 24	184
Walden	Caledonia	Davison S. Ferguson	J. La Point's	71
Wallingford	Rutland	Nicholas Cook	Bennett's, 20	80
Waltham	Addison	William W. Booth	Mrs. True's, 43	157
Wardsboro	Windham	Herbert E. Kidder	Mrs. True's, 31	44
Warren	Washington	Milo Bucklin	American, 83	110
Washington	Orange	Noah C. Taylor	American, 83	111
Waterbury	Washington	Edwin F. Palmer	Pavilion, 83	143
Waterford	Caledonia	Dennis May	Orrin Daley's	138
Waterville	Lamoille	Omar D. Rogers	Bennett's, 1	65
Weathersfield	Windsor	Justus Dartt	Mrs. True's, 21	2
Wells	Rutland	Allen C. Grover	Bishop's, 63	127
West Fairlee	Orange	Fred. W. Farnham	Bishop's, 1	180
West Haven	Rutland	Rodney C. Abell	Riverside, 23	151

West Windsor	Windsor	Marquis F. Morrison	Mrs. True's, 26	207
Westfield	Orleans	Wm. Wells Wood	Bishop's, 31	22
Westford	Chittenden	Ira Stevens	Mrs. True's, 16	130
Westminster	Windham	Fenelon Arnold	Bishop's, 39	94
Westmore	Orleans	Welcome B. Daniels	Hathaway's	46
Weston	Windsor	Adin E. Bryant	Mrs. Walling's	181
Weybridge	Addison	Samuel James	Huntington's	217
Wheelock	Caledonia	Charles Rogers	Mrs. Newcomb's	224
Whiting	Addison	Daniel Holmes	Bennett's, 19	28
Whitingham	Windham	A. Augustine Butterfield	Mrs. Hibbard's	209
Williamstown	Orange	Oliver S. Walker	Mrs. Hibbard's	188
Williston	Chittenden	Hiram A Clark	Riverside, 15	49
Wilmington	Windham	Charles D. Spencer	Mrs. True's, 28	239
Windham	"	James W. Gould	Mrs. Walling's	191
Windsor	Windsor	Ripley Clark	Pavilion, 59	230
Winhall	Bennington	Bainbridge C. Benson	D. W. Dudley's	169

Towns.	Counties.	Representatives.	Rooms.	No. of Seat.
Wolcott	Lamoille	Not represented.		
Woodbury	Washington	Carroll A. McKnight	J. Voodry's	163
Woodford	Bennington	Truman J. Mallory	Bishop's, 13	176
Woodstock	Windsor	Justin F. Mackenzie	Pavilion, 24	183
Worcester	Washington	Chauncey N. Hunt	G. E. Hunt's	93

OFFICERS OF THE HOUSE.

Names.	Towns.	Offices.	Rooms.
HENRY N. NEWELL,	Shelburne,	*Clerk,*	Smilie's.
WILLIAM W. STICKNEY,	Ludlow,	*First Ass't Clerk,*	American, 31.
OLIN MERRILL,	Enosburgh,	*Second* " "	American, 31.
SELDEN B. CURRIER,	Moretown,	*Chaplain,*	At Home.

HIRAM SKEELS,	Highgate,	*Doorkeeper*,	Morse's.
WAYNE BAILEY,	Rutland,	*Ass't Doorkeeper*,	Mrs. Walling's.
HERBERT E. WALKER,	Ludlow,	*Messenger*,	Mrs. Newcomb's.
JONATHAN C. ROSS,	St. Johnsbury,	*Messenger*,	Mrs. Newcomb's.
E. MENTON ROCKWELL,	Alburgh,	*Messenger*,	Morse's.
EARLE S. KINSLEY,	Burlington,	*Messenger*,	Morse's.

4*

REPORTERS.

HENRY OVIATT,	Montpelier,	At Home.
EDWARD DANA,	Rutland,	Mrs. Walling's.

COMMITTEES.

JOINT STANDING COMMITTEES.

ON JOINT RULES.

Of the Senate—Mr. Gleason, of Orange,
Dana, of Addison.
Of the House—Mr. Abell, of West Haven,
Mackenzie, of Woodstock,
Grout, of Newport.

ON THE LIBRARY.

Of the Senate—Mr. King, of Rutland,
Field, of Windsor.
Of the House—Mr. Parker, of Pownal,
Priest, of Barre,
Haskell, of Grafton.

ON THE HOUSE OF CORRECTION.

Of the Senate—Mr. Judevine, of Essex,
Woodhouse, of Chittenden,
Peck, of Orange.
Of the House—Mr. Skinner of Barton,
Mackenzie, of Woodstock,
Parker, of Pownal,
Button, of Richford,
Prouty, of Marlboro.

ON THE REFORM SCHOOL.

Of the Senate—Mr. Start, of Franklin.
Blodgett, of Caledonia,
Paul, of Windsor.
Of the House—Mr. Merrifield, of Newfane,
Chapin, of Middlesex,
Richmond, of Rochester,
Grout, of Concord,
Leach, of Sheldon.

ON GAME AND FISHERIES.

Of the Senate—Mr. Goodsell, of Grand Isle,
North, of Addison,
Safford, of Franklin.
Of the House—Mr. Howe, of Ludlow,
Brainerd, of St. Albans,
Damon, of Victory,
Turner, of Dover,
Colton, of Sherburne.

UNDER THE FOURTH JOINT RULE.

Of the Senate—Mr. Thatcher, of Bennington,
Pember, of Rutland,
Robinson, of Chittenden.
Of the House—Mr. Sumner, of Halifax,
James, of Weybridge,
St. John, of Hubbardton.

ON BILLS.

Of the Senate—Mr. Weed, of Chittenden,
Fuller, of Windham.
Of the House—Mr. Harvey, of Topsham,
Tiffany, of Pittsford.

STANDING COMMITTEES OF THE SENATE.

On Rules.

Mr. Gleed,
Dillingham,
Brown.

On Finance.

Mr. Fuller,
Thatcher,
Judevine.

On Judiciary.

Mr. Dunton,
Gleed,
Start,
Gleason,
Henry,
Safford,
Bridgman.

On Claims.

Mr. Field,
Lane,
Sykes,
Dwinell,
North.

On Education.

Mr. Robinson,
King,
Gleason,
Goodsell,
Start.

On Agriculture.

Mr. Paul,
Dwinell,
Pember.

On Manufactures.

Mr. Peck,
Brown,
Fuller.

On Elections.

Mr. Darling,
Cook,
Weed.

On Military Affairs.

Mr. Henry,
Fuller,
King.

On Railroads.

Mr. Dillingham,
Dana,
Weed,
Woodworth,
Gleason,
Darling,
Fuller.

On Highways & Bridges.

Mr. North,
Pember,
Peck.

On Banks.

Mr. Woodhouse,
Blodgett,
Thatcher.

On Land Taxes.

Mr. Brown,
Judevine,
Sykes.

On Printing.

Mr. Safford,
Goodsell,
Field.

General Committee.

Mr. Lane,
Woodworth,
Sykes.

On Federal Relations.

Mr. Bridgman,
Blodgett,
Dunton.

On State Prison.

Mr. Dana,
Paul,
Weed.

On Insane Asylum.

Mr. Cook,
Bridgman,
Safford.

On Grand List.

Mr. Dwinell,
Judevine,
Woodworth.

On Proposals of Amendment to the Constitution.

Mr. Henry,
Dana,
Gleed,
Cook,
Dillingham,
Darling,
Dunton.

STANDING COMMITTEES OF THE HOUSE.

ON RULES.

Mr. Hinckley, - - - - *of Chelsea,*
Smith, - - - - - *of St. Johnsbury,*
Brainerd, - - - - *of St. Albans.*

ON ELECTIONS.

Mr. Judevine, - - - *of Hardwick,*
Palmer, - - - - *of Jericho,*
Harvey, - - - - *of Topsham,*
Bryant, - - - - *of Weston,*
Arnold, - - - - *of Westminster,*
Woodard, - - - *of Sandgate,*
Holmes, - - - - *of Whiting.*

ON FEDERAL RELATIONS.

Mr. Shepard, - - - - *of Brookfield,*
May, - - - - - *of Waterford,*
Stevens, - - - - *of Westford,*
Chase, - - - - *of Somerset,*
Morrison, - - - - *of West Windsor,*
Woodard, - - - - *of Sandgate,*
Daniels, - - - - *of Westmore.*

ON WAYS AND MEANS.

Mr. Page, - - - - - - *of Rutland,*
Scranton, - - - - *of Vergennes,*
Clark, - - - - - *of Windsor,*
Soule, - - - - - *of Fairfield,*
Deming, - - - - - *of Arlington,*
Dutton, - - - - - *of Dummerston,*
Kimball, - - - - - *of Newbury,*
Shattuck, - - - - - *of Eden,*
Gould, - - - - - *of Cabot.*

ON MILITARY AFFAIRS.

Mr. Hooker, - - - - - *of Brattleboro,*
Moore, - - - - - *of Shoreham,*
Ely-Goddard, - - - - *of Ely,*
Rhodes, - - - - - *of Guildhall,*
Stone, - - - - - - - *of Danville,*
Allen, - - - - - - *of Hinesburgh,*
Chase, - - - - - *of Jay.*

ON JUDICIARY.

Mr. Fifield, - - - - - *of Montpelier,*
Hinckley, - - - - *of Chelsea,*
Taft, - - - - - - *of Burlington,*
Thompson, - - - - *of Irasburgh,*
Simpson, - - - - - *of Craftsbury,*
Palmer, - - - - - *of Waterbury,*
Dartt, - - - - - - *of Weathersfield,*
Butterfield, - - - - *of Whitingham,*
Briggs, - - - - - *of Brandon.*

ON EDUCATION.

Mr. Dartt, - - - - - *of Weathersfield,*
Priest, - - - - - *of Barre,*
Kent, - - - - - *of Bristol,*

Mr. Spear, - - - - - - *of Braintree,*
Ellis, - - - - - *of Huntington,*
Manning, - - - - - *of Johnson,*
Lane, - - - - - *of Mount Tabor.*

ON CLAIMS.

Mr. Leavens, - - - - - *of Berkshire,*
Harvey, - - - - - *of Topsham,*
Smith, - - - - - *of Rockingham,*
Denny, - - - - - *of Northfield,*
Wright, - - - - - *of Orwell,*
Hendrick, - - - - *of Hyde Park,*
Hapgood, - - - - - *of Peru,*
Davis, - - - - - *of Chester,*
Whitney, - - - - - *of Franklin.*

ON RAILROADS.

Mr. Rogers, - - - - - *of Wheelock,*
Palmer, - - - - - *of Jericho,*
Orcutt, - - - - - *of Roxbury,*
Smith, - - - - - *of Monkton,*
Hazard, - - - - - *of Castleton,*
Howe, - - - - - *of Ludlow,*
Brown, - - - - - *of Grand Isle,*
Templeton, - - - - *of Glover,*
Merrifield, - - - - - *of Newfane.*

ON HIGHWAYS, BRIDGES AND FERRIES.

Mr. Mott, - - - - - *of Alburgh,*
Battell, - - - - - *of Middlebury,*
Barney, - - - - - *of Guilford,*
Wilson, - - - - - *of Manchester,*
Hinsdill, - - - - - *of St. George,*
Adams, - - - - - *of Pomfret,*
Perry, - - - - - *of Ira.*

ON BANKS.

Mr. Scranton, - - - - *of Vergennes,*
Sargent, - - - - - *of Bethel,*
Ely-Goddard, - - - - *of Ely,*
Gray, - - - - - *of Middletown,*
Hodges, - - - - - *of Richmond,*
Clark, - - - - - *of Williston,*
Leonard, - - - - *of Calais.*

ON MANUFACTURES.

Mr. Brainerd, . - - - - *of St. Albans,*
Mackenzie, - - - - - *of Woodstock,*
Allen, - - - - - *of Fair Haven,*
Pike, - - - - - - *of Stowe,*
Thomas, - - - - - *of Leicester,*
Le Clair, - - - - - *of Colchester,*
Whitney, - - - - *of Dorset.*

ON AGRICULTURE.

Mr. Prindle, - - - - - *of Charlotte,*
Colburn, - - - - - *of Springfield,*
Fowler, - - - - - *of Randolph,*
Simpson, - - - - - *of Greensboro,*
Whitney, - - - - - *of Brookline,*
Tracy, - - - - - *of E. Montpelier,*
Booth, - - - - - *of Ferrisburgh,*
Beebe, - - - - - *of Rupert,*
Smith, - - - - - *of Newark,*
Pond, - - - - - *of Lunenburgh,*
Curtis, - - - - - *of Georgia,*
Wilcox, - - - - - *of Pawlet,*
Parker, - - - - - *of Elmore,*
Dillon, - - - - - *of South Hero.*

ON LAND TAXES.

Mr. Fitch, - - - - - *of Brunswick,*
Hinsdill, - - - - - *of St. George,*
Boyce, - - - - - *of Fayston,*
Horton, - - - - - *of Chittenden,*
West, - - - - - *of Royalton,*
Knight, - - - - - *of Stratton,*
Hutchinson, - - - - *of Orange,*
Joslyn, - - - - - *of Brownington,*
Rogers, - - - - - *of Waterville,*
Shepardson, - - - - *of Fairfax,*
Renfrew, - - - - - *of Ryegate,*
Goodell, - - - - - *of Readsboro,*
Witherell, - - - - *of Bridport,*
Fefee, - - - - - - *of North Hero.*

ON GRAND LIST.

Mr. Jones, - - - - - *of Waitsfield,*
Rankin, - - - - - *of Milton,*
Blair, - - - - - - *of Barnet,*
Davis, - - - - - *of Barnard,*
Walker, - - - - - *of Williamstown,*
Blaisdell, - - - - *of Cambridge,*
Allen, - - - - - *of Enosburgh,*
Foster, - - - - - *of Shrewsbury,*
Black, - - - - - - *of Coventry,*
Ware, - - - - - *of Townshend,*
Benson, - - - - - *of Winhall,*
Hudson, - - - - - *of East Haven,*
Bingham, - - - - - *of Cornwall,*
Hurst, - - - - - *of Isle La Motte.*

GENERAL COMMITTEE.

Mr. Booth, - - - - - *of Morristown,*
Hubbard, - - - - - *of Plymouth,*

Mr. Ingalls, - - - - of *Sheffield*,
Davis, - - - - - of *Putney*,
Brown, - - - - - of *Grand Isle*,
Giddings, - - - - of *Bakersfield*,
Chamberlain, - - - of *Bradford*,
Tiffany, - - - - - of *Pittsford*,
Sawyer, - - - - - of *Moretown*,
Chafey, - - - - - of *Albany*,
Pierce, - - - - - of *Shaftsbury*,
Doud, - - - - - of *New Haven*,
Nichols, - - - - - of *Essex*,
Morrill, - - - - - of *Canaan*.

DISTRIBUTING COMMITTEE.

Mr. Cushing, - - - - - of *Jamaica*,
Shattuck, - - - - of *Eden*,
Taylor, - - - - - of *Washington*,
Caswell, - - - - - of *Holland*,
Mott, - - - - - - of *Alburgh*,
Abbott, - - - - - of *Landgrove*,
McGettrick, - - - - of *Fletcher*,
Lovejoy, - - - - of *Andover*,
Griffin, - - - - - of *Sudbury*,
Bucklin, - - - - - of *Warren*,
Whalen, - - - - - of *Bolton*,
Whitford, - - - - - of *Addison*,
Bolton, - - - - - of *Peacham*,
Matthews, - - - - of *Granby*.

ON STATE PRISON.

Mr. Goodwin, - - - - of *Hartland*,
Platt, - - - - - - of *Swanton*,
Hopkinson, - - - - of *Salem*,
Bemis, - - - - - of *Lyndon*,

Mr. Cilley, - - - - - *of Tunbridge,*
Ripley, - - - - - *of Poultney,*
Wheelock, - - - - *of Berlin.*

ON CORPORATIONS.

Mr. Abbott, - - - - - *of Bennington,*
Buck, - - - - - *of Troy,*
Smith, - - - - - *of Shelburne,*
Currier, - - - - - *of Norwich,*
Spencer, - - - *of Wilmington,*
Cook, - - - - - *of Wallingford,*
Cameron, - - - - - *of Maidstone.*

ON TOWN LINES.

Mr. Strong, - - - - - *of Benson,*
Taylor, - - - - - *of Thetford,*
Preston, - - - - - *of Baltimore,*
Bemis, - - - - - *of Burke,*
Woodworth, - - - *of Underhill,*
Roby, - - - - - *of Bloomfield,*
Ober, - - - - - - *of Athens.*

ON MILEAGE AND DEBENTURES.

Mr. Babcock, - - - - *of Bridgewater,*
Welch, - - - - - *of Groton,*
Grout, - - - - - *of Concord,*
Harbour, - - - - - *of Glastenbury,*
Perry, - - - - - *of Hancock,*
Allen, - - - - - - *of Hinesburgh,*
Dix, - - - - - - *of Montgomery,*
Fefee, - - - - - *of North Hero,*
Gould, - - - - - *of Windham,*
Smith, - - - - - *of Fairlee,*
Atwood, - - - - - *of Pittsfield,*
Dolloff, - - - - - *of Charleston,*
McKnight, - - - - *of Woodbury,*
Potter, - - - - - *of Belvidere.*

ON PUBLIC BUILDINGS.

Mr. Hinckley, - - - - - *of Chelsea,*
Abell, - - - - - *of West Haven,*
Farnham, - - - - - *of West Fairlee,*
Hunt, - - - - - *of Worcester,*
Hooker, - - - - - *of Brattleboro,*
Goodwin, - - - - *of Derby,*
Dexter, - - - - - *of Reading.*

ON THE INSANE.

Mr. Allen, - - - - - *of Hartford,*
Adams, - - - - - *of Brighton,*
Smith, - - - - - *of Plainfield,*
Kidder, - - - - - *of Wardsboro,*
Judevine, - - - - *of Hardwick,*
Searle, - - - - - *of Highgate,*
Towsley, - - - - - *of Panton.*

ON REVISION OF LAWS.

Mr. Taft, - - - - - *of Burlington,*
Thompson, - - - - - *of Irasburgh,*
Page, - - - - - *of Rutland,*
Grout, - - - - - *of Newport,*
Fifield, - - - - - *of Montpelier,*
Abell, - - - - - *of West Haven,*
Fletcher, - - - - - *of Cavendish,*
Smith, - - - - - *of St. Johnsbury,*
Palmer, - - - - - *of Jericho.*

BIOGRAPHICAL NOTES.

BIOGRAPHICAL AND POLITICAL NOTES

OF THE

FEDERAL OFFICERS, CONGRESSIONAL DELEGATION, JUDICIARY, MEMBERS OF THE EXECUTIVE DEPARTMENT, SENATE AND HOUSE OF REPRESENTATIVES, CONSTITUTING THE CIVIL GOVERNMENT OF VERMONT.

FEDERAL OFFICERS.

Hon. HOYT H. WHEELER, of Jamaica, district judge, was born in Chesterfield, N. H., August 30, 1833; received an academical education at Chesterfield Academy and Newfane, Vt.; read law with the late Hon. Charles K. Field, then of Newfane, and with Bradley & Kellogg, of Brattleboro; was admitted to the bar of Windham county in 1859, and located in Jamaica the same year. Judge Wheeler represented Jamaica in 1867, and was a senator from Windham county in 1868–69. In the latter year he was elected a judge of the supreme court, which position he continuously occupied until March 31, 1877, when he resigned, having been appointed by President Hayes judge for the district of Vermont. Religious preference, Congregationalist, and in politics is a republican.

DISTRICT ATTORNEYSHIP—Vacant.

Hon. BRADLEY B. SMALLEY, of Burlington, clerk of the district of Vermont, was born in Jericho, Vt., Nov. 26, 1836, and removed to Burlington in 1839. Mr.

Smalley received a common school and academic education; studied law with his father, the late Hon. David A. Smalley; was appointed district clerk in 1861, and admitted to the bar of Chittenden county in 1863. He represented the city of Burlington in the legislature of 1874 and again in 1878, and has held various municipal offices in his adopted city. Religious preference, Episcopalian, and in politics is a democrat.

General WILLIAM WIRT HENRY, of Burlington, marshal, was born in Waterbury, Vt., Nov. 21, 1831; received a common school and academical education, located in Burlington in 1868, and engaged in the manufacture and sale of proprietary and other medicines. Gen. Henry was commissioned first lieutenant of Co. D, 2d Vt. Vols.; promoted successively major, lieutenant colonel, colonel of the 10th Vt. Vols., and for gallant services on the field was made brigadier general by brevet. He has held several municipal offices in both his native town and adopted city. In 1865-66-67 he was a member of the senate from the county of Washington, and in 1874-75 from the county of Chittenden, and was appointed marshal by President Hayes in 1879, *vice* Gen. George P. Foster, deceased. Religious preference, Congregationalist, and in politics is a republican.

General WILLIAM WELLS, of Burlington, collector of customs, was born in Waterbury, Vt., Dec. 14, 1837; received an academical education at Barre, Vt., and Kimball Union Academy, of Meriden, N. H., and engaged in mercantile life. Early in the war of the rebellion he enlisted as a private in Co. C, 1st Vt. Cav., received successive promotions as first lieutenant, captain, major, colonel, brevet brigadier, brigadier and brevet major general of volunteers. In 1865 and '66 he represented his native town in the legislature. In 1866 he was elected adjutant and inspector general, which position he held by successive elections till May, 1872, when he was appointed by President Grant collector of customs, and the same year located in Burlington. Religious preference, Episcopalian, and in politics is a republican.

Hon. CHARLES S. DANA, of Montpelier, collector of internal revenue, was born in Danville, Vt., Nov. 18, 1815; was a graduate of Dartmouth College, class of 1837; studied law and graduated at the Harvard Law School in 1840. He was judge of probate for the district of Caledonia from 1846 to 1854; removed to St. Johnsbury in 1856, and was appointed clerk of the county, which position he occupied for eight years; was a member of the house in 1862 and '63, and senator from Caledonia county in 1864. In 1864 Judge Dana was appointed collector of internal revenue by President Lincoln, which office he has since held. Religious preference, Episcopalian, and in politics is a republican.

CONGRESSIONAL DELEGATION.

SENATORS.

Hon. GEORGE F. EDMUNDS, of Burlington, senator, was born at Richmond, Vt., Feb. 1, 1828; received a common school education and the instruction of a private tutor; studied law with A. B. Maynard, Esq., of Richmond, in 1846 and '47,—with Messrs. Smalley & Phelps, of Burlington, in 1848 and '49; was admitted to the bar of Chittenden county in 1849; practiced law in Richmond till November, 1851, when he located in Burlington. In 1854, '55, '57, '58 and '59 he was a representative in the legislature, serving as speaker of of the house in 1857, '58 and 59; was a member and president *pro tempore* of the senate in 1861 and '62. He was appointed United States senator, to fill the vacancy occasioned by the death of the Hon. Solomon Foot, and took his seat April 5, 1866; was elected for the remainder of the term ending March 4, 1869, and has received two successive elections since; his present term will expire in 1881. He was a member of the electoral commission in 1876, and is the acknowledged leader of the United States senate. Religious preference, Episcopalian, and in politics is a republican.

Hon. JUSTIN S. MORRILL, of Strafford, was born at Strafford, Vt., April 14, 1810; received an academic education; was a merchant, and afterwards engaged in agricultural pursuits; was a representative in the 34th, 35th, 36th, 37th, 38th and 39th congresses. In 1866 he was elected to succeed the Hon. Luke P. Poland in the United States senate, took his seat March 4, 1867, and has received two successive elections since, his present term ending March 3, 1885. Religious preference, Congregationalist, and in politics is a republican.

REPRESENTATIVES.

FIRST DISTRICT.

Counties—Addison, Bennington, Rutland, and Washington.

Hon. CHARLES H. JOYCE, of Rutland, was born near Andover, England, Jan. 30, 1830, and emigrated to this country when a mere lad. He received an academical education, and commenced the study of law with John L. Buck, Esq., of Northfield, about the year 1850, reading also in the offices of F. V. Randall, Esq., and Hon. Ferrand F. Merrill, of Montpelier; was admitted to the bar of Washington county in 1852, and located in Northfield. In 1853 and '54 he held the office of state librarian. In 1856 he was elected state's attorney for Washington county, and re-elected in 1857. In 1861 he was commissioned major of the 2d reg't Vt. Vols., and was promoted to the rank of lieutenant colonel in 1862. In 1863 he removed to Rutland, which town he represented in 1870, serving as speaker the same year. Col. Joyce was elected from the first district of Vermont to the 44th, 45th, and 46th congresses, and re-elected to the 47th, as a republican, receiving 15,645 votes against 6,771 votes for Jean J. R. Randall, democrat; 358 votes for Carlos C. Martin, greenbacker; scattering, 37.

SECOND DISTRICT.

Counties—Caledonia, Orange, Windham, and Windsor.

Hon. JAMES M. TYLER, of Brattleboro, was born at Wilmington, Vt., April 27, 1835; received an academical education; studied law with Messrs. Keyes & Howe, of Brattleboro; was one year in the law department of the University of Albany, N. Y., and was admitted to the bar in 1860; practiced law in his native town till 1864, when he located in Brattleboro. Mr. Tyler has never mingled in political life, but has strictly and successfully devoted himself to the pursuits of his profession, never holding any office except that of trustee of the Vermont asylum for the insane. He was elected from the second district of Vermont to the 46th and re-elected to the 47th congress, as a republican, receiving 15,960 votes against 6,698 votes for Daniel Campbell, democrat; 411 votes for John B. Mead; scattering 53.

—

THIRD DISTRICT.

Counties—Chittenden, Essex, Franklin, Grand Isle, Lamoille and Orleans.

Hon. BRADLEY BARLOW, of St. Albans, was born in Fairfield, Vt., May 12, 1814, and until 1858 was engaged in agricultural and mercantile pursuits, when he removed to St. Albans, where he has since been engaged in banking and other large business pursuits; is now president of the Vermont National Bank of St. Albans, and is largely interested in various railroad enterprises; has been six times elected to the state house of representatives, and twice elected a state senator; has been twice elected a member of state constitutional conventions—of one of which he was assistant secretary; was for several years county treasurer, and was elected to the 46th congress, as a national republican, receiving 8,367 votes, against 4,330 for Wm. W. Grout, republican, 1,095 votes for George L. Waterman, democrat, and 55 scattering votes. His term of service will expire March 3, 1881.

Hon. WILLIAM W. GROUT, of Barton, representative elect from the third district, was born in Compton, P. Q., May 24, 1836. He received a liberal classical education; read law and took a course in the State and National Law Schools, Poughkeepsie, N. Y., graduating in 1857, and immediately entered upon the practice of his profession, locating at Barton in 1857. He served in the war of the rebellion as lieutenant colonel of the 15th regiment, Vt. Vols. In 1865 and '66 he was state's attorney for Orleans county, and was a delegate to the Chicago convention in 1868. He was a member of the general assembly from Barton in 1868, '69, '70, and 74,—a senator from Orleans county in 1876, and was president *pro tempore* of the senate. He was elected a member of the 47th congress, receiving 12,253 votes against 6,191 votes for John W. Currier, democrat; 1256 votes for Fletcher Tarble, greenbacker; 506 votes for H. Henry Powers, and 82 votes scattering. Religious preference, Liberal.

JUDICIARY.

Hon. JOHN PIERPOINT, of Vergennes, chief justice, republican, was born in Litchfield, Conn., Sept. 10, 1806. He read law, graduating at Judge Gould's law school, and located in Vergennes in 1832. Was educated at the public schools and academies. Was a member of the house in 1841, and of the senate from Addison county in 1855, '56, and '57. In 1857 he was elected fourth assistant justice, and in 1865 succeeded to the chief justiceship of the supreme court of Vermont, which position he has occupied by continuous elections since. Religious preference, Congregationalist.

Hon. JAMES BARRETT, of Woodstock, first associate justice, republican, was born in Strafford, Vt., May 31, 1814. He is a lawyer by profession, and located in Woodstock in 1839. Previous to 1832, when he entered Orange County Grammar School, preparatory for college, Judge Barrett worked in a wool carding and clothing mill. He entered college in 1833—but was obliged to suspend his studies one year, for want of means—and graduated at Dartmouth in 1838. He was a senator from Windsor county in 1844 and '45, serving as president *pro tempore* the latter year; was state's attorney in 1854 and '55, and was elected a judge of the supreme court in 1857; and has occupied a seat upon the bench through successive elections since that time. Religious preference, Congregationalist.

Hon. HOMER E. ROYCE, of St. Albans, second associate justice, republican, was born in Berkshire, Vt., in 1819. He is a lawyer by profession, and located in St. Albans in 1869. Was educated at the common schools. Was a member of the house from Berkshire in 1846, '47, and in 1861, and was a senator from Franklin county in 1849, '50 and '51. Held the office of state's attorney in 1846 and '47. Was elected a member of congress from the third district in 1856, '58, and '60, and elected a judge of the supreme court in 1870, and has received continuous elections since. Has held a number of town offices in Berkshire. Religious preference, Episcopalian.

Hon. TIMOTHY P. REDFIELD, of Montpelier, third associate justice, was born in Coventry, Vt., Nov. 3, 1812. He graduated at Dartmouth College, class of 1836; read law with his brother, the late Hon. Isaac F. Redfield, formerly chief justice of the supreme court, and was admitted to the bar of Orleans county in 1839, settled in Irasburgh, and practiced his profession till 1848, when he removed to Montpelier. In 1848 he was a senator from Orleans county. In 1870 was elected a judge of the supreme court, and has received successive elections since. In politics, Judge Redfield adheres to the "Constitution and the Law." Religious preference, Episcopalian.

Hon. JONATHAN ROSS, of St. Johnsbury, fourth associate justice, republican, was born in Waterford, Vt., April 30, 1826. He is a lawyer, having read for that profession in the office of the late Hon. Wm. Hebard, and located in St. Johnsbury in 1856. Was a graduate of Dartmouth College. Was a member of the house in 1865, '66, and 67, and a senator from the county of Caledonia in 1870. Was a member of the state board of education from 1866 to 1870. Was one of the council of censors in 1869, and was elected an associate justice of the supreme court in 1870, and has received successive elections since. Religious preference, Congregationalist.

Hon. H. HENRY POWERS, of Morristown, fifth associate justice, republican, was born in Morristown, Vt., May 29, 1835. Was a graduate of the University of Vermont, class of 1855. Read law with the late Hon. Thomas Gleed, of Morristown; was admitted to the bar of Lamoille county in 1858; commenced the practice of his profession in Hydepark, and represented that town in the general assembly of 1858, and he was state's attorney for Lamoille county in 1861 and '62; was a member of the council of censors in 1869, and of the constitutional convention in 1870. In 1872 he was a senator from Lamoille county. In 1874 he was representative from Morristown, serving that year as speaker of the house. Was elected to the supreme bench in 1874, and has received successive elections since. Religious preference, Liberal. P. O. address, Morrisville.

Hon. WHEELOCK G. VEASEY, of Rutland, sixth associate justice, republican, was born in Brentwood, N. H., Dec. 5, 1835. He graduated at Dartmouth; read law and graduated in his profession at the Albany, (N. Y.,) Law School. He enlisted as a private in Co. A, was successively promoted to the offices of captain of said company, to major and lieutenant colonel of the 3d, and afterwards made colonel of the 16th regiment Vermont Volunteers. He was reporter of the decisions of the supreme court from 1864 to '72; was senator from Rutland county in 1872 and '73; register in bankruptcy from 1875 to '78, and appointed by Gov. Proctor, sixth associate justice of the supreme court, Nov. 1, 1879, *vice* Judge Dunton, resigned. Religious preference, Episcopalian.

Hon. JOHN W. ROWELL, of Randolph, reporter, republican, was born in Lebanon, N. H., June 9, 1835. He is a lawyer by profession, and located in town in 1856. Was educated at West Randolph Academy. Was state's attorney of Orange county in 1862 and '63, representing the town of Randolph in 1861 and '62, and was senator from that county in 1874. Has held the office of director of the Northfield National bank, is now director and vice president of the Randolph National bank; was elected reporter of the decisions of the supreme court in 1872, and has held the office by continuous elections, and appointment since. Religious preference, Christian. P. O. address, West Randolph.

EXECUTIVE DEPARTMENT.

GOVERNOR.

His Excellency, ROSWELL FARNHAM,

of Bradford, was born in Boston, Mass., July 23, 1827, being the eighth generation in descent from Ralph Farnham who came from England and settled at Andover, Mass., in 1645,—on the maternal side, his lineage is traced back to the Mayflower. His immediate ancestors, on both sides, were of New Hampshire origin. When quite young, his parents removed to Haverhill, Mass., where they resided till 1837, when the great financial crash of that year swept away the fortune of his father who was extensively engaged in the wholesale manufacture of shoes. The next year the family removed to Bradford, Vt., where the subject of this sketch has since resided, with the exception of a comparatively short period. He fitted for college at the Bradford academy, working on his father's farm at the same time. Being unable to enter college, when fitted, for want of means, he continued his studies at the academy until he was enabled to enter the junior class, which he did at the University of Vermont in 1847, and graduated in 1849. He immediately commenced teaching in the academy at Dunham, P. Q., where he remained some more than a year; he then taught in the academy at Franklin, Vt., during the next three years, and closed his career as a teacher at Bradford academy, whose principal he had been for two years. He was admitted to the Orange county bar in January, 1857, located at Bradford, where he has since been engaged in a large and successful practice. In 1859, '60, and 61, he was elected state's attorney for Orange county. He held that office when he served his term as 2d lieutenant of Co. D, (Bradford Guards,) of the 1st regiment, Vt. Vols., and he resigned the position of state's attorney, to enter the 12th regiment, in the summer of 1862. While the 1st regiment was at Newport News, Gov. Farnham was appointed provost marshal of the forces then there. In 1862, when the 12th regiment was called for, he recruited the Bradford Guards to the number required by government; was elected captain, went to the field, was made lieutenant colonel, and held that position during the service of the regiment—being in command much of the time, as the colonel of the regiment was in command of the brigade. In 1868 and '69 Gov. Farnham was a senator from Orange county; he was a delegate to the national republican convention at Cincinnati, which nominated President Hayes, and was presidential elector the same year. He is one of the elective trustees of the University of Vermont and State Agricultural College. Religious preference, Congregationalist. He was elected governor, as a republican, receiving 47,848 votes against 21,245 votes for Edward J. Phelps, democrat; 1,578 votes for Madison O. Heath, greenbacker, and 13 votes scattering.

LESTER F. THURBER, of Bradford, Secretary of Civil and Military Affairs, republican, was born in Washington, Aug. 24, 1858. He is a teller in the Bradford Savings Bank and Trust Company, and located in town in 1876. Was educated at Goddard Seminary. Religious preference, Congregationalist.

FRANK H. BROWN, of Rockingham, Clerk in the Executive Department, republican, was born in Weathersfield, Feb. 13, 1854. Educated at Wesleyan Seminary, Springfield, and has been teller in the First National Bank of Springfield, for six years. Is now known as "Brownie," one of the Vermont correspondents of the Boston *Journal*. Religious preference, Episcopalian. P. O. address, Bellows Falls.

CHARLES C. FARNHAM, of Bradford, Messenger of the Governor, republican, was born in Bradford, May 9, 1864. He is a student. Religious preference, Congregationalist.

—

LIEUTENANT GOVERNOR.

His Honor, JOHN L. BARSTOW, of Shelburne, was born in Shelburne, Vt., Feb. 21, 1832. He is a farmer, and was educated in the schools of his native town. He served in the war of the rebellion as major of the 8th regiment Vt. Vols. In 1861 he was assistant clerk of the house of representatives, a member of the house in 1864 and '65, and a senator from Chittenden county in 1866 and '67. He was pension agent for many years, vacating the position only, when the office was consolidated with those of Maine and New Hampshire, and located at Concord in the latter state. He has been repeatedly honored by elections to various offices of trust and responsibility in his native town. Religious preference, Episcopalian. He was elected, as a republican, lieutenant governor, receiving 47,860 votes against 21,177 for George W. Gates, democrat, and 1,580 votes for Columbus F. Clough, greenbacker; scattering, 3 votes.

—

TREASURER.

Hon. JOHN A. PAGE, of Montpelier, was born in Haverhill, N. H., June 17, 1814. He is a son of the late Hon. John Page, governor of New Hampshire in 1839, '40 and '41, and received his education at the common schools and Haverhill academy. In September, 1837, he was appointed cashier of the Grafton bank in Haverhill, which institution was closed in 1844, when he removed to Danville, and was there engaged as cashier of the Caledonia county bank till November, 1848. In April, 1849, he removed to Montpelier, and became cashier of the Vermont bank. At the organization of the first national bank of Montpelier in 1865, he was elected president, which office he has held to the present time. He was repeatedly elected treasurer of Danville, and represented that town in the legislature of 1848. He was treasurer of Montpelier for many years. In 1853 he was elected state treasurer, and again in 1866, since which time he has held that office continuously. Religious preference, Congregationalist. He was elected as a republican, treasurer, receiving 47,904 votes against 21,177 votes for James H. Williams, democrat, and 1,583 votes for Samuel H. Soule, greenback; scattering, 3 votes.

Horace W. Kempton, of Montpelier, Clerk, republican, was born in Frankfort, Maine, Feb. 4, 1835. He is an ice dealer, and located in town in 1859. Was educated at the common schools. Religious preference, Episcopalian.

—

INSPECTOR OF FINANCE.

Hon. William H. DuBois, of Randolph, republican, was born in Randolph, March 24, 1835. He received a liberal academical education, and early in life entered into active business engagements in the city of Boston, which continued from 1852 to 1864, when he removed to the city of New York, where for the next five years he was engaged in a very extensive and successful business enterprise. In 1875 he organized the Randolph national bank, and has been its president since. He has held various positions of trust and responsibility, having been trustee of the endowment fund of the State normal school at Randolph for the last three years; treasurer of the graded school district, and the village of West Randolph since their incorporation; has been town auditor repeatedly, which office he now holds. In 1876, he was a member of the general assembly from Randolph; was appointed inspector of finance by Gov. Fairbanks in the same year, and re-appointed by Gov. Proctor in 1878. Religious preference, Baptist. P. O. address, West Randolph.

SECRETARY OF STATE.

Hon. GEORGE NICHOLS, of Northfield, republican, was born in that town, April 17, 1827. Graduated as physician and surgeon at the Vermont medical college (Woodstock) in 1851. He was surgeon of the 13th regiment Vt. Vols. He has repeatedly held the usual town offices. In 1868 he was elected director, and in 1874 president, of the Northfield national bank. In 1848 he was appointed state librarian by Gov. Coolidge, and received successive annual elections till 1853. In 1870 he was president of the constitutional convention. He was delegate to the national republican convention of 1872, and member of the national republican committee; has been a member of the republican state committee since that year, being secretary till 1880, when he was elected chairman of the same. Dr. Nichols was appointed secretary of state by Gov. Smith, to fill the vacancy occasioned by the death of Hon. Geo. W. Bailey, Jr., in 1865. Religious preference, Episcopalian.

CHARLES W. PORTER, of Montpelier, Deputy Secretary of State, republican, was born in Hartford, Vt., July 11, 1849. He is a lawyer, and located in town in 1872. Has been deputy since 1872, and was admitted to the bar in 1874. Religious preference, Congregationalist.

EUGENE W. J. HAWKINS, Starksboro, Engrossing Clerk, republican, was born in Starksboro, Vt., July 28, 1851. He is a lawyer, having been admitted to the bar of Addison county in 1873. Has held the offices of superintendent, agent, notary, and has been reporter for the Addison county court, and is a justice of the peace. Was appointed Engrossing Clerk in 1878. Religious preference, Methodist.

EVERETT C. BENTON, Messenger, was born in Guildhall, Sept. 25, 1862. He is a student. Was messenger in the Senate in 1878. Religious preference, Methodist.

AUDITOR OF ACCOUNTS.

Hon. E. Henry Powell, of Richford, republican, was born in Richford, Vt., Sept. 3, 1839. He read law, and was admitted to the bar in 1866. Was educated at Potsdam (N. Y.) and Fairfax academies. He held the office of inspector of customs in 1866, '67, and '68, and was state's attorney for Franklin county in 1872 and '73. In 1874 he was a member of the house from the town of Richford; in 1878 was a senator from the county of Franklin, and was elected auditor of accounts in 1878. Religious preference, Baptist.

Albert W. Ferrin, of Montpelier, Clerk, republican, was born in Johnson, Vt., July 4, 1851. He is treasurer of the Montpelier Savings Bank & Trust Company, and located in town in 1859. Was clerk in the auditor's office from 1870 to 1876, continuously, and again appointed in 1878. Religious preference, Unitarian.

—

SERGEANT-AT-ARMS.

Hon. Truman C. Phinney, of Montpelier, republican, was born in Middlesex, Vt., April 11, 1827, and removed to Montpelier in 1849, where he is successfully engaged as a bookseller and stationer. He was elected to the office of sergeant-at-arms in 1870. Religious preference, Episcopalian.

Arthur L. Jameson, Irasburgh, Clerk, republican, was born in Irasburgh, July 13, 1861. He is a student. Religious preference, Methodist.

Herman D. Hopkins, Jr., Montpelier, Messenger, republican, was born in Montpelier, July 24, 1864. He is a student—was a messenger in Auditor's office in 1876, and in this office in 1878. Religious preference, Congregationalist.

Harry C. Briggs, Brandon, Messenger, republican, was born in Brandon, Sept. 8, 1863. He is a student. Religious preference, Episcopalian.

ADJUTANT AND INSPECTOR GENERAL.

Gen. JAMES S. PECK, of Montpelier, republican, was born in that town, December, 1839, and graduated at the University of Vermont in 1860. He studied law, and was admitted to the bar in 1866. He was lieutenant and adjutant of the 13th, adjutant and major of the 17th regiment Vt. Vols. He was elected to the office of adjutant and inspector general in 1872. Religious preference, Episcopalian.

—

QUARTERMASTER GENERAL.

Gen. LEVI G. KINGSLEY, of Rutland, republican, was born in Shrewsbury, May 21, 1832, and is an alumnus of Norwich University, class of 1853. He removed to Rutland in 1857, and has since been engaged in mercantile business in that town. He was second lieutenant in the 1st, and captain and major in the 12th regiment Vt. Vols.; was made colonel of the Vermont state militia in 1864, and elected quartermaster general in 1874. Religious preference, Episcopalian.

—

JUDGE ADVOCATE GENERAL.

Gen. FRANKLIN G. BUTTERFIELD, republican, was born in Rockingham, May 11, 1842. He is a law student. Entered Middlebury College, class of 1863, but left in his junior year. Was second lieutenant in the 6th Vt. Vols., and was successively promoted to first lieutenant, captain, and lieutenant colonel of said regiment. Has been justice of the peace for the last seven years; was elected high bailiff of Windham county in 1878, and was clerk in the executive department, and elected Judge Advocate General the same year. In 1880 he was appointed supervisor of the 10th census for the district of Vermont. Religious preference, Congregationalist. P. O. address, Saxtons River.

STATE LIBRARIAN.

Hon. HIRAM A. HUSE, of Montpelier, republican, was born in Randolph, Vt., Jan. 17, 1843. He is a lawyer, and located in town in 1872. Was educated at Dartmouth College, graduating in the class of 1865. Was a resident of Wisconsin from 1845 to 1868. In 1862 he enlisted as a private in Co. F, 12th regiment Vt. Vols. In 1873 he was appointed state librarian to fill the vacancy occasioned by the death of the Hon. Charles Reed, and was a member of the house in 1878. Religious preference, Episcopalian.

THOMAS L. WOOD, of Montpelier, Assistant Librarian, republican, was born in Randolph, Aug. 1, 1839. He is a clerk, and was a member of the 10th regiment Vt. Vols. Was messenger in the library in 1876 and '78. Religious preference, Episcopalian.

EDWARD L. SMITH, Montpelier, Messenger, was born in Montpelier, April 6, 1865. He is a student. Was messenger in Sergeant-at-Arms' office in '78. Religious preference, Congregationalist.

—

STATE SUPERINTENDENT OF EDUCATION.

Hon. EDWARD CONANT, of Randolph, republican, was born in Pomfret, Vt., May 10, 1829. He is a teacher by profession, and located in town in 1861. Was educated at Dartmouth college, and received the honorary degree of A. M. from Middlebury college in 1866, and from the University of Vermont in 1867. He has held the office of town superintendent of schools; was a member of the state board of education in 1866–7; was a member of the constitutional convention in 1870, and has been state superintendent of education since 1874. Religious preference, Congregationalist.

—

STATE SUPERINTENDENT OF AGRICULTURAL AFFAIRS.

Hon. JOHN B. MEAD, of Randolph, republican, was born in Stratham, N. H., March 15, 1831. He is a farmer, and located in Randolph in 1841. Was educated at the Orange county grammar school, and the academy in Orford, N. H. Col. Mead was commissioned as second lieutenant of Co. G, 8th regiment Vt. Vols., and successively promoted to first lieutenant and captain of said company, to major, lieutenant colonel and colonel of the regiment. He was a member of the house in 1867; a senator from Orange county in 1878–9; was appointed state superintendent of agricultural affairs in 1878, and was a delegate to the national republican convention, held in Chicago, in 1880. Religious preference, Congregationalist.

—

STATE PRISON AND HOUSE OF CORRECTION.

Hon. WILLIAM H. H. BINGHAM, of Stowe, director, democrat, was born in Fletcher. Vt., April. 15, 1813. He is an attorney and also president of the Vermont Mutual Fire Insurance Company, and located in town in 1836. Was educated at the common schools and St. Albans academy. He was a member and secretary of the council of censors in 1862, and member of the constitutional convention of 1870; has held the offices of state's attorney of Lamoille county, county commissioner and pension agent. He has held the usual town offices, and is director of the Waterbury National Bank, National Life Insurance Company, Montpelier and Wells River, and the Central Vermont Railroads. In 1878 he was appointed director of the state prison and house of correction. Religious preference, Congregationalist.

Hon. NER P. SIMONS, of Rutland, director, republican, was born in Williamstown, Vt., Nov. 1, 1831. He is a lawyer and located in town in 1861. Was educated at the common schools, and Randolph and Meriden (N. H.) academies. He was a senator from Rutland county in 1876; was appointed one of the commissioners by Gov. Fairbanks—having in charge the construction of the house of correction, and was appointed director of the state prison and house of correction in 1878. He has held the office of superintendent of schools, deputy sheriff, and deputy marshal. Religious preference, Unitarian.

Hon. JOSEPH CHASE PARKER, of Hartford, director, republican, was born in Plainfield, N. H., Oct. 28, 1823. He is a farmer and manufacturer, and located in town in 1857. Was educated at the common schools. He was a member of the general assembly from the town of Barre in 1856, from Hartford in 1867 and '68, and a senator from Windsor county in 1874-5. He was appointed director of the state prison and house of correction in 1878. Religious preference, Unitarian. P. O. address, Quechee.

Hon. WENDELL P. RICE, of Windsor, superintendent of state prison, republican, was born in Hampden, Maine, Dec. 23, 1851, and located in town in 1878. Was educated at the common and high schools of Thomaston, Maine. He was an officer in the Maine state prison from 1869 to 1878—four years of which time was deputy warden. He was appointed superintendent of the state prison in 1878, and has held the office of justice of the peace. Religious preference, Universalist.

Hon. GEORGE N. EAYRES, of Rutland, superintendent of the house of correction, republican, was born in Rutland, Vt., Dec. 12, 1824. He is a farmer, and removed to Pittsford in 1855, and again located in Rutland in 1877. Was educated at the common schools and academy. He was selectman of Pittsford in 1868, '69, '73, '74, and '75, and lister for several years; was a member of the general assembly from the town of Pittsford in 1876, and was appointed by Gov. Proctor superintendent of the house of correction in 1878, *vice* Isaac M. Tripp, resigned.

—

VERMONT REFORM SCHOOL.

Hon. WILLIAM P. DILLINGHAM, of Waterbury, trustee. [See senate, Washington county, page —.]

Hon. CYRUS M. SPAULDING, of Burlington, trustee, republican, was born in Jericho, Vt., March 28, 1827.

He is a banker, and located in town in 1879. Was educated at the common schools and academies. During the last twenty-five years previous to his removal to Burlington, he was constantly engaged in the service of his native town, holding at different times nearly every office in the gift of his townsmen. He was elected a director of the state prison in 1876, and appointed trustee of the reform school in 1878.

Hon. DAVID M. CAMP, of Newport, trustee, republican, was born in Derby, Dec. 11, 1836. He is an editor, and located in town in 1866. Was educated at the academies of Derby and St. Johnsbury. Was assistant clerk of the house in 1868, and held the office of clerk of the house from 1869 to 1876. Was a member of the constitutional convention of 1870. Has held at different times the offices of selectman, constable, superintendent, and for a term of years was a member of the state board of education. In 1878 he represented the town of Newport in the general assembly, and was also appointed trustee of the reform school the same year. Religious preference, Congregationalist.

Hon. WILLIAM GOODNOW FAIRBANK, of Vergennes, superintendent of the reform school, republican, was born in Sterling, Mass., Feb. 24, 1840, and located in town in 1875. Was a graduate of the state normal school at Bridgewater, Mass. He has been teacher at farm school, Thompson's Island, Mass.; officer and teacher at the reform school, Westboro, Mass, and has been superintendent of the Vermont reform school since June 14, 1869. Religious preference, Baptist.

—

SUPERVISORS OF THE INSANE.

Hon. JOSEPH L. HARRINGTON, of Halifax, republican, was born in Jamaica, Vt., Aug. 5, 1840. He is a physician and surgeon, and located in town in 1866. Is a graduate in medicine of the University of Vermont. Was a member of Co. I, 4th regiment, and was subsequently commissioned assistant surgeon of the 1st Vermont heavy artillery. Was a member of the constitutional convention of 1870, and has held many town offices. He has been justice since 1867, and is town clerk and treasurer. He was a member of the general assembly from the town of Halifax in 1878, and was elected supervisor of the insane the same year. Religious preference, Unitarian.

Hon. WILLIAM HARRIS WALKER, of Ludlow, republican, was born in Windham, Vt., Feb. 2, 1832. He is an attorney-at-law, and located in town in 1860. Was educated at the Black River academy, and graduated at Middlebury college in the class of '58, and has been one of the trustees of the college for several years. He was a member of the House from Ludlow in 1860 and 1866, a senator from Windsor county in 1867 and '68, state's attorney in 1874–5, and was elected judge of probate for the district of Windsor in 1878, and also elected supervisor of the insane the same year; has held the usual town offices. Religious preference, Episcopalian.

Hon. JOSIAH O. CRAMTON, of Colchester, democrat, was born in Berkshire, Vt., July 7, 1839. He is a physician, and located in town in 1870. Was educated at Fairfax institute, and graduated in medicine at the Bellevue medical college, New York city, in 1862. Dr. Cramton represented the town of Fairfield in the legislature of 1865 and '66, was a member of the general assembly from the town of Colchester in 1878, and was elected supervisor of the insane the same year. Has been town superintendent for five years. Religious preference, Episcopalian. P. O. address, Winooski.

—

CURATOR OF CABINET.

Hon. HIRAM A. CUTTING, of Lunenburg, republican, was born in Concord, Vt., Dec. 23, 1832. He is a merchant, and located in Lunenburgh in 1854. He graduated in medicine at Dartmouth college, and received the honorary degree of Master of Arts at Norwich University. He was appointed geologist and curator in 1871. Religious preference, Methodist.

THE SENATE.

ADDISON COUNTY.

Hon. EDWARD S. DANA, of New Haven, republican, was born in Cornwall, Vt., April 27, 1834. He is a farmer and located in town in 1877. Received an academical education at Bakersfield, Vt., and elsewhere. Was selectman of Cornwall from 1873 to '77, and has held various other town offices. Was assistant clerk of the Vermont house of representatives in 1855, '60, and '61, and represented the town of Cornwall in 1874. Was clerk and examiner-in-chief in the U. S. pension office, at Washington, D. C., for several years, and assistant clerk of the U. S. House of Representatives from 1866 to '71. Religious preference, Congregationalist.

Hon. JULIUS N. NORTH, of Shoreham, republican, was born in Shoreham, Vt., Aug. 17, 1829. He is a farmer and was educated at the district schools and academy. He was a member of the general assembly, representing his native town, in 1869 and '70. He has held the usual town offices. Religious preference, Congregationalist.

BENNINGTON COUNTY.

Hon. GILBERT M. SYKES, of Dorset, republican, was born in Dorset, Vt., Nov. 20, 1834. He is a merchant. Was educated at the common schools. He has held the office of postmaster fifteen years; has been town treasurer and is a selectman. Religious preference, Congregationalist.

Hon. CHARLES THATCHER, of Bennington, republican, was born in Bennington, Vt., April 13, 1823. He is a banker; and was educated at Bennington academy. He has held the office of auditor, village and school trustee. Religious preference, Congregationalist. P. O. address, North Bennington.

CALEDONIA COUNTY.

Hon. JONATHAN R. DARLING, of Groton, republican, was born in Groton, Vt., Nov. 16, 1823. He is a farmer and lumberman. Was educated at the common schools and academies. He was an assistant judge of the county court of Caledonia county in 1869, '70, and '71; is now, and has been, town clerk since 1860; has been justice of the peace since 1851, continuously, and has held several other town offices of trust and responsibility. In 1857 and '58 was a member of the general assembly from the town of Groton. Religious preference, Liberal.

Hon. ELIJAH D. BLODGETT, of St. Johnsbury, republican, was born in Randolph, Vt., May 20, 1820. He is an accountant, and located in St. Johnsbury in 1853. Was educated at the common schools and academy. He was a member of the general assembly trom St. Johnsbury in 1874–75, and in 1876–77. Religious preference, Episcopalian.

CHITTENDEN COUNTY.

Hon. ASHER C. ROBINSON, of Westford, republican, was born in Fairfax, Vt., Feb. 15, 1839. He is a farmer, and located in town in 1867. Was educated at the common schools and academies, and was a member of the house from Westford in 1874. He has repeatedly held the usual town offices. Religious preference, Congregationalist. P. O. address, North Underhill.

Hon. CHARLES WILLIAMS WOODHOUSE, of Burlington, republican, was born in Brattleboro, Vt., Sept. 19, 1835. He is a banker, and located in town in 1854. Was educated at the common schools and academies. He was town and city treasurer from 1863 to '69. Religious preference, Unitarian.

Hon. WALTER A. WEED, of Shelburne, republican, was born in Hinesburgh, Vt., Sept. 15, 1833. He is a farmer, and located in town in 1860. Was educated at Hinesburgh and Swanton academies. He has held the usual town offices, and was a member of the general assembly from Shelburne in 1868 and '69. Religious preference, Episcopalian.

ESSEX COUNTY.

Hon. HARVEY JUDEVINE, of Concord, republican, was born in Concord, Vt., March 28, 1820. He is a farmer. Was educated at the common schools and academies. Has been postmaster, deputy sheriff, and has repeatedly been honored with elections to the usual town offices. He represented Concord in the general assembly of 1865 and '66. P. O. address, West Concord.

FRANKLIN COUNTY.

Hon. HENRY R. START, of Bakersfield, republican, was born in Bakersfield, Vt., Dec. 22, 1845. He is an attorney. Was educated at the common schools and academies. He was a member of Co. A, 3d regiment Vt. Vols., and was state's attorney of Franklin county from 1876 to '78. Religious preference, Congregationalist.

Hon. ARTHUR W. WOODWORTH, of Enosburgh, republican, was born in Berkshire, Vt., May 7, 1823. He is a farmer, and located in town in 1836. Was educated at the common schools. He has repeatedly held the offices of selectman, constable, grand juror, and justice of the peace. Religious preference, Methodist. P. O. address, Enosburgh Falls.

Hon. ALFRED GREELEY SAFFORD, of St. Albans, republican, was born in St. Albans, Vt., Aug. 17, 1844. He is a lawyer, and was educated at the University of Vermont, being a member of the class of '63. Was in the service of the government, during the rebellion, as chief operator of the military telegraphic corps. Has been member of the school board since 1878, and is chief engineer of the St. Albans fire department. Religious preference, Congregationalist.

GRAND ISLE COUNTY.

Hon. ELISHA R. GOODSELL, of Isle La Motte, republican, was born in Isle La Motte, Vt., Sept. 3, 1837. He is a farmer and quarryman, and with the exception of four years residence at North Hero, has always resided in town. He was educated at the common schools, and one term in an academy. Was selectman in 1867, '68, '74, and '79; lister in '70, '71, '75, '76, 77; has been auditor and grand juror several years; was clerk of Grand Isle county from 1862 to '71, continuously, and has been deputy clerk since; held the office of postmaster of North Hero in 1862 and '63. Was a member of the general assembly from Isle La Motte in 1865 and '66. Religious preference, Universalist.

LAMOILLE COUNTY.

Hon. PHILIP KING GLEED, of Morristown, republican, was born in Granby, P. Q., September 6, 1834. He is an attorney, and located in town in 1861. Was educated at Union college, Schenectady, N. Y,, graduating in the class of '59. He held the office of selectman for ten years. Was trustee of the Vermont reform school in 1869. Was assessor of internal revenue in the 3d district of Vermont from 1870 to '74. Religious preference, Congregationalist. P. O. address, Morrisville.

ORANGE COUNTY.

Hon. MARCUS PECK, of Brookfield, republican, was born in Brookfield, Vt., June 26, 1834. He is a fork manufacturer of the firm of Peck, Clark & Co. Received a liberal academical education, and has been repeatedly elected to the offices of selectman and lister. Religious preference, Congregationalist.

Hon. SAMUEL MILLS GLEASON, of Thetford, republican, was born in Thetford, Vt., June 28, 1833. He is a lawyer, and was educated at Dartmouth College, graduating in the class of '58. He has held the office of superintendent six years; was state's attorney for Orange county in 1864, '65, '68, and '69, and represented Thetford in the general assembly in 1864 and '65. Religious preference, Methodist. P. O. address, Thetford Centre.

ORLEANS COUNTY.

Hon. ELISHA LANE, of Derby, republican, was born in Newport, Vt., Dec. 26, 1835. He is a merchant, and located in town in 1858. Was educated at the common schools and Derby Academy. He was a member of the house from Derby in 1866 and '67, and has been lister, overseer, auditor and selectman from 1872 to '79. Religious preference, Congregationalist. P. O. address, West Derby.

Hon. JAMES BROWN, of Lowell, republican, was born in Morristown, Vt., Sept. 15, 1829. He is engaged in the manufacture of starch and lumber, and located in town in 1869, and was educated at the common schools and academies. He was a representative in the general assembly in 1864, '65, '72, and '74. Was selectman from 1857 to '61, lister 1863 to '66, and in Lowell from 1872 to the present time, and has held several minor offices. Religious preference, Universalist.

RUTLAND COUNTY.

Hon. WALTER C. DUNTON, of Rutland, republican, was born in Bristol, Vt., Nov. 29, 1830. He is a lawyer, and located in Rutland in 1861. Was educated at Franklin Academy, Malone, N. Y., and graduated at Middlebury College in 1857. Read law with Messrs. Dillingham & Durant, of Waterbury, and Linsley & Prout, of Rutland, and was admitted to the bar of Rutland county in 1858. He was commissioned and served as captain of Co. H. 14th regiment Vt. Vols. Judge Dunton resided for two years in Kansas prior to its admission as a state, and was a member of the last territorial legislature in 1861. He was a member of the constitutional convention in 1870. Was elected judge of probate for the district of Rutland in 1865, and held that office by continuous elections till April 14, 1877, when he was appointed by Gov. Fairbanks, judge of the supreme court, to fill the vacancy occasioned by the appointment of Hon. Hoyt H. Wheeler as judge for the district of Vermont. He was elected to the same position in 1878, but resigned Nov. 1, 1879, on account of ill health. Religious preference, Congregationalist.

Hon. ROYAL DANIEL KING, of Benson, republican, was born in Benson, Vt., Nov. 17, 1825. He is a farmer, and fitted for and entered the University of

Vermont, and graduated, class of 1846. Was a private in Co. D. 14th regiment Vt. Vols. Was lister in 1859, selectman in 1862, '64, and '65; superintendent of schools in 1860, '61, '62, and since 1870, continuously. Was a member of the general assembly from Benson in 1852 and 1854. Religious preference, Congregationalist.

Hon. OREL COOK, of Mendon, republican, was born in Rutland, Vt., Dec 7, 1813. He is a physician and surgeon, and located in town in 1870. Was educated at the Bangor classical school, graduated at Dartmouth College, class of '41, read medicine and graduated in his profession at the University of Pennsylvania. During the war of the rebellion he was acting surgeon in hospitals at Louisville and Lebanon, Ky. Has held the usual town offices, and was a member of the general assembly, from the town of Mendon, in 1872 and '74. Religious preference, Congregationalist.

Hon. EMMETT R. PEMBER, of Wells, republican, was born in Wells, Vt., Sept. 21, 1846. He is a farmer. Received a liberal academic education, and was engaged in teaching in earlier life. He has held the office of lister, auditor, and superintendent of schools; was enumerator of census the present year. Religious preference, Methodist.

WASHINGTON COUNTY.

Hon. WILLIAM PAUL DILLINGHAM, of Waterbury, republican, was born in Waterbury, Vt., Dec. 12, 1843, and was educated at the common schools and academy. He read law in the office of his father, the Hon. Paul Dillingham, and was admitted to the bar of Washington county in 1867. Was appointed secretary of civil and military affairs in 1866, to fill the vacancy occasioned by the resignation of Charles M. Gay, Esq., and again in 1874. He was elected state's attorney for Washington county in '72 and '74. Was a member of the house from Waterbury in 1876, and a senator from Washington county in 1878, serving on the committees of joint rules, the judiciary, railroads, and insane asylum. Was appointed a trustee of the Vermont reform school in 1878. Religious preference, Methodist.

Hon. ALBERT DWINELL, of Calais, republican, was born in Calais, Vt., Jan. 15, 1823. He is a farmer. Was educated at the common schools and academies. Was a member of the general assembly from Calais in 1860 and '61. Has held various town offices. Was a member of the first state board of equalization in 1874, and in 1878 a senator from Washington county, serving on the committees of agriculture, land taxes, and the grand list. Religious preference, Congregationalist. P. O. address, East Calais.

WINDHAM COUNTY.

Hon. LEVI K. FULLER, of Brattleboro, republican, was born in Westmoreland, N. H., Feb. 24, 1841. He is engaged in the manufacture of the celebrated Estey organs, and located in town in 1860. Was educated at the schools of Bellows Falls and Brattleboro. He is commander of the Fuller light battery, national guards of Vermont. Religious preference, Baptist.

Hon. JABEZ DELANO BRIDGMAN, of Rockingham, republican, was born in Grafton, Vt., June 10, 1828. He is a lawyer, and located in town in 1849. Was educated at the common schools and academies. He was adjutant of the 16th regiment Vt. Vols., and was a member of the general assembly, representing the town of Rockingham in 1857 and '58. P. O. address, Bellows Falls.

WINDSOR COUNTY.

Hon. ORA PAUL, of Pomfret, republican, was born in Pomfret, Vt., June 25, 1836. He is a farmer and received an academical education. He was a member of Co. B, 1st regiment, and captain of Co. B, 12th regiment Vt. Vols. Was elected selectman in 1865, '72, '73, '74, '79, and 80; was lister in 1870 and '78, and was a member of the state board of agriculture in 1876 and '77. He represented Pomfret in the general assembly of 1865, '66, and '76–77. Religious preference, Christian. P. O. address, Woodstock.

Hon. FREDERIC GRISWOLD FIELD, of Springfield, republican, was born in Springfield, Vt., Jan. 1, 1842. He is engaged in mercantile pursuits, and was educated at the common schools and Springfield Wesleyan Seminary. He was a member of the general assembly from the town of Springfield in 1870 and 1872, and has held minor town offices. Religious preference, Baptist. P. O. address, North Springfield.

Hon. HUGH HENRY, of Chester, republican, was born in Chester, Vt., March 21, 1838. He is a lawyer, and received a liberal academical education. He was a member of the general assembly from the town of Chester in 1870, '72, '74 and '76, and was lieutenant of Co. I, 16th regiment Vt. Vols. He has held the minor town offices. Religious preference, Unitarian.

OFFICERS OF THE SENATE.

CHAUNCEY W. BROWNELL, Jr., *Burlington*, Secretary, republican, was born in Williston, Oct. 7, 1847. He is a lawyer, and located in Burlington in 1873. Is a graduate of the University of Vermont, class of 1870, and of the Law University of Albany in 1872. Was assistant secretary of the Senate from 1874 to 1880. Religious preference, Congregationalist.

FRANK A. DWINELL, *Plainfield*, Assistant Secretary, republican, was born in Calais in 1847. He is a merchant, and located in town in 1873. Was educated at the common schools and Barre Academy, and is town clerk and treasurer. Was a member of the general assembly from Plainfield in 1878. Religious preference, Congregationalist.

EDWIN WHEELOCK, *Cambridge*, Chaplain, republican, was born in Cambridge, Nov. 17, 1822. He is a graduate of the University of Vermont, class of '49. Has repeatedly held the office of superintendent of schools. Was a member of the house in 1866-'67, and a senator from Lamoille county in 1876. Religious preference, Congregationalist.

ALVIN D. WHITE, *Huntington*, Door-Keeper, republican, was born in Huntington in 1841. He is a farmer. Was a member of Co. F, 13th regiment Vt. Vols. Was assistant door-keeper of the senate in 1878. Religious preference, Universalist.

CHARLES S. DANA, *New Haven*, Assistant Door-Keeper, republican, was born in New Haven, Sept. 13, 1862. He is a student. Religious preference, Congregationalist.

WILLIAM G. STEARNS, *Bethel*, Messenger, was born in Northfield, July 1, 1857. He was educated at St. John's school, Poultney, Vt., and is a law student. Religious preference, Episcopalian.

JULIUS B. NORTH, *Shoreham*, Messenger, was born in Shoreham, Feb. 24, 1868, and is a student. Religious preference, Congregationalist.

ROBERT ROBERTS, *Burlington*, Reporter, republican, was born in Manchester, Jan. 1, 1848. He is a lawyer, and located in Burlington in 1857. Graduated at the University of Vermont, class of '69, and at the Columbia Law School in 1871. He held the office of Senate Reporter in 1874 and 1878. Religious preference, Congregationalist.

RECAPITULATION.

The Senate is composed of thirty Republicans. Messrs. Dillingham and Dwinell, of Washington county, were members in 1878, and are the only gentlemen who have been members of the senate before. Twenty-two have been members of the house and eight are new members.

The oldest Senator is the Hon. ORREL COOK, and the youngest is the Hon. EMMETT R. PEMBER—both of Rutland county.

Seventeen reside in the town where they were born.

The following table exhibits the place of birth, occupation, and religious preference.

PLACE OF BIRTH.

Vermont	28	Canada	1
New Hampshire	1		

OCCUPATION.

Farmers	11	Bankers	2
Lawyers	8	Farmer and Lumberman	1
Manufacturers	3	Farmer and Quarryman	1
Merchants	3	Physician	1
Total			30

RELIGIOUS PREFERENCE.

Congregationalists	14	Universalists	2
Methodists	4	Christian	1
Episcopalians	2	Liberal	1
Baptists	2	No preference	2
Unitarians	2		
Total			30

THE HOUSE.

ADDISON COUNTY.

GIDEON W. WHITFORD, *Addison*, republican, was born in Addison, Aug. 10, 1828. He is a farmer. Was educated at the public schools. He has held several town offices. Religious preference, Baptist. P. O. address, East Addison.

JOHN HARRIS WITHERELL, *Bridport*, republican, was born in Bridport in 1841. He is a farmer. Was educated at the common schools. He has held the office of selectman since 1878. Religious preference, Congregationalist. P. O. address, West Bridport.

ERASMUS M. KENT, *Bristol*, republican, was born in Lincoln in 1842. He is a physician and druggist, and located in town in 1866. Was educated at the Bristol Academy, and graduated in his profession at the University of Vermont, class of 1866. He has held the office of town clerk since 1874, and is lister. Religious preference, Congregationalist.

WILLIAM HARRISON BINGHAM, *Cornwall*, republican, was born in Cornwall, Jan. 9, 1843. He is a farmer. Was educated at the common schools. He was corporal of Co. D, 14th regiment Vt. Vols. He held the office of selectman in 1872 '73 and '74, and was elected town treasurer in 1879 and '80. Religious preference, Congregationalist. P. O. address, West Cornwall.

JARED BOOTH, *Ferrisburgh*, republican, was born in Ferrisburgh, May 27, 1839. He is a farmer. Was educated at the common and high schools. Religious preference, Congregationalist. P. O. address, Vergennes.

GEORGE E. DUTTON, *Goshen*, republican, was born in Pittsford in 1835. He is a mechanic, and located in town in 1845. Was educated at the common schools. Religious preference, Methodist. P. O. address, Brandon.

ALVIN FORD, *Granville*, republican, was born in Braintree in 1816. He is a farmer, and located in town in 1821. Was educated at the common schools. He has held town offices of minor importance. Religious preference, Liberal.

HIRAM R. PERRY, *Hancock*, republican, was born in Hancock, Jan. 28, 1842. He is a farmer. Was educated at the common schools, and was a member of Co. E, 14th regiment Vt. Vols. He held the office of selectman in 1877, and was elected lister in 1873, again in 1876 and continuously since. Religious preference, Universalist.

WALTER J. THOMAS, *Leicester*, republican, was born in Salisbury, Jan. 31, 1841. He is a farmer and mechanic, and located in town in 1866. Was educated at the common schools. He was a member of Co. E, 14th regiment Vt. Vols. He has held the usual town offices, and is one of the selectmen. Religious preference, Congregationalist.

SAMUEL DORVILLE O. BRYAN, *Lincoln*, republican, was born in Middlebury, April 24, 1824. He is a farmer, and located in town in 1859. Was educated at the common schools. He was a selectman in 1870, '71 and '79; lister in 1869, '70, '71, '72, '79 and '80; was justice of the peace in 1869 and '70. Religious preference, Methodist.

JOSEPH BATTELL, *Middlebury*, republican. He located in town in 1879. He was a member of the general assembly from the town of Ripton in 1872 and 1876; was a senator from the county of Addison in 1878, serving on the committee on rules, on railroads, and on the grand list.

LUCIUS E. SMITH, *Monkton*, republican, was born in Monkton in 1824. He is a farmer, and was educated at Joliette College, Canada. He was a member of the general assembly from Monkton in 1858, '59, '61, '62, and was a senator from Addison county in 1867 and '68. He has held the usual town offices. Religious preference, Roman Catholic.

EDSON A. DOUD, *New Haven*, republican, was born in New Haven, Nov. 18, 1832. He is a farmer. Received an academical education. He has held the office of auditor, lister, trustee, treasurer, and is a justice of the peace. Religious preference, Congregationalist.

WILLIAM BOTTUM WRIGHT, *Orwell*, republican, was born in Orwell, June 28, 1848. He is a merchant. Was educated at the Highland Military School, Worcester, Mass. Is a director of the First National bank of Orwell. Religious preference, Congregationalist.

NORMAN J. TOWSLEY, *Panton*, republican, was born in Rupert, Aug., 1815. He is a physician, and located in town in 1846. Was educated at Poultney Seminary, and graduated in his profession at Castleton Medical College, class of 1844. He has held the office of town superintendent, and was postmaster from 1848 to 1859. Religious preference, Methodist.

WILLIAM NOMLAS COBB, *Ripton*, republican, was born in Springfield, Nov. 28, 1820. He is a farmer, and located in town in 1845. Was educated at the public schools. He was selectman in 1853–'54, and justice of the peace in 1853 and '59. Religious preference, Congregationalist. P. O. address, Bread Loaf.

LOYAL N. WATERHOUSE, *Salisbury*, republican, was born in Middlebury, July 11, 1826. He is a farmer, and located in town in 1827. Was educated at the public schools. He has been town clerk and lister since 1876, and was elected a justice of the peace in 1878. Religious preference, Congregationalist.

FRANKLIN MOORE, *Shoreham*, republican, was born in Shoreham in 1815. He is a farmer, and was educated at the common schools and academy. He was a captain of Co. K, first Vermont cavalry, and has been selectman, overseer, and justice of the peace at sundry times.

J. SYLVESTER HILL, *Starksboro*, republican, was born in Starksboro, Dec. 21, 1824. He is a farmer, and was educated at the common schools. He has held the office of selectman. Religious preference, Freewill Baptist.

WALTER SCRANTON, *Vergennes*, republican, was born in Scranton, Pa., Aug. 12, 1849. He is engaged in a general business, and located in town in 1875. Was educated at Stockbridge, Mass. He was a member of the general assembly in 1878, from Vergennes, serving on the committee of ways and means; the same year he was appointed aid-de-camp on the staff of Gov. Proctor. He is president of the Farmers' National bank. Religious preference, Presbyterian.

WILLIAM WHALEY BOOTH, *Waltham*, republican, was born in Ferrisburgh, May 26, 1841. He is a farmer, and located in town in 1875. Was educated at the public and high schools. Is a selectman, and has been trustee of public money since 1879. Religious preference, Episcopalian. P. O. address, Vergennes.

SAMUEL JAMES, *Weybridge*, republican, was born in Weybridge, Aug. 13, 1822. He is a farmer, and was educated at the public schools and Middlebury Academy. He has held the offices of selectman, lister, justice of the peace, and other minor positions. Religious preference, Congregationalist. P. O. address, Middlebury.

DANIEL HOLMES, *Whiting*, republican, was born in Hubbardton, Vt., March 7, 1837. He is a farmer, and located in town in 1873. Fitted for and entered Middlebury College, class of '63; but left at the expiration of the sophomore year. Was sergeant in Co. F, 14th Vt. Vols. He has held the usual town offices, and was a member of the general assembly from the town of Hubbardton in 1865 and '66. Religious preference, Congregationalist.

BENNINGTON COUNTY.

MARTIN HYDE DEMING, *Arlington*, republican, was born in Arlington, Aug. 25, 1844. He is a merchant. Was educated at the Vermont Episcopal Institute at Burlington, and by private instruction. He held the office of selectman from 1875 to '78. Religious preference, Episcopalian.

LYMAN FREDERIC ABBOTT, *Bennington*, republican, was born in Holden, Mass, Jan. 13, 1839. He is a manufacturer of knit underwear, and located in town in 1854. Was educated at the common schools and academies. He is a member of the extensive manufacturing firm of H. E. Bradford & Co., of Bennington, and since the death of Mr. Bradford, April, 1878, has been the general manager of the company. Religious preference, Episcopalian.

ORREN EMERSON WHITNEY, *Dorset*, republican, was born in Rutland, Vt., Nov. 31, 1833. He is a marble worker, and located in town in 1840. Was educated at the common schools. He was a justice of the peace from 1869 to 1874. Religious preference, Congregationalist. P. O. address, North Dorset.

TRENOR PARK HARBOUR, *Glastenbury*, republican, was born in Woodford, July 29, 1853. He is a sawyer. Was educated at the common schools. He was a selectman in 1879, and is a lister.

JAMES H. ABBOTT, *Landgrove*, republican, was born in Landgrove, Jan. 4, 1848. He is a farmer and manufacturer. Was educated at the common schools. He was first constable from 1871 to 1879, and is a selectman. Religious preference, Methodist.

DAVID SEYMOUR WILSON, *Manchester*, republican, was born in Townshend, March 16, 1836. He is a cabinet-maker, and located in town in 1846. Was educated at the common schools. P. O. address, Factory Point.

MARSHALL JAY HAPGOOD, *Peru*, republican, was born in Peru, January 13, 1850. He was educated at Williams College and Harvard University; also attended the Harvard law school one year. He located permanently at Peru in 1874, since which time he has had charge of a general store, spending the most of his individual time in travel, lecturing, and in the pursuit of general literature. He was "elected on a printed platform." Religious preference, Liberal.

ABRAHAM GARDNER PARKER, *Pownal*, republican, was born in Pownal, Oct. 3, 1815. He is a merchant. Was educated at the common schools of Pownal and the Union Academy at Bennington. Was postmaster from 1849 to 1859, and re-appointed in 1861; was justice of the peace from 1842 to 1848 inclusive, and was a member of the Constitutional Convention in 1870. Religious preference, Baptist.

TYLER D. GOODELL, *Readsboro*, republican, was born in Readsboro, Nov. 10, 1849. He is a mail-carrier, and was educated at the common schools. He is lister. Religious preference, Universalist.

EDGAR H. BEEBE, *Rupert*, republican, was born in Sandgate, March 8, 1843. He is a carpenter and joiner, and located in town in 1864. Was educated at the district schools. He has held the office of town grand juror for the last three years. Religious preference, Church of the Disciples. P. O. address, West Rupert.

CRAWFORD R. WOODARD, *Sandgate*, democrat, was born in Sandgate, Oct. 21, 1836. He is a farmer. Was educated at the common school. He was a member of the general assembly from Sandgate in 1868, and '69 ; was lister in 1865 ; and from 1870 to '74 inclusive ; justice from 1874 to '78 ; constable and collector in 1866–'67, and again in 1877–'78 and '79. Religious preference, Methodist.

ROZEL HYDE STANLEY, *Searsburgh*, republican, was born in Halifax, Nov. 23, 1831. He is a farmer and mechanic, and located in town in 1865. Was educated at the common schools. He has held the office of lister, constable and collector, and several minor town offices. Religious preference, Universalist.

MILO PIERCE, *Shaftsbury*, republican, was born in Shaftsbury, July 22, 1830. He is superintendent of a manufactory, and was educated at the common schools. He was a selectman in 1857 and 1861. Was a member of the general assembly from the town of Shaftsbury in 1869. Religious preference, Universalist. P. O. address, South Shaftsbury.

WHEELER C. BRATTON, *Stamford*, democrat, was born in Stamford, Sept. 18, 1828. He is a farmer, and was educated in the common schools. He has held the office of constable, and has been overseer since 1872. Religious preference, Universalist.

ARNOLD R. WEBB, *Sunderland*, democrat, was born in Sunderland, April 1, 1842. He is a farmer, and was educated at the common schools. He was a member of Co. G, 1st. Vt. Cav., and has been town clerk for ten years.

BAINBRIDGE C. BENSON, *Winhall*, republican, was born in Winhall, April, 1836. He is a farmer. Was educated at the common schools. Has held the office of lister several times, and is constable and collector. Was a member of the house in 1878, serving on the committee on the grand list. Religious preference, Universalist. P. O. address, Bondville.

FREEMAN C. MALLORY, *Woodford*, democrat, was born in Bennington, in 1852. He is a lumberman, and located in town in 1860. Was educated at the common schools. He has held some town offices.

CALEDONIA COUNTY.

GEORGE P. BLAIR, *Barnet*, republican, was born in Scotland, April 2, 1836. He is a merchant, and located in town in 1870. Was educated at the common schools. He was a member of Co. D, 1st Vt. Cav., and successively promoted to company, and to regimental quartermaster sergeant. He has held the office of selectman of Peacham in 1867, '68, and '69; lister in Barnet in 1876, '77, '78, and '79, and had been justice of the peace several years, both in Peacham and Barnet. Religious preference, Presbyterian. P. O. address, West Barnet.

JOHN S. J. BEMIS, *Burke*, republican, was born in Lyndon, Nov. 9, 1810. He is a carriage-maker, and located in town in 1832. Was educated at the common schools. He has held the office of constable, and is town treasurer. Religious preference, Universalist.

SILAS H. STONE, *Danville*, republican, was born in St. Johnsbury, July 29, 1838. He is a railroad station and express agent, and located in town in 1856. Was educated at the common schools and Phillips Academy. He was sergeant of Co. H, 4th regiment Vt. Vols, and promoted to 1st lieutenant of Co. G, of the same regiment. He has held the office of justice of the peace since 1874. Religious preference, Methodist.

SAMUEL P. WELCH, *Groton*, republican, was born in Groton, Dec. 18, 1843. He is a merchant, and was educated at the district schools. Religious preference, Baptist.

ALDEN EDSON JUDEVINE, *Hardwick*, republican, was born in Concord, Aug. 4, 1811. He is a merchant and farmer, and located in town in 1839. Received a liberal academical education. Was a member of the constitutional conventions of 1850, 1857, and 1870; represented Hardwick in the general assembly of 1853 and '54, and again in 1878—serving on the committee of ways and means;—was a senator from Caledonia county in 1860 and '61. Held the office of deputy sheriff and constable in Concord; also high bailiff of Essex county. Was elected assistant judge of the county court of Caledonia county in 1850 and '51; county commissioner in 1854. Has been repeatedly honored by election to the various town offices, holding that of town clerk, seven years; selectman, ten years; and held the office of postmaster for twenty-three years. Religious preference, Liberal.

HENRY RANNEY, *Kirby*, democrat, was born in Kirby, July 4, 1843. He is a farmer, and was educated at the public schools. Religious preference, Congregationalist. P. O. address, East St. Johnsbury.

WELCOME ARNOLD BEMIS, *Lyndon*, republican, was born in Lyndon, in 1828. He is a farmer. Was educated at the district schools and Newbury Seminary. He has held the office of overseer for the last ten years, and has been lister and justice of the peace. Religious preference, Universalist. P. O. address, Lyndonville.

JABEZ SMITH, *Newark*, republican, was born in Canaan, N. H., Oct. 1812. He is a farmer, and located in town in 1840. Was educated at the common schools. He has held the office of selectman, lister and justice of the peace, and was a member of the general assembly from Newark in 1846, '47, and in 1850, '51. Religious preference, Methodist. P. O. address, West Burke.

PLYNN BOLTON, *Peacham*, republican, was born in Danville, in 1824. He is a farmer, and located in town in 1865. Was educated at the common schools. He held the office of lister in 1870, 1871 and 1872, and was elected a selectman in 1879, which office he now holds. Religious preference, Congregationalist.

JEFFERSON RENFREW, *Ryegate*, republican, was born in Ryegate, April 28, 1836. He is a farmer, and was educated at the common schools. He has held several town offices, and offices of trust in different benevolent and religious societies. Religious preference, Baptist. P. O. address, South Ryegate.

CHARLES INGALLS, *Sheffield*, democrat, was born in Sheffield, May 5, 1834. He is a farmer. Was educated at the common schools. He was a member of the general assembly from the town of Sheffield in 1878, serving on the general committee. Religious preference, Baptist.

WALTER PERRIN SMITH, *St. Johnsbury*, republican, was born in Hardwick, Nov. 4, 1841. He is an attorney, and located in town in 1869. Was a graduate of the University of Vermont, class of 1867. Was state's attorney for Caledonia county from 1874 to 1876, superintendent of schools in 1874, and is agent and auditor. Religious prefence, Congregationalist.

ALVAH SUEL AYER, *Stannard*, republican, was born in Brunswick, April 6, 1848. He is a farmer, and located in town in 1852. Was educated at the common schools. He has held the office of first constable since 1878.

CHARLES W. WILLEY, *Sutton*, republican, was born in Sutton, August 25, 1830. He is a farmer. Was educated at the district schools. He was selectman in 1870, '71 and 1880; he has been lister and justice of the peace. Religious preference, Freewill Baptist.

DAVISON S. FERGUSON, *Walden*, republican, was born in Springfield, N. Y., in 1835. He is a farmer, and located in town in 1868. Was educated at the district schools. He has held the office of lister for the last three years. Religious preference, Methodist. P. O. address, So. Walden.

DENNIS MAY, *Waterford*, republican, was born in Concord, Feb. 27, 1807. He is a farmer and located in town in 1832. Was educated at the public schools and Essex County Grammar School. He was lister from 1851 to '54 inclusive; again in '58, '60 and '65: was selectman from 1862 to 1867 inclusive, except in '65, and a member of the house, from the town of Waterford, in 1845, '46 and '55. Religious preference, Universalist. P. O. address, Lower Waterford.

CHARLES ROGERS, *Wheelock*, republican, was born in Alton, N. H., Aug. 28, 1823. He is a farmer, and located in town in 1829. Was a member of the general assembly from Wheelock in 1852, '54, '61, '62, and in 1878, serving on the committee on railroads; was also a senator from Caledonia county in 1872 and '74. Was assistant judge of the county court in 1868 and '69; has held the usual town offices for many years, and was one of the trustees of the Vermont reform school from 1874 to 1878. Religious preference, Methodist.

CHITTENDEN COUNTY.

THOMAS BARTHOLOMEW WHALEN, *Bolton*, democrat, was born in Bolton, Jan. 13, 1855. He is a farmer, and was educated at the common schools and academy. Has been constable and collector since 1878. Religious preference, Roman Catholic.

RUSSELL S. TAFT, *Burlington*, republican, was born in Williston, Jan. 28, 1835, and located in town in 1853. He was educated at the common schools and academies. He is a lawyer; was selectman from 1861 to 1864, and alderman of the city of Burlington from 1865 to 1869; was state's attorney of Chittenden county in 1862, '63 and '64; a senator from that county in 1865, '66, and lieutenant governor in 1872. Religious preference, Universalist.

CHARLES D. PRINDLE, *Charlotte*, republican, was born in Charlotte, April 25, 1814. He is a farmer. Was educated at the district schools. He has held the offices of selectman and lister. Religious preference, Spiritualist. P. O. address, East Charlotte.

FRANCIS LECLAIR, *Colchester*, democrat, was born in St. John Baptiste, P. Q., August 5, 1818. He is a merchant and brick manufacturer, and located in town in 1828. Is self educated. He has held several town and village offices of trust, and is chairman of the board of selectmen. Religious preference, Roman Catholic. P. O. address, Winooski.

CHARLES H. NICHOLS, *Essex*, republican, was born in Richmond, in 1820. He is a farmer, and located in town in 1836. Was educated at the common schools. He was selectman in 1862, '63, '64, '72 and '73; overseer in 1877, '78, '79 and '80, and is director of the Union Poor Farm Association. Religious preference, Methodist.

JOHN HAMILTON ALLEN, *Hinesburgh*, republican, was born in Hinesburgh, in 1838. He is a harness-maker. Was educated at the common school and academy. He was 1st lieutenant of Co. G, 14th Vt. Vols. He held the office of 2d constable in 1878. Religious preference, Baptist.

ORVIS H. ELLIS, *Huntington*, republican, was born in Huntington, Oct. 31, 1839. He is a farmer. Was educated at the common schools and academies. He was superintendent of schools from 1861 to 1865, and from 1868 to 1872; lister in 1868–9; selectman from 1872 to '74, and has held minor town offices. Religious preference, Baptist. P. O. address, Huntington Centre.

CORNELIUS SOLOMON PALMER, *Jericho*, republican, was born in Underhill, Nov. 2, 1844. He is a lawyer, and located in town in 1871. Was educated at the common schools and academy. An incident in his life is here worthy of record. S. M. Palmer, a brother, enlisted as a private in Co. F, 13th reg't. Vt. Vols., having its rendezvous at Richmond, Vt. The morning of the day that the company left for Brattleboro, the brother, becoming dissatisfied with camp life, expressed so earnest a desire to remain at home, that the subject of this sketch assumed the responsibility. An exchange of clothing was hastily made, and away to the front went the new recruit, serving the full period of enlistment, and promptly answering to the name and discharging all the duties of Simeon M. Palmer. He held the office of state's attorney for Chittenden county from 1876 to 1878. Religious preference, Congregationalist.

HENRY HOLMES RANKIN, *Milton*, republican, was born in Georgia, Vt., April 15, 1846. He is a merchant, and located in town in 1865. Was educated at the common schools and academies. He has held the office of town clerk since 1873; was selectman in 1878 and '79, and is lister. Religious preference, Congregationalist.

HENRY A. HODGES, *Richmond*, republican, was born in Richmond, April 27, 1821. He is a merchant. Was educated at the common school and academy. He was town clerk from 1852 to 1864 continuously.

DAVID C. SMITH, *Shelburne*, republican, was born in Shrewsbury, Jan. 12, 1840. He is a farmer, and located in town in 1865. Was educated at the common schools. Religious preference, Methodist.

SEYMOUR ELI THAYER, *South Burlington*, democrat, was born in South Burlington, July 1, 1829. He is a farmer, and was educated at the common schools. He was a lister in 1869 and '70, and selectman in 1870, '71, '79 and '80. Religious preference, Methodist. P. O. address, Burlington.

MITCHELL W. HINSDILL, *St. George*, republican, was born in St. George, April, 1845. He is a farmer. Was a member of Co. K, 17th reg't Vt. Vols. Has held the office of constable and collector since 1876, and was a member of the general assembly from St. George in 1878, serving on the committee on land taxes.

GEORGE W. WOODWORTH, Jr., *Underhill*, democrat, was born in Underhill, Feb. 11, 1851. He is deputy sheriff and collector, and was educated at the district schools. He was town clerk from 1872 to 1877; constable and collector in 1878–'79, and is collector of taxes; has been deputy sheriff since 1878. P. O. address, Underhill Centre.

IRA STEVENS, *Westford*, republican, was born in Williston, in 1809. He is a farmer, and located in town in 1855. Was educated at the common schools. He was selectman from 1865 to 1870, and again from 1872 to 1874. Religious preference, Congregationalist.

HIRAM A. CLARK, *Williston*, republican, was born in Williston, Aug. 31, 1836. He is a farmer and was educated at the common schools and academy. He has held the offices of selectman and lister. Religious preference, Methodist.

ESSEX COUNTY.

FRED. A. ROBY, *Bloomfield*, republican, was born in Clarksville, N. H., Feb. 22, 1843. He is a harness maker, and located in town in 1874. Was educated at the district schools. He was a member of Co. E, 9th regiment Vt. Vols. Religious preference, Universalist. P. O. address, Coos, N. H.

CEPHAS GARDNER ADAMS, *Brighton*, republican, was born in Holland, March 13, 1829. He is a physician, and located in town in 1859. Received an academical education; read medicine and graduated in his profession at the University of Vermont, medical department, class of 1855. Was contract surgeon, serving in the 6th army corps. He has held the usual town offices. Religious preference, Congregationalist. P. O. address, Island Pond.

WILLIAM W. FITCH, *Brunswick*, republican, was born in Sebago, Maine, Oct. 5, 1826. He is a farmer, and located in town in 1874. Was educated at the public schools. He was a member of the house from Brunswick in 1876. He has held the offices of selectman, treasurer, etc. Religious preference, Universalist. P. O. address, Stratford, N. H.

WILLIAM MORRILL, *Canaan*, republican, was born in Canaan, Sept. 18, 1826. He is a farmer, and was educated at the public schools. He has held the office of selectman twelve, lister ten, and justice of the peace fifteen years. Religious preference, Unitarian.

SELIM E. GROUT, *Concord*, republican, was born in Kirby, June 11, 1836. He is railroad station agent, and located in town in 1847. Was educated at the common schools. He has been deputy sheriff since 1869, with the exception of 1874 and '75, when he was sheriff of Essex county. P. O. address, West Concord.

SOLOMON S. HUDSON, *East Haven*, republican, was born in Athens, July 22, 1836. He is a farmer, and located in town in 1857. Was educated at the common schools. He was a member of Co. A, 10th reg't. Vt. Vols. He has held the offices of selectman, lister, overseer, superintendent of schools, justice of the peace, and several minor positions of trust and responsibility. Religious preference, Freewill Baptist.

CHARLES W. MATTHEWS, *Granby*, republican, was born in Granby, Aug. 31, 1851. He is a farmer, and was educated at the common schools. He was a lister in 1875, 1877 and 1880; selectman in 1879, and was elected town clerk in 1877, which office he now holds. Religious preference, Congregationalist.

ELDAD A. RHODES, *Guildhall*, republican, was born in Northumberland, N. H., in 1842. He is a farmer and teacher, and located in town in 1876. Received a liberal academical education. He was a member of Co. B, 5th reg't. N. H. Vols.; was promoted to sergeant, served in the 2d Army Corps under Hancock, was wounded at Malvern Hill, shot through the chest at Antietam, was subsequently promoted to lieutenant, but by reason of severe disability was soon after mustered out. Religious preference, Congregationalist.

BARNARD O. NEIL, *Lemington*, democrat, was born in Lemington, Dec. 16, 1842. He is a farmer, and was educated at the district schools. P. O. address, Columbia, N. H.

Martin Joslin Pond, *Lunenburgh*, republican, was born in Lunenburgh, Sept. 6, 1826. He is a farmer, and was educated at the common schools. He was a musician of Co. K, 8th regiment Vt. Vols. Religious preference, Congregationalist.

Ira C. Cameron, *Maidstone*, democrat, was born in Moretown, Aug. 26, 1833. He is a farmer, and located in town in 1865. Was educated at the common schools. He was a member of Co, K, 6th regiment Vt. Vols. Was a justice of the peace in 1867, '77 and '78, and was a lister in 1874 and '78. P. O. address, Guildhall.

Charles Damon, *Victory*, independent, was born in Kirby, Jan. 9, 1824. He is a farmer, and located in town in 1874. Was educated at the public schools. Has held offices of honor and trust, both in Canada and the States. He was a member of the house from Victory in 1878, serving on the joint committee "on game and fisheries."

FRANKLIN COUNTY.

William H. Giddings, *Bakersfield*, republican, was born in Bakersfield, Oct. 24, 1840. He is a physician. Was educated at the common schools and academy, and graduated in his profession at the University of Vermont, class of 1866. He was a member of the constitutional convention of 1870. Religious preference, Congregationalist.

Leander Cushman Leavens, *Berkshire*, republican, was born in Berkshire, March 29, 1841. He is a merchant, and is also extensively engaged in the manufacture of leather. Was educated at the common schools. He was a member of Co. I, 10th Vt. Vols.; promoted to 1st lieutenant, U. S. infantry, and served as commissary of subsistence and assistant quartermaster upon the staff of Brig. Gen. Litchfield, and was mustered out August 22, 1865. He held the office of selectman in 1878 and '79, and justice from 1876 to 1880. Religious preference, Universalist. P. O. address, West Berkshire.

Charles Allen, *Enosburgh*, republican, was born in Enosburgh, in 1834. He is a farmer, and was educated at the common schools. He has held the usual town offices. Religious preference, Congregationalist. P. O. address, East Berkshire.

David A. Shepardson, *Fairfax*, republican, was born in Fairfax, in 1822. He is a farmer, and was educated at the common schools. Has been overseer, grand juror, and has been constable since 1876. Religious preference, Universalist.

SAMUEL HUNGERFORD SOULE, *Fairfield*, greenbacker, was born in Fairfield, Sept. 4, 1824. He is a farmer, and was educated at the common schools. He was trustee of school fund from 1862 to 1869; selectman from 1874 till 1879, and was lister in 1870, '71 and '78.

PETER MCGETTRICK, *Fletcher*, democrat, was born in Fletcher, September 5, 1849. He is a farmer, and was educated in the common and high schools. He has held some of the town offices, and is lister. Religious preference, Roman Catholic.

BART WHITNEY, *Franklin*, republican, was born in Franklin, March 8, 1826. He is a farmer, and received an academical education at St. Armand, P. Q., and Bakersfield, and has held the usual town offices. Religious preference, Methodist. P. O. address, West Berkshire.

JAMES KNOX CURTIS, *Georgia*, republican, was born in Burlington, Feb. 20, 1845. He is a farmer, and located in town in 1850. Was educated at the common school and Williston Academy. Has been lister since 1878. Religious preference, Methodist. P. O. address, St. Albans.

OSCAR S. SEARLE, *Highgate*, republican, was born in Berkshire, Jan. 19, 1820. He is a physician and surgeon, and located in town in 1847. Was educated at the common schools and academies, and graduated in his profession at the Castleton (Vt.) Medical College, class of 1846. He has held several town offices, and has been justice of the peace. Religious preference, Universalist. P. O. address, Highgate Centre.

SAMUEL NEVINS DIX, *Montgomery*, republican, was born in Troy, May 4, 1839. He is a mercantile clerk, and located in town in 1870. Was educated at the common schools. He was a member of Co. I, 15th Vt. Vols. Religious preference, Baptist. P. O. address, Montgomery Centre.

ALONZO BUTTON, *Richford*, republican, was born in Swanton, in 1834. He is a farmer, and located in town in 1874. Was educated at the common schools. He was lister in 1878, and selectman in 1879 and '80. Religious preference, Methodist.

ALBERT S. LEACH, *Sheldon*, republican, was born in Fairfield, Dec. 31, 1840. He is a farmer, and located in town in 1868. Was educated at the common schools. He was town treasurer in 1878 and '79, and has been selectman since 1878. Religious preference, Methodist.

HERBERT BRAINERD, *St. Albans*, republican, was born in St. Albans. He is treasurer of the St. Albans iron and steel works. Was educated at the common schools, and at Allentown, Pa. He was a member of Co. L, 1st Vt. cavalry and subsequently promoted to quartermaster of the regiment. Religious preference, Congregationalist.

HIRAM PLATT, *Swanton*, republican, was born in Swanton, April 24, 1826. He is a farmer, and was educated at the common schools. He was captain of Co. F, 10th regiment Vt. Vols. He has held the office of selectman for the last three years.

GRAND ISLE COUNTY.

HENRY MOTT, *Alburgh*, republican, was born in Alburgh, June 7, 1837. He is a farmer and speculator. Was educated at the common schools, and was a member of the general assembly from the town of Alburgh in 1878, serving on the committee on claims. Religious preference, Protestant.

JAMES A. BROWN, *Grand Isle*, democrat, was born in Grand Isle, Nov. 23, 1840. He is a lawyer, and was educated at the University of Vermont, graduating in the class of '63. He has held the office of selectman, and has been state's attorney of Grand Isle County.

JAMES HURST, *Isle La Motte*, republican, was born in Canada in 1842. He is a farmer and quarryman, and located in town in 1862. Was educated at the common schools in Canada. He held the office of justice of the peace in 1872 and '73; selectman in 1874 and 1879, and auditor in 1878. Religious preference, Episcopalian.

HOLLAND J. FEFEE, *North Hero*, republican, was born in North Hero, Nov. 14, 1853. He is a farmer. Was educated at the common schools. Religious preference, Methodist.

DAVID S. DILLON, *South Hero*, democrat, was born in Ireland, in 1837. He is a farmer, and located in town in 1849. Was educated at the common schools of South Hero. He was a member of Co. K, First Vt. Cavalry. Religious preference, Roman Catholic.

LAMOILLE COUNTY.

THOMAS M. POTTER, *Belvidere*, republican, was born in Belvidere, Nov. 11, 1843. He is a farmer, and was educated in the common schools. He has been constable for the last four, and deputy sheriff for the last two years. Religious preference, Good Samaritan.

LOWELL A. BLAISDELL, *Cambridge*, republican, was born in Cambridge, Nov. 22, 1848. He is a farmer, and was educated at the common schools and academy. He is a justice of the peace and selectman. Religious preference, Congregationalist.

MARTIN SHATTUCK, *Eden*, republican, was born in Belvidere, Feb. 5, 1842. He located in town in 1871. Was educated at the public schools. Religious preference, Congregationalist.

JUDSON T. PARKER, *Elmore*, republican, was born in Elmore, in 1826. He is a farmer, and was educated at the common schools. He has held the office of selectman. Religious preference, Methodist.

HARRISON W. HENDRICK, *Hyde Park*, republican, was born in Fairfield, Nov. 4, 1848. He is a physician, and located in town in 1872. Received a liberal academical education, read medicine, attending medical lectures at the University of Michigan and the University of Vermont, and graduated in his profession from the latter institution, class of '72. He has held the office of county auditor, and other minor positions. Religious preference, Methodist.

ISAAC A. MANNING, *Johnson*, republican, was born in New Boston, N. H., Jan. 24, 1819. He is a farmer, and located in town in 1824. Was educated at the common schools and academy. Was elected selectman in 1852, 1876, '77, '78 and 1880, and has held several other town offices. He was a member of the general assembly in 1869. Religious preference, Baptist.

ISAAC P. BOOTH, *Morristown*, republican, was born in Union, Conn., Sept. 10, 1843. He is a clergyman, and located in town in 1876. Received a classical education, read law, and was admitted a member of the bar of Summit county, Ohio, in Sept., 69—practiced but a limited time and engaged in the occupation of teaching. He has held the office of town superintendent since 1876, and also other minor positions. Religious preference, Universalist. P. O. address, Morrisville.

PAPHRO D. PIKE, *Stowe*, republican, was born in Morristown, Dec. 1, 1835. He is a tub manufacturer, and located in town in 1860. Was educated at the common schools and Johnson Academy. He was a member of Co. D. 11th Vt. Vols.; was promoted successively to corporal, quartermaster sergeant, and 2d lieutenant, but was not mustered into the latter office. He has held the office of lister and auditor. Religious preference, Unitarian.

OMAR D. ROGERS, *Waterville*, republican, was born in Bakersfield, May 22, 1845. He is a blacksmith, and located in town in 1871. Was educated at the schools and academy of Stanbridge, P. Q. Was selectman in 1874 and '75, and has held several minor town offices.

WOLCOTT—not represented.

ORANGE COUNTY.

MOSES REMEMBRANCE CHAMBERLAIN, *Bradford*, democrat, was born in Newbury, April 28, 1816. He is a farmer, and located in town in 1821. Was educated at the district school and Bradford Academy. He has held the usual town offices, and also deputy sheriff. Religious preference, Methodist.

VICTOR I. SPEAR, *Braintree*, republican, was born in Braintree, Sept. 20, 1852. He is a farmer, and was educated at Dartmouth College, graduating in the scientific department, class of 1874. Was elected member of the examining board of teachers in 1878, '79; has been superintendent of schools since 1875, auditor since 1874, and is selectman.

ALMON SHEPHERD, *Brookfield*, republican, was born in Brookfield, Dec. 6, 1811. He is a clergyman, and was educated at the common schools. He was a member of the legislature of New Hampshire in 1855. Religious preference, Freewill Baptist. P. O. address, East Brookfield.

LYMAN G. HINCKLEY, *Chelsea*, republican, was born in Thetford, April 13, 1832, and located in town in 1857. He is a lawyer. Fitted for and entered Dartmouth College, and graduated in the class of 1856. Has held the office of county clerk of Orange county since 1860; was assistant clerk of the house of representatives from 1856 to 1859, inclusive; was a member of the house in 1862, '63, '68, '69, '70; was a senator from Orange county in 1872–'73, and was lieutenant governor in 1874–'75. Has also been justice of the peace since 1870. Religious preference, Baptist.

CORINTH—not represented.

ELY ELY-GODDARD, *Ely*, republican, was born in the city of New York in 1855. He is not at present engaged in any business. He located in West Fairlee in 1876, and represented that town in the general assembly of 1878, serving on the committee on banks; in 1879 he removed to Ely. Was educated at the institutions of learning in Europe, graduating at Ecole des Sciences Diplomatique, Paris. Religious preference, Roman Catholic.

MYRON W. SMITH, *Fairlee*, republican, was born in Fairlee, in 1834. He is a farmer. Was educated at the common schools. He was a member of Co. A, 15th regiment Vt. Vols. He holds the office of town superintendent. Religious preference, Congregationalist.

DANIEL PUTNAM KIMBALL, *Newbury*, republican, was born in Haverhill, N. H., July 25, 1824. He is a farmer, and located in town in 1867. Was educated at the common schools. Religious preference, Congregationalist.

LEWIS HUTCHINSON, *Orange*, republican, was born in Washington, January 14, 1836. He is a farmer, and located in town in 1866. Was educated at the public schools. He was a lister in 1877–'78, and is one of the board of selectmen. Religious preference, Methodist. P. O. address, East Orange.

JAMES GIFFORD FOWLER, *Randolph*, republican, was born in Bethel, May 27, 1824. He is a farmer, and located in town in 1866. Was educated at the common schools, academies and at the State Normal School at Randolph. Has held minor town offices. Religious preference, Baptist. P. O. address, East Bethel.

NATHAN B. COBB, *Strafford*, republican, was born in Strafford, Oct. 14, 1827. He is a farmer, and was educated at Norwich University, receiving the degree of A. M. in course. He has held the office of town clerk since 1863; jnstice of the peace, since 1866, and was school superintendent from 1872 to 1880. Was associate justice of Orange county court in 1874, and was a member of the general assembly from Strafford in 1870. Religious preference, Congregationalist.

JEDUTHAN TAYLOR, *Thetford*, republican, was born in Thetford, April 25, 1817. He is a farmer, and was educated at the common schools. He was a selectman in 1869, '79 and '80. Religious preference, Congregationalist. P. O. address, East Thetford.

RONEY M. HARVEY, *Topsham*, republican, was born in Topsham, May 20, 1843. He is a lawyer, and was educated at the common schools and academies. He has held several town offices, and was elected state's attorney for Orange county in 1878. Religious preference, Protestant. P. O. address, West Topsham.

ORVIS P. CILLEY, *Tunbridge*, republican, was born in Tunbridge, Sept. 23, 1816. He is a farmer. Was educated at the common schools. Religious preference, Methodist.

NOAH CLINTON TAYLOR, *Washington*, republican, was born in Washington, June 24, 1845. He is a farmer, and was educated at the public schools. He was superintendent of schools in 1876, '77; selectman in 1877, '78, '80, and is lister. Religious preference, Universalist.

FRED. W. FARNHAM, *West Fairlee*, democrat, was born in Tunbridge, Dec. 12, 1839. He is a hotel keeper, and located in town in 1866. Was educated at the common schools and academies. He was a selectman in 1875, '76 and '77. Religious preference, Universalist.

OLIVER SMITH WALKER, *Williamstown*, republican, was born in Williamstown, Nov. 4, 1818. He is a farmer, and was educated at the district schools. He was sealer of weights and measures and inspector of leather for twenty years; lister in 1868, '69, '73; first selectman in 1870; has been auditor; treasurer in 1876, '77, '78; and has held several minor offices at different times. Religious preference, attends meetings at the Methodist Episcopal church.

ORLEANS COUNTY.

HIRAM W. CHAFEY, *Albany*, republican, was born in Brookfield, Oct. 22, 1830. He is a merchant and farmer, and located in town in 1867. Was educated at the district schools. He held the office of postmaster in Craftsbury under Lincoln; is town clerk, and has repeatedly held the usual town offices. Religious preference, Baptist.

RICHARD BAXTER SKINNER, *Barton*, republican, was born in Barnet, May 1, 1834. He is a physician and surgeon, and located in town in 1853. Was educated at the common schools and academies; read medicine and graduated in his profession with distinguished honor at Harvard medical college in 1858. Was town superintendent in 1863, '64, and has held other offices of trust and honor. Religious preference, Congregationalist.

AHIRA OTHNIEL JOSLYN, *Brownington*, republican, was born in Brownington, June 17, 1842. He is a manufacturer, and was educated at the common schools and academy of Brownington, and attended a commercial course at Burlington, Vt. He has held the offices of auditor, lister, treasurer, justice of the peace in 1879, and selectman in 1878 and '79. Religious preference, Congregationalist.

THOMAS L. DOLLOFF, *Charleston*, republican, was born in Sutton, November, 1821. He is a farmer, and located in town in 1853. Was educated at the common schools. He has held the usual town offices. Religious preference, Freewill Baptist. P. O. address, East Charleston.

HENRY FAYETTE BLACK, *Coventry*, republican, was born in Coventry, June 28, 1842. He is a farmer, and was educated in the district schools and academy. He has held several town offices, and is 1st selectman. P. O. address, East Coventry.

JAMES W. SIMPSON, *Craftsbury*, republican, was born in Scotland, in 1822. He is a merchant, and located in town in 1847. Was educated at the district schools of Greensboro and Craftsbury. He has held the usual town offices. He was a senator from Orleans county in 1867 and '68. Religious preference, Presbyterian. P. O. address, East Craftsbury.

WARREN GOODWIN, *Derby*, republican, was born in Sheffield, in 1830. He is a farmer, and located in town in 1853. Was educated at the public schools. He has held the office of selectman and other minor offices. Religious preference, Congregationalist. P. O. address, Beebe Plain.

WILBUR FISK TEMPLETON, *Glover*, republican, was born in Tilton, N. H., Feb. 9, 1836. He is a physician, and graduated at the Eclectic Medical College of the City of N. Y. in 1857. Served as surgeon on detached service in the civil war. Was a member of the general assembly from Glover in 1876, and again in 1878, serving the latter year on the committee on the insane. Religious preference, Rationalist.

JOHN SIMPSON, *Greensboro*, republican, was born in Scotland, Mar. 4, 1826. He is a farmer, and located in town in 1829. Was educated at the common schools and academies. He has held the office of overseer and lister more or less for the last twenty-five years. Religious preference, Presbyterian.

George R. Caswell, *Holland*, republican, was born in Stanstead, P. Q., May 26, 1833. He is a lumberman, and located in town in 1872. Was educated at the schools of Stanstead. Religious preference, Methodist. P. O. address, Derby Line.

Laforrest H. Thompson, *Irasburgh*, republican, was born in Bakersfield, Jan. 6, 1848. He is a lawyer, and located in town in 1871. Was educated at the Johnson (Vt.) Normal School, and Kimball Union Academy of Meriden, N. H. Was state's attorney of Orleans County in 1874, and has been judge of probate for the district of Orleans since 1876. Religious preference, Congregationalist.

Jonathan E. Chase, *Jay*, republican, was born in Fletcher, Nov. 3, 1838. He is a farmer, and located in town in 1849. Was educated at the common schools and academy. He was a member of Co. H, 2d Vt. Vols, and Co. F, U. S. S. S., extending over a time from April 25, 1861, to Aug. 31, 1866. Was selectman in 1876, '77; lister several years, and has been justice of the peace, and was superintendent of schools from 1871 to 1879. Religious preference, Baptist.

Carlos Farman, *Lowell*, republican, was born in Lowell, July 16, 1838. He is a farmer, and was educated at the common schools. He was a lister in 1878, and has been town agent for several years.

Jeremiah S. Wilcox, *Morgan*, republican, was born in Salem in 1824. He is a farmer, and located in town in 1826. Was educated at the common schools. Religious preference, Congregationalist.

Theophilus Grout, *Newport*, republican, was born in Compton, P. Q., Sept. 3, 1848. He is a lawyer, and located in town in 1870. Received a liberal academical education He has held various offices of public trust and responsibility, and is state's attorney for Orleans county. Religious preference Episcopalian.

David Hopkinson, *Salem*, republican, was born in Salem, Nov. 23, 1826. He is a farmer, and was educated at the common schools and academies. He was assistant justice of Orleans county court' in 1876–'77, a representative from the town of Salem in 1859 and '60. He has held the offices of selectman, lister and town clerk. Religious preference, Congregationalist. P. O. address, Derby.

Daniel H. Buck, *Troy*, republican, was born in Westford, April 27, 1827. He is a manufacturer of lumber, and located in town in 1866. Was educated at the public schools and Bakersfield Academy. He formerly resided in Westfield, and there was selectman and superintendent of schools in 1855 and '56; was postmaster from 1860 to '64; lister in 1865 and '66, and was a member of the house from Westfield in 1864 and '65. Religious preference, Universalist.

WILLIAM WELLS WOOD, *Westfield*, republican, was born in Newport, N. Y., Nov. 25, 1841. He is a farmer, and lolated in town in 1866. Was educated at the common schools. He was a member of Co. I, 2d regiment N. H. Vols.—was detailed as wagon master of Gen. Hooker's headquarters train, afterwards transferred to 3d army corps as wagon master of the ammunition train. He held the office of lister in 1876, '77 and '78. Religious preference, Liberal.

WELCOME B. DANIELS, *Westmore*, republican, was born in Wheelock, March 24, 1814. He is a farmer, and located in town in 1854. Was educated at the public schools. He held the office of selectman in 1855, '56, and again in 1876; was justice of the peace in 1857 and '58.

RUTLAND COUNTY.

WILLARD EZRA STRONG, *Benson*, republican, was born in Benson, Oct. 14, 1832. He is a carriage maker, and was educated at the common schools. He was selectman in 1872 and '73, and has held minor town offices. Religious preference, Congregationalist.

GEORGE BRIGGS, *Brandon*, republican, was born in Brandon, April 26, 1844. He is a lawyer, and was educated at Hobart college, Geneva, N. Y., graduating in the class of '66, and from the Albany law school in 1867. He has been town clerk for the last thirteen years. Religious preference, Episcopalian.

SAMUEL L. HAZARD, *Castleton*, republican, was born in Liverpool, England, where his parents were temporarily residing, June 16, 1814. He is a manufacturer, and located in town in 1864. Was educated at the common schools. Has been justice of the peace for the last ten and selectman for the last two years. Religious preference, Congregationalist. P. O. address, West Castleton.

EDWIN HORTON, *Chittenden*, republican, was born in Clarendon, Aug. 25, 1843. He is a farmer, and located in town in 1858. Was educated at the common and select schools of Clarendon and Black River Academy at Ludlow. He was a private in Co. G, 22d reg't. N. Y. Vols., and was corporal in Co. C, 4th reg't. Vt. Vols. He has held the office of constable and collector since 1871, except one year, and has held several minor town offices.

NOEL POTTER, *Clarendon*, republican, was born in Clarendon, Jan. 19, 1841. He is a farmer, and was educated at the common schools. He was a member of Co. F, Berdan's reg't. sharpshooters. He has held the office of lister and auditor. P. O. address, Clarendon Springs.

ERASTUS KELLEY, *Danby*, republican, was born in Danby, July 19, 1835. He is a mechanic, and was educated at Troy Conference Academy. He was justice of the peace in 1874, and has been lister for the last four years. Religious preference, Methodist.

EDWARD L. ALLEN, *Fair Haven*, republican, was born in Hartford, N. Y., Feb. 24, 1835. He is a manufacturer, and located in town in 1836. Was educated at Castleton Seminary. He has held town and village offices. Religious preference, Congregationalist.

ALLEN ST. JOHN, *Hubbardton*, republican, was born in Hubbardton, May, 1840. He is a farmer, and was educated at the common and high schools. He has held the office of lister since 1879. P. O. address, East Hubbardton.

EBEN B. PERRY, *Ira*, republican, was born in Ira, Aug. 1, 1852. He is a farmer, and was educated at the common and high schools. Has held the office of first constable since 1875. Was a member of the general assembly from Ira in 1878, serving on the distributing committee. Religious preference, Congregationalist.

HENRY HARRISON SHEDD, *Mendon*, republican, was born in Sherburne, June 5, 1841. He is a farmer, and located in town in 1850. Was educated at the common schools. Was selectman in 1874, '76, '79; lister in 1872, '78; and has held minor town offices. Religious preference, Methodist.

LEONIDAS GRAY, *Middletown*, republican, was born in Middletown, Dec. 10, 1834. He is a member of the firm of A. W. Gray's Sons, manufacturers of horse powers. He was educated in the common schools and academies. P. O. address, Middletown Springs.

CHARLES W. PRIEST, *Mount Holly*, republican, was born in Mount Holly, Feb. 27, 1843. He is a merchant, and was educated at the district schools. He was a member of Co. I, 2d regiment Vt. Vols. He held the office of constable and collector from 1870 to 1875. Religious preference, Methodist. P. O. address, Mechanicsville.

DANIEL H. LANE, *Mount Tabor*, republican, was born in Ireland, March 18, 1831. He is a teacher and farmer, and located in town in 1868, and was educated at the common schools and academies. He was a musician of Co. B, 14th and Co. I, 17th, and sergeant and 2d lieutenant of Co. A, 17th regiments, Vt. Vols. He has repeatedly held the offices of selectman, superintendent of schools, justice of the peace, lister, and auditor. P. O. address, Danby.

AMOS W. WILCOX, *Pawlet*, republican, was born in Pawlet in 1836. He is a farmer, and was educated at the public schools. He has held the office of selectman for the last three years. Religious preference, Baptist. P. O. address, Granville, N. Y.

EDWARD ATWOOD, *Pittsfield*, republican, was born in Bridgewater, Sept. 27, 1844. He is a mechanic, and located in town in 1868. Was educated at the common schools. He was a member of Co. E, 2d regiment United States sharp shooters, was elected one of the selectmen in 1879 and '80. Religious preference, Congregationalist.

AMOS D. TIFFANY, *Pittsford*, republican, was born in Pittsford in 1841. He is a railroad station agent, and was educated at the common schools. He has been a member of the republican town committee since 1872. Religious preference, Congregationalist.

CHARLES RIPLEY, *Poultney*, republican, was born in Poultney, April 10, 1838. He is a manufacturer, and was educated at the common schools. He was town clerk in 1870. Religious preference, Baptist.

JOHN B. PAGE, *Rutland*, republican, was born in Rutland, Feb. 25, 1826. He is a banker, and is connected with various railroad enterprises, besides being actively engaged in extensive manufacturing industries. Was educated at the public schools. He was a member of the general assembly from his native town in 1852, '53 and '54. In 1860 he was elected to the office of state treasurer and received successive annual elections till 1866, and during this time was allotment commissioner, by appointment of President Lincoln. In 1867 he was elected governor of the state, and reelected the following year. He has been repeatedly honored with various offices of trust and responsibility, both of town and the benevolent institutions of the day. Religious preference, Congregationalist.

EDWIN S. COLTON, *Sherburne*, republican, was born in Sherburne, June 29, 1846. He is a farmer, and was educated at the public schools. He was constable and collector in 1873, '74, '75, '78, '79, and selectman in 1876 and '77. Was a member of the house from Sherburne in 1874. Religious preference, Universalist.

GEORGE WELLINGTON FOSTER, *Shrewsbury*, republican, was born in Shrewsbury, April 10, 1840. He is a merchant, and was educated at the common schools. He was a musician of Co. B, 14th reg't. Vt. Vols, and captain in the state militia. P. O. address, Cuttingsville.

BENONI GRIFFIN, *Sudbury*, republican, wae born in Sudbury, March 20, 1819. He is a farmer, and was educated at the public schools. He held the office of selectman during the war of the rebellion, and has held most of the minor town offices at different times. Religious preference, Methodist. P. O. address, Brandon.

ISAAC D. TUBBS, *Tinmouth*, republican, was born in Clarendon, December 25, 1839. He is a farmer, and located in town in 1870. Was educated at the common schools. He has held the office of town clerk since 1873, is one of the selectmen, and has frequently been elected lister.

NICHOLAS COOK, *Wallingford*, republican, was born in Wallingford, March 4, 1816. He is a butcher, and was educated at the common schools. He has repeatedly held the usual town offices. Religious preference, Universalist. P. O. address, South Wallingford.

ALLEN CRAIN GROVER, *Wells*, democrat, was born in Wells, March 31, 1837. He is a physician, and was educated at the Albany Medical College, graduating in his profession in the class of '66, but is not in practice. He held the office of selectman in 1871, '72 and '73. Religious preference, Episcopalian.

RODNEY C. ABELL, *West Haven*, republican, was born in Benson, Oct. 17, 1831. He is an attorney and farmer, and located in town in 1856. Was educated at Union College, graduating in the class of 1854. He was a member of the general assembly from the town of West Haven in 1859, '60, '68, '69, '74 and '76; a senator from Rutland County in 1870, and has held the usual town offices. Was a member of the state board of equalization tn 1874 and 1878. Religious preference, Christian.

WASHINGTON COUNTY.

HENRY PRIEST, *Barre*, republican, was born in Mount Holly, May 5, 1847. He is a teacher, and located in town in 1874. Was educated at Tufts college, graduating in the class of '74. He has been principal of Goddard Seminary for the last six years. Religious preference, Universalist.

MARTIN W. WHEELOCK, *Berlin*, republican, was born in Montpelier, March 18, 1853. He is a bookbinder, and located in town in 1854. Was educated at the Washington county grammar school. Was superintendent of schools in 1875, and has been town clerk, treasurer and justice of the peace for the last five years, and has held minor offices of trust and responsibility. Religious preference, Methodist. P. O. address, Montpelier.

GEORGE GOULD, *Cabot*, republican, was born in Cabot, July 1, 1840. He is a farmer, and was educated at the common schools. He was a selectman in 1879. Religious preference, Congregationalist.

JOSEPH W. LEONARD, *Calais*, republican, was born in Calais, April, 1828. He is a farmer, and was educated at the common schools. He was a member of Co. I, 11th Vt. Vols. Held the office of justice of the peace in 1863, '64, '67, '68, '69; lister in '63, '64; selectman in 1874, '75 and '80. Religious preference, Spiritualist. P. O. address, East Calais.

DUXBURY—not represented.

ANDREW AVERILL TRACY, *East Montpelier*, republican, was born in Stowe, August 17, 1823. He is a farmer, and located in town in 1867. Was educated at the common schools. He has held the office of selectman, justice of the peace in the town of Middlesex, where he formerly resided. Religious preference, Universalist. P. O. address, Montpelier.

NATHAN BOYCE, *Fayston*, republican, was born in Fayston, April 30, 1836. He is a farmer and lumberman, and was educated at the common schools and academy. He has held the office of lister and justice of the peace, and other minor town offices. Religious preference, Congregationalist. P. O. address, Moretown.

MARK MEARS, *Marshfield*, republican, was born in Marshfield, in 1840. He is a farmer, and was educated at the common schools and Peacham Academy. He has held the office of constable and collector since 1878. P. O. address, Plainfield.

WILLIAM CHAPIN, *Middlesex*, republican, was born in Middlesex, Dec. 7, 1831. He is a farmer, and was educated at the common schools. He was constable in 1858, '59; lister in 1860, '70, '75, '76, '79, '80; selectman in 1871, '72; has been town agent since 1876, and has held various other town offices of minor importance. Religious preference, Good Samaritan.

BENJAMIN F. FIFIELD, *Montpelier*, republican, was born in Orange, Nov. 18, 1832; graduated at the University of Vermont, class of 1855; studied law with Peck & Colby, succeeding to their business after his admission to the bar of Washington County, which took place in 1859, and from that time Montpelier has been his permanent residence. In 1869 he was appointed by President Grant district attorney for the District of Vermont, which office he resigned in Sept., 1880. Religious preference, Episcopalian.

RUSSELL SAWYER, *Moretown*, republican, was born in Middlesex, Sept. 4, 1826. He is a farmer, and located in town in 1867. Was educated at the common schools. He was constable and collector in 1872, '73, '75, '76, and first selectman in 1878, '79.

ANDREW E. DENNY, *Northfield*, republican, was born in Northfield, August 4th, 1832. He is engaged in the manufacture of lumber and leather, and was educated at the common schools. He was a member of the general assembly from the town of Northfield in 1876. Religious preference, Congregationalist.

DUDLEY B. SMITH, *Plainfield*, republican, was born in Williamstown, Dec. 15, 1832. He is a physician and surgeon, and located in town in 1856. Was educated at the common schools and academies; read medicine, and graduated in his profession at the University of Vermont (medical deparment) in the class of '56. Religious preference, Unitarian.

WILLIAM B. ORCUTT, *Roxbury*, republican, was born in Roxbury, Jan. 15, 1820. He is a farmer, and was educated at the common schools. He was a member of the general assembly from his native town in 1859, '60 and '78, serving the latter year on the committee on grand list. He has held the office of assistant judge of the Washington county court, and has repeatedly been chosen selectman, lister, and to other minor town offices. Religious preference, Congregationalist.

WALTER A. JONES, *Waitsfield*, republican, was born in Waitsfield, July 27, 1840. He is a merchant. Received a liberal academical education; read medicine, and graduated in his profession at the Berkshire (Mass.) medical college, class of '65. Has been auditor since 1873; chairman of the board of school directors, and superintendent of schools, under the town system, since 1875. Religious preference, Congregationalist.

MILO BUCKLIN, *Warren*, republican, was born in Warren, March 1, 1843. He is a farmer, and was educated at the district schools. He was a member of Co. A, 8th regiment Vt. Vols. Religious preference, Congregationalist.

EDWIN FRANKLIN PALMER, *Waterbury*, republican, was born in Waitsfield in 1836. He is a lawyer, and located in town in 1865. Was educated at Dartmouth College, graduating in the class of '62. Was second lieutenant of Co. B, 13th regiment Vt. Vols. He has held minor town offices. Religious preference, Congregationalist.

CALEB A. MCKNIGHT, *Woodbury*, republican, was born in Calais, March 1, 1840. He is a carpenter and joiner, and located in town in 1867. Was educated at the common schools. He was a member of Co. C, 11th regiment Vt. Vols. Religious preference, Universalist.

CHAUNCEY NATHAN HUNT, *Worcester*, republican, was born in Worcester, April 17, 1851. He is a physician, and was educated at the common schools and academies, and graduated in his profession at the University of Vermont, class of 1875. Religious preference, Methodist.

WINDHAM COUNTY.

GEORGE N. OBER, *Athens*, republican, was born in Rockingham in 1826. He is a farmer, and located in town in 1856. Was educated at the common schools. He was a member of the general assembly from Athens in 1868 and '69. Religious preference, Baptist.

GEORGE W. HOOKER, *Brattleboro*, republican, was born in Salem, N. Y., Feb. 6, 1838. He is a manufacturer, and located in town in 1875. Received a liberal classical education. He was a member of the 4th Vermont and assistant adjutant general of volunteers. He was chief of governor's staff in 1878; Commander of the Grand Army of the Republic, department of Vermont, in 1879; delegate at large to the national republican convention at Chicago in 1880; was a member of the national republican committee of 1880; member of the executive board, and assistant secretary of the same. Religious preference, Universalist.

ERASTUS WHITNEY, *Brookline*, republican, was born in Brookline, Dec. 6, 1815. He is a farmer, and was educated at the common schools. He was selectman from 1851 to 1864 inclusive; was a member of the general assembly from Brookline in 1869 and '70, and was also a member of the constitutional convention in 1870. Religious preference, Universalist.

HENRY J. TURNER, *Dover*, republican, was born in Putney, in 1824. He is a farmer, and located in town in 1856. Was educated at the common schools. He has held the usual town offices. Religious preference, Baptist. P. O. address, East Dover.

STEPHEN LYMAN DUTTON, *Dummerston*, republican, was born in Dummerston, June 8, 1827. He is a farmer, and was educated at the common and select schools. He was a member of the general assembly from the town of Dummerston in 1869 '70 and '72; is one of the board of selectmen, and has held several minor offices of responsibility. P. O. address, Brattleboro.

CHARLES WARREN HASKELL, *Grafton*, republican, was born in Westford, Nov. 5, 1836. He is a farmer and book agent, and located in town in 1875. Was educated at the common schools and academies. He was a member of Co. D, 9th regiment Vermont volunteers; appointed 1st sergeant July, 1862, promoted November, 1862 and May, 1863, and continued as company commander, except when on detached service as provost marshal, until expiration of service in 1865. He has held the office of justice of the peace since '77; was selectman in 1877–'78, and is lister. Religious preference, Liberal. P. O. address, Cambridgeport.

WILLIAM W. BARNEY, *Guilford*, republican, was born in Guilford, in 1821. He is a farmer, and was educated at the common schools. He was a member of the house in 1862 and in 1874. He held the office of selectman from 1864 to 1874, and has been justice of the peace for the last eight years. Religious preference, Universalist. P. O. address, Guildford Centre.

LEWIS WORDEN SUMNER, *Halifax*, republican, was born in Halifax, Sept. 8, 1839. He is a farmer and lumberman, and was educated at the common schools. He was selectman in 1868, '79, and again elected in 1880. Religious preference, Universalist. P. O. address, West Halifax.

WARREN C. CUSHING, *Jamaica*, republican, was born in Newfane, in 1839. He is a farmer, and located in town in 1869. Was educated at the common schools. He was a lister in 1870-'71, and is one of the selectmen. Religious preference, Congregationalist. P. O. address, Wardsboro.

JAMES LOREN MARTIN, *Londonderry*, republican, was born in Landgrove, Sept. 13, 1846. He is an attorney, and located in town in 1869. He was representative from Londonderry in 1874, 1876 and in 1878—the latter year he was elected speaker of the house; in 1876 he was state's attoreny for Windham County. Religious preference, Baptist. P. O. address, South Londonderry.

ALBERT M. PROUTY, *Marlboro*, republican, was born in Oakham, Mass., in 1842. He is a farmer, and located in town in early childhood. Was educated at the common and select schools. He is town clerk, treasurer and justice of the peace. Religious preference, Universalist.

JOHN H. MERRIFIELD, *Newfane*, republican, was born in Newfane, June, 12, 1847. He is a farmer, and was educated at the common schools and Springfield Wesleyan Seminary. He held the office of engrossing clerk in 1874 and '76; was superintendent of schools in 1870, '71 and '72, and lister in 1873, '74 and '75. He was a member of the general assembly from Newfane in 1878, serving on the committee on state prison. Religious preference, Methodist. P. O. address, Williamsville.

DENISON DAVIS, *Putney*, republican, was born in Putney, May 3, 1819. He is a farmer, and was educated at the public schools. He has repeatedly held the usual town offices, having been one of the selectmen for the last twenty years.

CHARLES SMITH, *Rockingham*, democrat, was born in Rockingham, May 29, 1825. He is a dealer in soap stone, and was educated at Saxton's River seminary. He has been selectman for the last six years. P. O. address, Saxton's River.

FRANKLIN DANIEL CHASE, *Somerset*, republican, was born in Dummerston, June 21, 1839. He is a lumberman, and located in town in 1878. Was educated at the district schools and West Townshend Academy. Religious preference, Baptist.

ANDREW DEXTER KNIGHT, *Stratton*, republican, was born in Marlboro, in 1840. He is a farmer, and located in town in 1869. Was educated at the public schools. Has held the office of lister, and was a member of the general assembly from Stratton in 1878, serving on the distributing committee. P. O. address, West Wardsboro.

JOSEPH B. WARE, *Townshend*, republican, was born in Putney, in 1809. He is a farmer and drover, and located in town in 1822. Was educated at the public schools. Religious preference, Congregationalist. P. O. address, East Townshend.

JOSIAH M. MORRILL, *Vernon*, republican, was born in Danville, Dec. 29, 1841. He is a railroad conductor, and located in town in 1870. Was educated at the common schools and Peacham Academy. He was a member of Co. B, 13th regiment Mass. Vols. Religious preference, Universalist.

HERBERT EMERSON KIDDER, *Wardsboro*, republican, was born in Wardsboro, April 12, 1840. He is a merchant, and was educated at the common schools and Leland & Gray seminary. Religious preference, Congregationalist. P. O. address, South Wardsboro.

FENELON ARNOLD, *Westminster*, republican, was born in Westminster, Jan. 25, 1817. He is a farmer, and was educated at the common schools. He has held the usual town offices. Religious preference, Liberal.

A. AUGUSTINE BUTTERFIELD, *Whitingham*, republican, was born in Wilmington, June 25, 1844. He is a lawyer, and located in town in 1868. Was educated at the common schools and Wilmington Academy. He has held various town offices, and has been officially connected with many of the benevolent enterprises of the day. Religious preference, Baptist. P. O. address, Jacksonville.

CHARLES DAVID SPENCER, *Wilmington*, republican, was born in Brattleboro, Sept. 26, 1854. He is a salesman, and located in town in 1865. Was educated at the common and high schools. Religious preference, Methodist.

JAMES W. GOULD, *Windham*, republican, was born in Windham, July 7, 1842. He is a farmer, and was educated at the district and select schools. He has held the office of justice of the peace six years, and selectman seven years. Religious preference, Congregationalist.

WINDSOR COUNTY.

ISAIAH LOVEJOY, *Andover*, republican, was born in Weston, July 30, 1827. He is a farmer, and located in town in 1853. Was educated at the common schools. He has held the office of selectman since 1874.

THOMAS PRESTON, *Baltimore*, republican, was born in Weathersfield in 1819. He is a farmer, and located in town in 1825. Was educated at the common schools. He was selectman in 1849, '50, '63, '64, '71, '72, '75, '76; lister in 1852, '53, '56, '64, '70, '71, '78; constable in 1870, '71, '79; overseer from 1853 to 1867 inclusively. Has been justice of the peace since 1874; superintendent since 1875, and has held other town offices. Religious preference, Baptist. P. O. address, North Springfield.

ISAAC DANFORTH DAVIS, *Barnard*, republican, was born in Barnard, Feb. 27, 1811. He is a farmer, and was educated at the common schools and academies. He was lister from 1836 to '40; was selectman in 1843–'44, and from 1856 to '64, again from 1869 to '71 inclusive, was also agent from 1855 to '59. Has held the office of justice of the peace several years. Religious preference, Congregationalist.

JOSEPH GRANT SARGENT, *Bethel*, republican, was born in Bethel, Aug. 6, 1841. He is a merchant, and was educated at the common schools and academies. He was postmaster from 1868 to '75. Religious preference, Congregationalist.

CHARLES BABCOCK, *Bridgewater*, republican, was born in Bridgewater, Nov. 21, 1808. He is a merchant, and was educated at the common schools. He has held the office of treasurer for the last fourteen years. Religious preference, Advent. P. O. address, Bridgewater Corners.

HENRY A. FLETCHER, *Cavendish*, republican, was born in Cavendish, Dec. 11, 1839. He is a farmer. Was educated at the common schools and academies. Was first sergeant of Co. C, 16th regiment Vt. Vols.; promoted to sergeant major, and second lieutenant of his company, April 2, 1863. Was a member of the house in 1867 and '68, and again in 1878, serving on the general committee. He is aid-de-camp on the staff of Gov. Proctor. Has held a few town offices. Religious preference, Baptist. P. O. address, Proctorsville.

DANIEL W. DAVIS, *Chester*, republican, was born in Londonderry, Feb. 24, 1844. He is a mercantile clerk, and located in town in 1870. Was educated at the common schools and academies of Londonderry and Townshend, and Eastman's Commercial College in Poughkeepsie, N. Y. He was a private in Co. D, 16th regiment Vt. Vols. Religious preference, Congregationalist.

SAMUEL J. ALLEN, *Hartford*, republican, was born in Newport, N. H., Jan. 8. 1819. He is a physician and surgeon, and located in town in 1847. Received a liberal education, read medicine and graduated in his profession at Castleton Medical College, class of '42. Was surgeon 4th regiment Vt. Vols. After expiration of three years service was appointed acting staff surgeon U. S. army, and assigned to 6th corps as medical inspector. Religious preference, Presbyterian. P. O. address, White River Junction.

ELAM M. GOODWIN, *Hartland*, republican, was born in Plainfield, December 22, 1828. He is a farmer, and located in town in 1862. Was educated at the common schools and academies at Morrisville and South Woodstock. He has held the office of county commissioner since 1878, and was a member of the general assembly from Hartland in 1874. Religious preference, Universalist.

ELWIN A. HOWE, *Ludlow*, republican, was born in Londonderry, Sept. 18, 1843. He is agent and superintendent of the Ludlow Toy Manufacturing Company, and located in town in 1869. Was educated at the common schools and West River Academy. Was a private of Co. G, 11th regt. Vt. Vols.; promoted corporal Jan. 1864; was first lieutenant Co. I, 108th U. S. C. I.; aide-de-camp to Gen. James Oakes, and captain Co. K, 108th C. I. Was superintendent of schools in Londonderry. Has been constable and collector in Ludlow. Was a member of the house in 1878, serving on the committee on military affairs. Religious preference, Congregationalist.

SAMUEL HAMMOND CURRIER, *Norwich*, republican, was born in Norwich, June 7, 1835. He is a physician, and was educated at Norwich University; read medicine, and graduated at the University of Vermont, medical department class of '58. Was assistant surgeon of the 8th reg't. Vt. Vols. He has held the office of school superintendent in both West Fairlee and Norwich. Religious preference, Congregationalist.

ALONZO F. HUBBARD, *Plymouth*, republican, was born in Plymouth, Nov. 28, 1843. He is a farmer and merchant, and was educated at the common schools and academy. He was a member of the house in 1878, serving on the committee on the insane. He has held the office of justice of the peace for eight years. Religious preference, Spiritualist. P. O. address, Tyson Furnace.

WILLIAM H. ADAMS, *Pomfret*, republican, was born in Pomfret, April 7, 1841. He is a farmer, and was educated at the common schools. He was sergeant of Co. G, 16th reg't. Vt. Vols., and has been selectman since 1879. Religious preference, Congregationalist. P. O. address, North Pomfret.

ELEAZER DEXTER, *Reading*, republican, was born in Hardwick, Mass., July 7, 1813. He is a farmer, and located in town in 1843. Was educated at the district schools. Religious preference, Episcopalian.

ALBERT RICHMOND, *Rochester*, republican, was born in Rochester, April 3, 1844. He is a physician and surgeon, and was educated at Barre Academy. He was superintendent of schools from 1873 to 1877. Religious preference, Congregationalist.

CHARLES WEST, *Royalton*, republican, was born in Norwich, Aug. 1826. He is a farmer, and located in town in 1867. Was educated at the common schools. He has held the office of selectman from 1872 to '76. Religious preference, Congregationalist. P. O. address, South Royalton.

AMMI FOLLETT, *Sharon*, republican, was born in Enosburgh, Feb. 12, 1825. He is a farmer, and located in town in 1867. Was educated at the common schools. He was constable and collector in 1849'-50; lister in 1864, '65, '72, '73, '78; selectman 1870, '71, '72, '79, '80, and is agent. Religious preference, Congregationalist.

ROBERT MORRIS COLBURN, *Springfield*, republican, was born in Springfield, Dec. 6, 1844. He is a farmer, and was educated at the common schools and Kimball Union Academy, Meriden, N. H., and at Andover, Mass. He has held several offices of trust and responsibility. Religious preference, Congregationalist.

ORLANDO J. RICHARDSON, *Stockbridge*, republican, was born in Roxbury, Nov. 5, 1840. He is a farmer, and located in town in 1860. Was educated at the common schools and Randolph Academy. He was a member of Co. A, 16th regiment Vt. Vols., and was selectman in 1876, '77, '78, '79. Religious preference, Methodist. P. O. address, Gaysville.

JUSTUS DARTT, *Weathersfield*, republican, was born in Weathersfield, Feb. 17, 1836. He was formerly a teacher, but is now a farmer. Was educated at the Springfield Wesleyan and Newbury Seminaries. Was second lieutenant of Co. D, 9th regiment Vt. Vols. Was a member of the house in 1874 and in 1878—serving the latter year on the committee on rules, on education, and was elected a trustee of the University of Vermont and State Agricultural College in the same year. Has been superintendent, lister, auditor and selectman. Religious preference, Congregationalist. P. O. address, Ascutneyville.

ADIN E. BRYANT, *Weston*, republican, was born in Weston, Sept. 11, 1847. He is a manufacturer, and was educated at the common schools. . He has held the usual town offices. Religious preference, Universalist.

MARQUIS F. MORRISON, *West Windsor*, republican, was born in West Windsor, March 2, 1825. He is a farmer, and was educated at the district schools. He was a member of the general assembly from West Windsor in 1864 and 1865. He has held town offices since 1856 as follows: Selectman fourteen years, overseer eight years, and lister two years. Religious preference, Universalist. P. O. address, Hartland 4-Corners.

RIPLEY CLARK, *Windsor*, republican, was born in Strafford, July 23, 1817. He is a physician, and located in town in 1861. Received a liberal academical education, read medicine, and graduated in his profession at the medical department of Dartmouth College. Religious preference, Baptist.

JUSTIN F. MACKENZIE, *Woodstock*, republican, was born in Woodstock, May 5, 1816. Was educated in common schools. In 1836 he assisted in building the woolen mills at the head of Quechee gulf, in Hartford, where he was engaged in the different departments, most of the time until the spring of 1858, when he became partner in the firm of A. G. Dewey & Co., which connection he still retains. The mill has six sets of woolen machinery, all modern. Has held the usual town offices. Religious preference, Unitarian.

OFFICERS OF THE HOUSE.

HENRY NELSON NEWELL, *Shelburne*, Clerk, republican, was born in Charlotte, June 18, 1843. He is a farmer, and located in town in 1844. Received a liberal academical education. Was assistant clerk in 1868, '69 and '70; clerk of the house in 1878, and was a member of the general assembly from Shelburne in 1874. Has held the usual town offices. Religious preference, Methodist.

WILLIAM WALLACE STICKNEY, *Ludlow*, First Assistant Clerk, republican, was born in Plymouth, March 21, 1853. Was educated at Phillips' Exeter Academy, class of 1877. He is a lawyer, and located in town in 1877. Was second assistant clerk of the house in 1872, and first assistant in 1878. Religious preference, Baptist.

OLIN MERRILL, *Enosburgh*, Second Assistant Clerk, republican, was born in Plainfield, March 11, 1854. He studied law, but is now a partner in the firm of B. J. Kendall & Co., proprietary medicines, and located in town in 1873. Was educated at the Vermont Methodist Seminary, and was second assistant clerk of the house in 1878. Religious preference, Methodist. P. O. address, Enosburgh Falls.

SELDON B. CURRIER, *Moretown*, Chaplain, republican, was born in Berlin, Maine, Oct. 12, 1835. He is a clergyman, and located in town in 1880. Was educated at the Vermont Conference Seminary, Newbury. He was a member of Co. B, 4th Vt. Vols. He has held the office of superintendent of schools in Orange, and in Irasburgh, Vt. Religious preference, Methodist.

HIRAM SKEELS, *Highgate*, Door-Keeper, republican, was born in Highgate, April 21, 1830. He is a farmer. Was educated at the common schools and academy. Was a member of the general assembly in 1876. Was inspector of customs in 1868, '69, '70; deputy collector of customs from 1870 to '72; consular agent at Stanbridge, P. Q., from 1873 to 1875, and was door-keeper of the house in 1878. Religious preference, Liberal. P. O. address, Highgate Centre.

WAYNE BAILEY, *Rutland*, Assistant Door-Keeper, republican, was born in Rupert in 1845. He is a lawyer, and was educated at the common schools and academies. He has repeatedly held the offices of lister, constable and collector of Rupert; was clerk of the municipal court of Rutland in 1876, and is register of probate for the district of Rutland. In 1876 was door-keeper of the Senate. Religious preference, Congregationalist.

HERBERT E. WALKER, *Ludlow*, Messenger, was born in Ludlow, May 13, 1866. He is a student.

JONATHAN C. ROSS, *St. Johnsbury*, Messenger, was born in St. Johnsbury, March 22, 1867. He is a student.

E. MENTON ROCKWELL, *Alburgh*, Messenger, was born in Alburgh, Nov. 8, 1868. He is a student. P. O. address, Alburgh Centre.

EARLE S. KINSLEY, *Burlington*, Messenger, was born in Burlington, Nov., 1869. He is a student.

HENRY OVIATT, *Montpelier*, Reporter, was born in Dunbarton, New Hampshire, on the 13th of May, 1847. He is an Episcopalian in religion, an independent in politics, and a stenographer by profession.

EDWARD DANA, *Rutland*, Assistant Reporter, republican, was born in Woodstock, May 6, 1852, and located in town in 1867. He is a lawyer, and was educated at Middlebury College, graduating in the class of '76. Was reporter in the house in 1878. Religious preference, Congregationalist.

RECAPITULATION OF THE HOUSE.

The House of Representatives consists of 238 members, of which 217 are Republicans, 19 are Democrats, 1 Greenbacker and 1 Independent: three towns, Wolcott, Corinth and Duxbury, are not represented. Nineteen representatives were members of the House in the last General Assembly. Forty-one have been representatives before; four have previously been members of the House and Senate, and three have been Senators, one has been Governor, and Treasurer, and two have been Lieut.-Governors of the State; one has been Assistant Clerk, and one Engrossing Clerk. One hundred and eighteen represent their native towns; DENNIS MAY, of Waterford, is the oldest, and ELY ELY-GODDARD, of Ely, is the youngest member of the House.

PLACES OF BIRTH.

Vermont	207	Ireland	2
New Hampshire	8	Connecticut	1
New York	6	Pennsylvania	1
Canada	4	England	1
Massachusetts	3	Maine	1
Scotland	3	Not given	1

OCCUPATIONS.

Farmers	128	Teacher	1
Merchants	17	Blacksmith	1
Physicians	15	Butcher	1
Lawyers	13	Cabinet Maker	1
Manufacturers	12	Mail Carrier	1
R. R. Employes	4	Soap-Stone Dealer	1
Lumber Dealers	3	Bookbinder	1
Mechanics	3	Hotel Keeper	1
Clerks	3	Marble Dealer	1
Bankers	2	Sawyer	1
Clergymen	2	Treasurer	1
Carpenters	2	Farmer and Lawyer	1
Harness Makers	2	Farmer and Manufacturer	1
Superintendents	2	Farmer and Drover	1
Carriage Makers	2	Farmer and Speculator	1
Farmer & Lumber Dealer	2	Farmer and Quarryman	1
Farmer and Merchant	2	Deputy Sheriff	1
Farmer and Teacher	2	Salesman	1
Farmer and Mechanic	2	Not classified	2

RELIGIOUS PREFERENCES.

Congregationalists	65	Unitarians	4
Methodists	34	Spiritualists	3
Universalists	33	Good Samaritans	2
Baptists	24	Protestants	2
Episcopalians	9	Adventists	2
Liberals	6	Christian	1
Catholics	6	Church of the Disciples	1
Presbyterians	5	Rationalist	1
Freewill Baptists	4	No preference	37

ARRIVAL AND DEPARTURE OF MAILS.

WESTERN closes at 9.40 A. M., 3.30 and 9 P. M.

NORTHERN closes at 3.30 and 9 P. M.
Arrives at 10.30 A. M. and 11.30 P. M.

SOUTHERN AND EASTERN closes at 9.40 A. M. and 9 P. M.
Arrives at 7 A. M. and 5 P. M.

NEW YORK closes at 9.40 A. M. 3.30 and 9 P. M.
Arrives at 7 A. M. and 5 P. M.

BARRE MAIL arrives at 6 P. M. and 11 A. M.
Leaves at 9.30 A. M. and 3.30 P. M.

MONTPELIER & WELLS RIVER MAIL closes at 8.45 A.M.
Arrives at 6 P. M.

MORRISVILLE STAGE arrives every day (except Sundays) at 4 P. M. Leaves every day (except Sundays) at 9.30 A. M.

CALAIS arrives and departs three times a week—Tuesdays Thursdays and Saturdays. Arrives at 12 M., and departs at 4 P. M.

BERLIN, arrives and departs every day, (except Sundays.) Arrives at 3 P. M., and departs at 4.30 P. M.

☞ All matter for the above mails, by railroad, must be in the office promptly at the hour of closing.

OFFICE HOURS—7 A. M. to 8 P. M. Sundays—12 M. to 1 P. M.

JOHN W. CLARK, *Postmaster*.

MONTPELIER, October, 1880.

☞ Stamps of 1, 2, 3, 5, 6, 10, 15, and 30 cents, stamped envelopes and stamped paper wrappers, always on hand. Treasury notes, specie and government currency only, received for stamps. Stamps must be put on letters and papers by the forwarder.

RAILROAD TIME TABLE.

CENTRAL VERMONT RAILROAD.

Trains going SOUTH AND EAST leaves Montpelier as follows:

Mail Train.......................................9.50 A. M.
Day Express....................................11.35 A. M.
Mixed Train to W. R. Junction.......................6.55 P. M.
Night Express...................................11.10 P. M.

NORTH AND WEST.

Night Express.....................................3.10 A. M.
Accommodation....................................8.50 A. M.
Local Passenger.................................10.50 A. M.
Express Mail.......................................3.55 P. M.
Accommodation....................................6.00 P. M.

FOR BARRE.

Leave Montpelier at 7.00 A. M., 10.05 A. M., and 4.30 P. M.

MONTPELIER & WELLS RIVER RAILROAD.

Trains leave Montpelier as follows:

Mail...9.00 A. M.
Express Passenger..................................2.00 P. M.
Mixed..4.30 P. M.

RELIGIOUS SERVICES.

EACH SUNDAY.

At Bethany Church, (Congregationalist,) corner of Main and School Streets, Rev. Mr. Hincks, at 10.30 A. M. and 7 P. M. Lecture and Social Meeting Wednesday evening.

Christ Church, (Episcopal,) State Street, Rev. Mr. Hill, at 10.30 A. M. and 7 P. M.

Trinity M. E. Church, Main Street, Rev. Mr. Fellows, at 10.30 A. M. and 7 P. M. Prayer Meeting on Tuesday evening, and Class Meeting on Thursday evening at 7 o'clock.

Church of the Messiah, (Independent,) Main Street, Rev. Mr. Wright, at 10.30 A. M. and 7 P. M.

Baptist Church, School Street, Rev. Mr. Rogers, at 10.30 A. M. and 7 P. M. Prayer Meeting on Thursday evening, at 7 o'clock.

St. Augustine, (Roman Catholic,) Court Street, Rev. Father Dugluе. High Mass at 10.30 A. M.; Vespers at 3.30 P. M.

ALPHABETICAL INDEX TO HOUSE DIAGRAM.

Member.	*Seat.*
Abbott, of Bennington	235
Abbott, of Landgrove	97
Abell, of West Haven	151
Adams, of Brighton	60
Adams, of Pomfret	123
Allen, of Hinesburgh	148
Allen, of Enosburgh	38
Allen, of Fair Haven	13
Allen, of Hartford	149
Arnold, of Westminster	94
Atwood, of Pittsfield	164
Ayer, of Stannard	74
Babcock, of Bridgewater	227
Barney, of Guilford	190
Battell, of Middlebury	206
Beebe, of Rupert	208
Bemis, of Burke	8
Bemis, of Lyndon	144
Benson, of Winhall	169
Bingham, of Cornwall	199
Black, of Coventry	140
Blair, of Barnet	222
Blaisdell, of Cambridge	200
Bolton, of Peacham	33
Booth, of Ferrisburgh	203
Booth, of Waltham	157
Booth, of Morristown	92
Boyce, of Fayston	134
Brainerd, of St. Albans	135
Bratton, of Stamford	173
Briggs, of Brandon	237
Brown, of Grand Isle	128
Bryant, of Weston	181
Buck, of Troy	213
Bucklin, of Warren	110
Butterfield, of Whitingham	209
Button, of Richford	126
Cameroh, of Maidstone	79
Caswell, of Holland	129
Chafey, of Albany	141
Chamberlain, of Bradford	178
Chapin, of Middlesex	216
Chase, of Jay	125
Chase, of Somerset	107
Cilley, of Tunbridge	154
Clark, of Williston	49
Clark, of Windsor	230
Cobb, of Ripton	109
Cobb, of Strafford	24
Colburn, of Springfield	182
Colton, of Sherburne	90
Cook, of Wallingford	80
Currier, of Norwich	105
Curtis, of Georgia	85
Cushing, of Jamaica	153
Damon, of Victory	53
Daniels, of Westmore	46
Dartt, of Weathersfield	2
Davis, of Putney	212
Davis, of Barnard	106
Davis, of Chester	232
Deming, of Arlington	236
Denny, of Northfield	219
Dexter, of Reading	23
Dillon, of South Hero	172
Dix, of Montgomery	37
Dolloff, of Charleston	69
Doud, of New Haven	152

Member.	*Seat.*
Dutton, of Goshen	103
Dutton, of Dummerston	215
Ellis, of Huntington	10
Ely-Goddard, of Ely	19
Farman, of Lowell	84
Farnham, of West Fairlee	180
Fefee, of North Hero	118
Ferguson, of Walden	71
Fifield, of Montpelier	24
Fitch, of Brunswick	211
Fletcher, of Cavendish	231
Follett, of Sharon	155
Ford, of Granville	78
Foster, of Shrewsbury	18
Fowler, of Randolph	5
Giddings, of Bakersfield	47
Goodell, of Readsboro	192
Goodwin, of Derby	17
Goodwin, of Hartland	124
Gould, of Cabot	39
Gould, of Windham	191
Gray, of Middletown	201
Griffin, of Sudbury	186
Grout, of Concord	36
Grout, of Newport	210
Grover, of Wells	127
Hapgood, of Peru	195
Harbour, of Glastenbury	122
Harvey, of Topsham	40
Haskell, of Grafton	182
Hazard, of Castleton	14
Hendrick, of Hyde Park	43
Hill, of Starksboro	108
Hinckley, of Chelsea	150
Hinsdill, of St. George	228
Hodges, of Richmond	202
Holmes, of Whiting	28
Hooker, of Brattleboro	187
Hopkinson, of Salem	139
Horton, of Chittenden	29
Howe, of Ludlow	189
Hubbard, of Plymouth	214
Hudson, of East Haven	62
Hunt, of Worcester	23
Hurst, of Isle La Motte	119
Hutchinson, of Orange	41
Ingalls, of Sheffield	102

Member.	*Seat.*
James, of Weybridge	217
Jones, of Waitsfield	184
Joslyn, of Brownington	218
Judevine, of Hardwick	225
Kelley, of Danby	159
Kent, of Bristol	63
Kidder, of Wardsboro	44
Kimball, of Newbury	177
Knight, of Stratton	112
Lane, of Mount Tabor	114
Leach, of Sheldon	11
Leavens, of Berkshire	58
LeClair, of Colchester	52
Leonard, of Calais	116
Lovejoy, of Andover	83
Mackenzie, of Woodstock	183
Mallory, of Woodford	176
Manning, of Johnson	68
Martin, of Londonderry	*Chair.*
Matthews, of Granby	137
May, of Waterford	138
McGettrick, of Fletcher	121
McKnight, of Woodbury	162
Mears, of Marshfield	96
Merrifield, of Newfane	240
Moore, of Shoreham	197
Morrill, of Canaan	100
Morrill, of Vernon	170
Morrison, of West Windsor	207
Mott, of Alburgh	120
Nichols, of Essex	45
Ober, of Athens	56
OBrian, of Lincoln	70
O. Neil, of Lemington	229
Orcutt, of Roxbury	15
Page, of Rutland	185
Palmer, of Jericho	147
Palmer, of Waterbury	143
Parker, of Pownal	20
Parker, of Elmore	54
Perry, of Hancock	88
Perry, of Ira	76
Pierce, of Shaftsbury	193
Pike, of Stowe	67
Platt, of Swanton	166
Pond, of Lunenburgh	81
Potter, of Belvidere	66

Member.	*Seat.*
Potter, of Clarendon	162
Preston, of Baltimore	42
Priest, of Mount Holly	30
Priest, of Barre	21
Prindle, of Charlotte	101
Prouty, of Marlboro	25
Rankin, of Milton	160
Ranney, of Kirby	233
Renfrew, of Ryegate	73
Rhodes, of Guildhall	196
Richardson, of Stockbridge	82
Richmond, of Rochester	99
Ripley, of Poultney	118
Roby, of Bloomfield	174
Rogers, of Wheelock	224
Rogers, of Waterville	65
Sargent, of Bethel	226
Sawyer, of Moretown	133
Scranton, of Vergennes	4
Searle, of Highgate	35
Shattuck, of Eden	104
Shedd, of Mendon	89
Shepardson, of Fairfax	86
Shepherd, of Brookfield	27
Simpson, of Craftsbury	95
Simpson, of Greensboro	221
Skinner, of Barton	98
Smith, of Monkton	3
Smith, of Newark	9
Smith, of St. Johnsbury	223
Smith, of Shelburne	50
Smith, of Fairlee	48
Smith, of Plainfield	59
Smith, of Rockingham	179
Soule, of Fairfield	87
Spear, of Braintree	6
Spencer, of Wilmington	239
St. John, of Hubbardton	161
Stanley, of Searsburgh	117
Stevens, of Westford	130
Stone, of Danville	12
Strong, of Benson	32
Sumner, of Halifax	26
Taft, of Burlington	1
Taylor, of Thetford	75
Taylor, of Washington	111
Templeton, of Glover	238
Thayer, of South Burlington	51
Thomas, of Leicester	136
Thompson, of Irasburgh	142
Tiffany, of Pittsford	7
Towsley, of Panton	64
Tracy, of East Montpelier	16
Tubbs, of Tinmouth	158
Turner, of Dover	31
Walker, of Williamstown	188
Ware, of Townshend	55
Waterhouse, of Salisbury	91
Webb, of Sunderland	175
Welch, of Groton	72
West, of Royalton	156
Whalen, of Bolton	61
Wheelock, of Berlin	77
Whitford, of Addison	204
Whitney, of Dorset	115
Whitney, of Franklin	57
Whitney, of Brookline	171
Wilcox, of Morgan	131
Wilcox, of Pawlet	220
Willey, of Sutton	146
Wilson, of Manchester	194
Witherell, of Bridport	198
Wood, of Westfield	22
Woodard, of Sandgate	205
Woodworth, of Underhill	145
Wright, of Orwell	234

NUMERICAL INDEX TO HOUSE DIAGRAM.

Seat.	*Member.*
1	Taft, of Burlington.
2	Dartt, of Weathersfield.
3	Smith, of Monkton.
4	Scranton, of Vergennes.
5	Fowler, of Randolph.
6	Spear, of Braintree.
7	Tiffany, of Pittsford.
8	Bemis, of Burke.
9	Smith, of Newark.
10	Ellis, of Huntington.
11	Leach, of Sheldon.
12	Stone, of Danville.
13	Allen, of Fair Haven.
14	Hazard, of Castleton.
15	Orcutt, of Roxbury.
16	Tracy, of East Montpelier.
17	Goodwin, of Derby.
18	Foster, of Shrewsbury.
19	Ely-Goddard, of Ely.
20	Parker, of Pownal.
21	Priest, of Barre.
22	Wood, of Westfield.
23	Dexter, of Reading.
24	Cobb, of Strafford.
25	Prouty, of Marlboro.
26	Sumner, of Halifax.
27	Shepherd, of Brookfield.
28	Holmes, of Whiting.
29	Horton, of Chittenden.
30	Priest, of Mount Holly.
31	Turner, of Dover.
32	Strong, of Benson.
33	Bolton, of Peacham.
34	Fifield, of Montpelier.
35	Searle, of Highgate.
36	Grout, of Concord.
37	Dix, of Montgomery.
38	Allen, of Enosburgh.
39	Gould, of Cabot.
40	Harvey, of Topsham.
41	Hutchinson, of Orange.
42	Preston, of Baltimore.
43	Hendrick, of Hyde Park.
44	Kidder, of Wardsboro.
45	Nichols, of Essex.
46	Daniels, of Westmore.
47	Giddings, of Bakersfield.
48	Smith, of Fairlee.
49	Clark. of Williston.
50	Smith, of Shelburne.
51	Thayer, of South Burlington.
52	LeClair, of Colchester.
53	Damon, of Victory.
54	Parker, of Elmore.
55	Ware, of Townshend.
56	Ober, of Athens.
57	Whitney, of Franklin.
58	Leavens, of Berkshire.
59	Smith, of Plainfield.
60	Adams, of Brighton.
61	Whalen, of Bolton.
62	Hudson, of East Haven.
63	Kent, of Bristol.
64	Towsley, of Panton.
65	Rogers, of Waterville.
66	Potter, of Belvidere.
67	Pike, of Stowe.
68	Manning, of Johnson.

Seat.	*Member.*
69	Dolloff, of Charleston.
70	OBrian, of Lincoln.
71	Ferguson, of Walden.
72	Welch, of Groton.
73	Renfrew, of Ryegate.
74	Ayer, of Stannard.
75	Taylor, of Thetford.
76	Perry, of Ira.
77	Wheelock, of Berlin.
78	Ford, of Granville.
79	Cameron, of Maidstone.
80	Cook, of Wallingford.
81	Pond, of Lunenburgh.
82	Richardson, of Stockbridge.
83	Lovejoy, of Andover,
84	Farman, of Lowell.
85	Curtis, of Georgia.
86	Shepardson, of Fairfax.
87	Soule, of Fairfield.
88	Perry, of Hancock.
89	Shedd, of Mendon.
90	Colton, of Sherburne.
91	Waterhouse, of Salisbury.
92	Booth, of Morristown.
93	Hunt, of Worcester.
94	Arnold, of Westminster.
95	Simpson, of Craftsbury.
96	Mears, of Marshfield,
97	Abbott, of Landgrove.
98	Skinner, of Barton.
99	Richmond, of Rochester.
100	Morrill, of Canaan.
101	Prindle, of Charlotte.
102	Ingalls, of Sheffield.
103	Dutton, of Goshen.
104	Shattuck, of Eden.
105	Currier, of Norwich.
106	Davis, of Barnard.
107	Chase, of Somerset.
108	Hill, of Starksboro.
109	Cobb, of Ripton.
110	Bucklin, of Warren.
111	Taylor, of Washington.
112	Knight, of Stratton.
113	Ripley, of Poultney.
114	Lane, of Mount Tabor,
115	Whitney, of Dorset.

Seat.	*Member.*
116	Leonard, of Calais.
117	Stanley, of Searsburgh.
118	Fefee, of North Hero.
119	Hurst, of Isle La Motte.
120	Mott, of Alburgh.
121	McGettrick, of Fletcher.
122	Harbour, of Glastenbury.
123	Adams, of Pomfret.
124	Goodwin, of Hartland.
125	Chase, of Jay.
126	Button, of Richford.
127	Grover, of Wells.
128	Brown, of Grand Isle.
129	Caswell, of Holland.
130	Stevens, of Westford.
131	Wilcox, of Morgan.
132	Colburn, of Springfield.
133	Sawyer, of Moretown.
134	Boyce, of Fayston.
135	Brainerd, of St. Albans.
136	Thomas, of Leicester.
137	Matthews, of Granby.
138	May, of Waterford.
139	Hopkinson, of Salem.
140	Black, of Coventry.
141	Chafey, of Albany.
142	Thompson, of Irasburgh.
143	Palmer, of Waterbury.
144	Bemis, of Lyndon.
145	Woodworth, of Underhill.
146	Willey, of Sutton,
147	Palmer, of Jericho.
148	Allen, of Hinesburgh.
149	Allen, of Hartford.
150	Hinckley, of Chelsea,
151	Abell, of West Haven.
152	Doud, of New Haven.
153	Cushing, of Jamaica.
154	Cilley, of Tunbridge.
155	Follett, of Sharon.
156	West, of Royalton.
157	Booth, of Waltham.
158	Tubbs, of Tinmouth.
159	Kelley, of Danby.
160	Rankin, of Milton.
161	St. John, of Hubbardton.
162	Potter, of Clarendon.

Seat.	Member.
163	McKnight, of Woodbury.
164	Atwood, of Pittsfield.
165	
166	Platt, of Swanton.
167	
168	
169	Benson, of Winhall.
170	Morrill, of Vernon.
171	Whitney, of Brookline.
172	Dillon, of South Hero.
173	Bratton, of Stamford.
174	Roby, of Bloomfield.
175	Webb, of Sunderland.
176	Mallory, of Woodford.
177	Kimball, of Newbury.
178	Chamberlain, of Bradford.
179	Smith, of Rockingham.
180	Farnham, of West Fairlee.
181	Bryant, of Weston.
182	Haskell, of Grafton.
183	Mackenzie, of Woodstock.
184	Jones, of Waitsfield.
185	Page, of Rutland.
186	Griffin, of Sudbury.
187	Hooker, of Brattleboro.
188	Walker, of Williamstown.
189	Howe, of Ludlow.
190	Barney, of Guilford.
191	Gould, of Windham.
192	Goodell, of Readsboro.
193	Pierce, of Shaftsbury.
194	Wilson, of Manchester.
195	Hapgood, of Peru.
196	Rhodes, of Guildhall.
197	Moore, of Shoreham.
198	Witherell, of Bridport.
199	Bingham, of Cornwall.
200	Blaisdell, of Cambridge.
201	Gray, of Middletown.
202	Hodges, of Richmond.
203	Booth, of Ferrisburgh.
204	Whitford, of Addison.
205	Woodard, of Sandgate.
206	Battell, of Middlebury.
207	Morrison, of West Windsor.
208	Beebe, of Rupert.
209	Butterfield, of Whitingham.
210	Grout, of Newport.
211	Fitch, of Brunswick.
212	Davis, of Putney.
213	Buck, of Troy.
214	Hubbard, of Plymouth.
215	Dutton, of Dummerston.
216	Chapin, of Middlesex.
217	James, of Weybridge.
218	Joslyn, of Brownington.
219	Denny, of Northfield.
220	Wilcox, of Pawlet.
221	Simpson, of Greensboro.
222	Blair, of Barnet.
223	Smith, of St. Johnsbury.
224	Rogers, of Wheelock.
225	Judevine, of Hardwick.
226	Sargent, of Bethel.
227	Babcock, of Bridgewater.
228	Hinsdill, of St. George.
229	O. Neil, of Lemington.
230	Clark, of Windsor.
231	Fletcher, of Cavendish.
232	Davis, of Chester.
233	Ranney, of Kirby.
234	Wright, of Orwell.
235	Abbott, of Bennington.
236	Deming, of Arlington,
237	Briggs, of Brandon.
238	Templeton, of Glover.
239	Spencer, of Wilmington.
240	Merrifield, of Newfane.

www.ingramcontent.com/pod-product-compliance
Lightning Source LLC
Chambersburg PA
CBHW021125270326
41929CB00009B/1055

* 9 7 8 3 3 3 7 2 1 3 8 3 1 *